Understanding & Expressing Sexuality

DATE DUE			
APR. 19.1993			
APR. 03.1995			
GAYLORD			PRINTED IN U.S.A.

This book is printed on recycled paper.

Understanding & Expressing Sexuality

Responsible Choices for Individuals with Developmental Disabilities

**Rosalyn Kramer Monat-Haller, M.Ed.,
LISW, LPC, CCC-SLP, AASECT**
Certified Sex Educator/Sex Counselor
Allied Therapeutic Services
Summerville, South Carolina

·P·A·U·L·H·
BROOKES
PUBLISHING CO.

Baltimore • London • Toronto • Sydney

Paul H. Brookes Publishing Co.
P.O. Box 10624
Baltimore, Maryland 21285-0624

Typeset by Brushwood Graphics, Inc., Baltimore, MD.
Manufactured in the United States of America by
The Maple Press Company, York, PA.

Permission to reprint the following quotations is gratefully
acknowledged:
Pages 58 and 59:   Quotations from Schepp, K.F. (1986). *Sexuality
counseling: A training program.* Muncie, IN: Accelerated
Development, Inc. Reprinted by permission.

Situations described in this book come from composite multiple case
studies of this author and her counterparts throughout the United
States. The names of individuals, places, and organizations are
pseudonyms. Any similarity to actual individuals or circumstances is
coincidental and no implications should be inferred.

Rosalyn Kramer Monat-Haller offers workshops and lectures about
sexuality issues for individuals with developmental disabilities
and mental retardation. To arrange one of these in-service training
workshops, please write the author at the following address: Rosalyn
Kramer Monat-Haller, Allied Therapeutic Services, P.O. Box 2103,
Summerville, SC 29484-2103.

Library of Congress Cataloging-in-Publication Data
Monat-Haller, Rosalyn Kramer, 1945--
    Understanding and expressing sexuality : responsible choices for
individuals with developmental disabilities / by Rosalyn Kramer
Monat-Haller.
        p.   cm.
    Includes bibliographical references and index.
    ISBN 1-55766-073-5
    1. Sex instruction for the mentally handicapped—United States.
2. Mentally handicapped—United States—Sexual behavior.
3. Developmentally disabled—United States—Sexual behavior.
I. Title.
HQ54.3.M663   1992
306.7'087'4—dc20   91-33624
                                                             CIP

Contents

◇◇◇◇◇◇◇◇◇◇◇◇◇◇◇◇◇◇◇◇◇◇◇◇◇◇◇◇◇◇◇◇

About the Author

Rosalyn Kramer Monat-Haller, who holds a master's degree in education from Boston University, expanded and refocused her role from that of a licensed speech-language pathologist to that of a family therapist. For more than 24 years, Rosalyn has directed a multi-therapy department in an agency serving individuals with developmental disabilities and mental retardation while spearheading a statewide Very Special Arts program and coordinating a multidisciplinary cleft lip and cleft palate center. During this period, she has focused her therapeutic work on individuals and families that include a person with a developmental disability or mental retardation. Using her background in communication disorders, she has increasingly devoted her time to sexuality education and sexuality counseling, becoming certified in both areas by the American Association of Sex Educators, Counselors, and Therapists.

As her work progressed, Rosalyn obtained advanced training in family therapy with Dr. Virginia Satir, one of the founders of family therapy. Rosalyn became licensed as a professional counselor and independent social worker in the state of South Carolina. Since the 1982 publication of her book, *Sexuality and the Mentally Retarded: A Clinical and Therapeutic Guidebook* and her copyrighted 1983 videotape, *Sexuality and the Mentally Retarded*, Rosalyn has presented workshops internationally to train parents and professionals. She has several journal articles to her credit and is a recognized authority on sexuality and developmental disability; she has appeared on the Phil Donahue show and other television and radio programs, addressing sexuality issues for persons with developmental disabilities and mental retardation.

Rosalyn is married and the proud parent of two sons, David and Adam; "Magic," a therapy dog; and "Rainbow," therapy parrot in training.

Foreword

There are few issues in this society that polarize community, caregivers, families, and individuals as dramatically and definitively as the subjects of human sexuality, sex education, sexual health, and sexual counseling. As professionals in these areas, we all strive to obtain current and relevant information that will assist us in improving our skills for the benefit of our clients.

Information and materials on sexuality and sexual health have been developed over the last 25 years and have reached beyond the fundamentals into areas of expertise. Many of us tailor our work to specific populations while others of us remain generalists in the field of sexual health.

An important goal is to continue to grow, develop, and keep abreast of societal times and contemporary issues of sexual health. It is toward this end that Rosalyn Monat-Haller has revised her earlier text on sexuality and mental retardation. She has provided us with a useable and comprehensive presentation of human needs, professional skills, and contemporary and controversial issues—coupled with specific programmatic planning, recommendations, and counseling options for our work with persons with developmental disabilities and mental retardation.

The responsibility is ours as professionals to expand the definition of sexuality to include feelings integrated with knowledge and behavior. This comprehensive approach will be beneficial to all involved. As Monat-Haller states, it is crucial to acknowledge that all "sexual behavior is affected by one's disabilities and is also governed and influenced by rules and attitudes of the society in which one lives." She has summarized her personal viewpoints in light of her experiences and skills, which include successes and disappointments. She urges us to improve the tools we already have and to add our own successful techniques. In essence, she encourages us to continue to challenge ourselves to work in most creative ways.

Readers will not find this book a testimony to what is "appropriate and correct" but rather, a working, hands-on sharing (citing case examples) of what has been effective from the author's unique experiences. Monat-Haller's nonjudgmental, nonmanipulative writing style is helpful in stirring personal imagination, creativity, and skills of her readers.

Straightforward and helpful suggestions include stressing sex-positive messages of being a "person with a disability" instead of a "disabled person." In addition, examples of education, counseling, and interaction with individuals with varying degrees of mental retardation and physical limitations are given. This helps in assisting the reader to gauge the range of professional competency necessary to address the wide variation of common life issues.

Sexuality is always a concern to families and community, particularly as it relates to individuals with intellectual limitations. Monat-Haller stresses and reminds us throughout her book that knowledge enables self-esteem and independence and empowers individuals to maintain their personal dignity and integrity. Participation in the process of enabling personal growth in individuals is an opportunity, privilege, and responsibility for all of us as professionals.

The reader will appreciate the graphic step-by-step examples and exercises that are helpful in the training of professionals. Discussion regarding the identification and integration of community resources and potential is beneficial, as are the great many examples of teaching self-help skills to persons with mental retardation. Such training includes responsible sexual behaviors and safer sex.

I am very pleased to see that contemporary issues such as sexually transmitted diseases (STDs and AIDS) are recognized and included specifically in sexual health and risk assessment recommendations. Also, and equally as poignant, Monat-Haller points out that there is no easy technique for teaching integrity of personal choice, natural expression, and responsibility during these difficult times in society when STDs and AIDS preclude responsible, spontaneous, curious sexual expression and instead indicate caution and precautionary measures.

Of particular importance, and infrequent appearance in the literature, is the awareness that sexual ignorance, sexual repression, and sexual exploitation can be the ingredients that could develop into sexual offense. Few people have experienced working with sexual offenders with mental retardation and, again, bringing these issues into the foreground so that we may more readily understand, interact, and help these individuals is one step further toward creating a healthy environment.

For professionals working with persons with developmental disability and mental retardation, these issues are complex and perplexing. There are no easy answers. Monat-Haller stresses that programming, organization, and structure of training, as well as service delivery, must always include administrative support, family awareness, and community education.

Most importantly, I agree with the viewpoint that professionals need to be trained and comfortable, and must demonstrate flexible skills with sexuality—a subject that has such a profound effect on all of us. The ability to work as a team in transdisciplinary support of one another, as well as with clients and patients, creates an environment wherein the highest standards of ethics in sexual health education and counseling can be provided. Toward that end, this book is a confirmation of professional competence.

Sandra S. Cole, Ph.D.
Professor
Director, Sexuality Training Center
Department of Physical Medicine and Rehabilitation
University of Michigan Medical Center
Ann Arbor

Preface

"If it's a boy, I'll name him Johnny. If it's a girl, I'll name her Jill. Oh, it doesn't matter—just as long as the baby's normal."

"Oh, a boy—six pounds. Is he O.K.? Let's see—ten fingers, ten toes, penis, and everything looks fine. I guess that's that. He seems healthy."

"Look how fast he's growing! Before you know it, he'll be ready for college. Retarded—what's retarded? He's my child. He can't be!!"

These are some of the familiar and common thoughts of all parents who have discovered that their child has a developmental disability or mental retardation. Producing a baby with developmental problems is something that always happens to the "other person." When it happens to one's self, the whole situation seems to be unrealistic. It can take a great deal of time before the parents can adjust to the fact that this "horrible" situation is actually happening.

The adjustment to having a child with a disability is difficult in itself. To further realize that this child has a developmental disability or mental retardation, with all its attendant problems regarding education, independent living skills, and the like, is still more difficult. To then go one step further and accept the idea that some aspects of the child's personality will develop the same as children without disabilities is almost impossible.

When one comes right down to it, acknowledging the existence and development of sexuality in a child with a disability is extremely difficult for the parents and for society. There is a great tendency to infantilize the individual with a disability regardless of his or her chronological age. Included in this infantilization is the concept of asexuality, or lack of sexuality, which extends to the lack of necessity for learning about one's self, one's sexuality, or one's psychosocial-sexual development. Therefore, as they go through the process of maturation, many individuals with developmental disabilities or mental retardation find themselves in a position where no one in their environment is willing to deal with or even recognize their developing sexuality.

In residential facilities for persons with developmental disabilities and mental retardation, community programs, or sheltered workshops or work assignments, the subject of sexuality seems to be a very threatening, taboo topic. Staff and administrators approach the subject as if it is one that will automatically cause problems. It is the hope of most parents, staff, and administrators that, with regard to sexuality in persons with developmental disabilities and mental retardation, everything will just be "O.K." and nothing will have to be handled or discussed.

As I have developed my skills in the field of sexuality counseling with persons with developmental disabilities and mental retardation, I have been through many processes beneficial to others in the fields of developmental disability and counseling who are dealing with this topic. I hope that this book will be an aid to those parents, administrators, educators, and staff members in gaining the necessary skills and abilities to accept the sexual needs and feelings of individuals with developmental disabilities and mental retardation, and to provide these individuals with education and counseling so that they in turn are able to understand and express their own developing sexuality. I believe that it is the right of all persons to have such acknowledgment, help, and support. This book is written as a tribute to those individuals with developmental disabilities and mental retardation who have enabled me to gain knowledge of their sexuality.

This book is not a technical or research adventure. Neither is it designed to incorporate all the present research into one volume. I have found that there is a need for a sharing of experiences and knowledge from a very pragmatic point of view. I offer suggestions, not solutions—techniques that have been tried, some with success, some with failure. There is a need for thought and for a willingness to examine the field. To all those involved with persons with developmental disabilities and mental retardation, I say that these individuals have the right to express and develop their own sexuality and to feel comfortable with it. I believe it is the responsibility of everyone in the environment of these individuals to acknowledge, recognize, and offer support systems for them so they can develop control and maturity in this aspect of their personality. We need to acknowledge that the development of the sexuality "skills" of persons with disabilities is as important as the development of adaptive, communicative, academic, or other personal social skills.

As you progress through this book, I hope that you will become comfortable with its ideas and philosophy so that you, the reader, will become you, the doer, and you, the support system, for the person with developmental disabilities and mental retardation. In this way, we will improve the world in which these individuals live and function. Any seeming generalizations regarding persons with developmental disabilities and mental retardation reflect my feelings and perceptions, which stem from my experiences in the real "clinical world" of sexuality education and counseling. The case histories reflect my experiences and those of my fellow professionals throughout the nation. Names used are fictitious.

This material is presented as a sharing of ideas, feelings, and experiences in hopes that it will allow others to use it as a sounding board to explore their own creativity and to pursue specific areas of interest in as much depth as will be meaningful to any specific reader. The ideas and techniques discussed in this book should aid adults in helping all persons with special needs develop healthy psychosocial-sexual attitudes and personalities. Because of the variety of circumstances and needs of these individuals, and in keeping with my emphasis on creativity and flexibility, this book is not intended to be a programmed, step-by-step final solution. It is instead proposed as a catalyst for the development of individualized responses to the sexuality problems of persons with developmental disabilities and mental retardation.

Acknowledgments

My appreciation is extended to my children, David and Adam, my mother, Irma Kramer, and my husband, Ralph, who showed me support, patience, and understanding for the time taken from them and who encouraged me to develop this book. I acknowledge the loving memory of my father, Izzy Kramer, by honoring his love for learning.

In the past 25 years of my professional life, I have received tremendous support, stimulation, and knowledge from the following people who have offered me the gift of information and the opportunity to explore and grow as "me." I am indebted with gratitude to each and every one of them: Dr. Erbert F. Cicenia, Dr. W. Bruce Newton, Jr., Mariana Roberts, Dr. Judy Johnson, Dr. Jack Howell, Dr. Phil Massey, Dr. Charles Barnett, Dr. Robert F. Hagerty, Muriel Offerman, the late Dr. Virginia Satir, Dr. Sol Gordon, Winifred Kempton, Dr. Sandra Cole, Dr. Jane Gerber, Dr. George Moskowitz, James Hill, Esq., Aphrodite Karvelas, Esq., Dr. Sara Schuh, Dr. Libby Ralston, Mary Mueller, Dr. Oliver Bjorkson, Dr. Tom Shipp, Dr. Brent Koyle, Ken Ward, June Sullivan, Dr. John Stine, Dr. John Abess, Dr. James Semens, the late Dr. Paul Fleming, Dr. and Mrs. J. Chambers, Dr. Sandra Catoe, Richard Henderson, Dr. Conrad Kottak, Dr. Albert Warshauer, Dr. Ron Kirschner, Dr. James McLean, and Dr. Margot Kopley. All of these people and all of my colleagues, in their own and special way, have entered my professional path, offering caring support and feedback to my process of professional growth.

In writing this particular book, I have received tremendous professional support from Paul H. Brookes Publishing Company, especially from Sarah B. Cheney, Acquisitions Editor, and Megan Westerfeld, Copyeditor. I applaud their efforts to enter the world of sexuality issues for individuals with developmental disabilities and mental retardation.

For proofreading, typing, and "getting it all together," I am indebted to Charlotte Bright, Ralph Haller, Patty Cartin, and Jo Ann Spangler. When time was tight, they helped make it happen.

I perceive my exploration of the issues in this book as a journey of discovery. I deeply appreciate each and every person who has entered this journey with me. Thanks!

In loving appreciation to my mother, Irma Kramer, and my husband, Ralph Haller, and as a challenge to my sons, David and Adam, as they go off to college: Use my love to search for the rainbows, bathe in the moon's glow, and capture your dreams in the rays of the sun! Enjoy and contribute to life—you both have so much to offer!

Understanding & Expressing Sexuality

Chapter 1

Overview

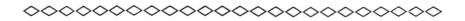

SEXUALITY AS A CONCEPT

A definition of sexuality encompasses many concepts: maleness/femaleness, sensuality, sense of self, ego, perception of self in relationship to the world and others, the quality or state of being sexual, the condition of having sexual activity or intercourse, and expressing or receiving an expression of sexual interest. For most people, sexuality has a very personal definition, and the specific meanings and thoughts associated with sexuality derive from experiences they have had from birth to their present stage of psychosexual (PS) development.

Sexuality is an evolving, instinctive type of behavior, and an individual's sexual responses are not related to his or her level of intellect. In the population with average intelligence, it is well accepted that people have sexuality that they may choose to express or not express within certain societal constraints. The expression of sexuality is inhibited, restricted, and defined by societal rules that do not readily recognize the population of individuals with mental retardation and developmental disabilities as having positive, responsible sexual development. However, individuals with mental retardation can effectively express their sexuality to explore and enjoy themselves in ways acceptable to their living environments and to society.

In this book, individuals with mental retardation or developmental disabilities will be considered as sexual human beings with various levels of development, adaptive behavior, and coping skills. Impairment in adaptive functioning will most directly affect the development and expression of sexuality among individuals with mental retardation or developmental disabilities. Determining the adaptive behavior skills of such individuals prior to counseling will help foster the development of appropriate and acceptable psychosocial-sexual (PSS) interactions within the family, society, and the community at large. All individuals with mental retardation or developmental disabilities can be counseled in ways that meet their specific needs. Consideration of the specific personality traits of each individual ensures that he or she will receive the type of service to which he or she is entitled.

Sexuality Education versus Sexuality Counseling

I prefer the term "sexuality education" to the typically used term "sex education." The word "sexuality" is more inclusive of the total person and suggests a more humanistic approach to the education and counseling processes. In the context of this book, I use the term "sexuality education" to mean the giving of information about such topics as anatomy and physiology, birth control, sexually transmitted diseases, marriage and parenthood, types of sexual expression, and inappropriate sexual behavior. The term "sexuality counseling" refers to an approach that includes dealing with feelings about sexuality and the integration of feelings, thoughts, and behavior into the ego structure and self-concept of the individual receiving the counseling. The role of the sexuality counselor is to explore such feelings, thoughts, and behaviors in the counseling sessions.

Sexuality counseling uses techniques such as role-playing and psychotherapy to help the individual develop some of his or her inner thoughts about the problems involved in feeling sexual and the complications these feelings raise in the eyes of society. With regard to developing sexuality, sexual feelings about oneself, and sexual feelings about others, the individual with mental retardation or developmental disabilities should be counseled to feel and behave as an adult with disabilities rather than an asexual or sexually incompetent person. However, it is important to understand that sexual behavior is affected by one's disabilities and is also governed and influenced by the rules and attitudes of the society in which one lives. The expression of sexuality by individuals with mental retardation and developmental disabilities in socially approved ways and in appropriate environments will ensure that their rights to sexuality are given the same weight and respect as are those of the rest of society. Various clinical and therapeutic approaches are used during sexuality counseling to help the individual understand and cope with this process of PSS development.

HISTORICAL PERSPECTIVE ON SEXUALITY

A Personal History

In reading a book such as this, many readers will be interested in the historical perspective on sexuality and persons with mental retardation or developmental disabilities. However, my purpose is not to present an overall historical view but rather to explore my own growth and learnings beginning in the mid-1960s as a professional in the field of mental retardation and developmental disabilities. In the early 1970s, I expanded from my background in speech-language pathology and communication theory to begin exploring counseling techniques, methods, and processes for providing sexuality education/counseling to persons with mental retardation and developmental disabilities. I have read, studied, and traveled extensively, trying to learn from all the professional resources I have encountered, with the goal of integrating information that was meaningful to me.

When I began my work in this field in the 1970s, it quickly became obvious to me that there were limited resources and references that I thought would work for my purpose. I remember attempting to evaluate the sexual knowledge of individuals with mental retardation by carefully asking them the questions on published questionnaires, such as, "Do you know the meaning of sexual intercourse?" or "What is your vagina?" When these questions met with little or no response, I decided they were too abstract for the work that I was doing. Most sexuality questionnaires available then seemed to link an individual's knowledge base concerning sexuality with the egg's trip down the Fallopian tubes or the ejaculation of semen during intercourse. However, I was working with individuals who had no knowledge of or interest in the Fallopian tubes or the meaning of ejaculation. I also did not feel that the materials I found supported or encouraged open discussions, especially about the topics of interpersonal communication, dating, and forming meaningful relationships. Finally, the resources did not seem sufficiently practical or pragmatic and often required the purchase of very expensive materials.

It was at this point that I made the decision to create my own educational/counseling procedures and techniques. The challenge then became to develop new, innovative ways to approach sexuality issues within many different environments with individuals of any level of mental retardation or developmental disability. I was convinced that sexuality education could be provided without a large expenditure of money for slide presentations and other materials. This goal led to the development of the "sexuality education with colored chalk" method, a pragmatic approach that is described in Appendix A. I wanted to develop a simple, portable, easy-to-use program that any parent, family member, or caregiver could use and that required only a limited financial outlay. I also wanted to develop a competency-based program, operating from the premise that a professional or parent trained in sexuality education that involved simple techniques to be used with any individual would be a beneficial contribution to the process of sexuality education for individuals with mental retardation or developmental disabilities.

In the 1970s my counseling approach was constrained by the methodology that was current at that time. What I do today is based primarily on my professional development, stemming from thousands of hours of experience in actual sexuality education and counseling sessions, including crisis intervention and consultation at a local and national level, and in workshops where feedback from other professionals has helped shape and solidify my procedures and techniques. By bringing together the unique combined backgrounds of speech-language pathology, sex education, sex counseling, and family therapy, I am in a position to provide PSS education and counseling that would address the needs of those individuals with mental retardation or developmental disabilities. I have a commitment to combine informative sexuality education with counseling on feelings and sexual behavior in individualized programs designed to meet specific and meaningful goals set down by individuals, families, and interdisciplinary teams in various living, learning, and working environments in the community.

In reading this book, one will likely find that there are many thoughts, perceptions, and premises that seem congruent with his or her own philosophy and might be worth exploring further. There will doubtless be other opinions, feelings, and thoughts that do not meet the philosophical needs of the reader. It is valuable to remember that this book is one person's viewpoint of how to conduct counseling on sexuality issues for persons with mental retardation or developmental disabilities within certain environments and situations.

This book is a compilation of my experiences—what has worked and what has not worked for me. This work is therefore not to be considered as a statement of the only or best way to approach sexuality issues. Rather, it is the author's personal and professional approach to dealing with these issues with persons with mental retardation or developmental disabilities. The reader is invited to participate in the process and use anything that fits his or her personal approach. The reader is encouraged to develop his or her own percepts that allow him or her to feel comfortable in tackling this difficult process. (For those readers interested in more in-depth study, the Bibliography and Related Materials found at the end of this book lists a wealth of diverse resources on various topics in sexuality education and counseling.)

Changes in Response to Normalization Movement

Normalization has been defined as "providing the same services, risks, and opportunities to persons with developmental special needs as are provided to everyone else" (N. E. S. Gardner, 1986, p. 47). The concepts of normalization as they apply to the lives of persons with mental retardation have been recently discussed by J. F. Gardner and Chapman (1990). Careful thought needs to be given to these concepts in relation to sexuality issues for persons with mental retardation and developmental disabilities. I support the notion of "normalization" for all individuals, but in the 1990s what is "normal" in reference to sexual behavior must take into account the problem of sexually transmitted diseases, particularly AIDS—at least until a cure or a vaccine is found. The AIDS virus complicates the task of the counselor who is committed to assisting individuals with mental retardation in achieving a "normalized" sexuality.

The normalization movement has had a profound impact on the lives of persons with mental retardation and developmental disabilities in many areas, including living environments, employment, legal rights, and self-determination. The 1980s brought many changes in these areas, and the role of the sexuality educator/counselor has altered in response to these changes. I believe that much of what is being done to assist persons with mental retardation and developmental disabilities in the areas of legal and working environments will be harder to accomplish in the personal and living sectors. This is because desires for rights cannot be responsibly fulfilled without accompanying responsible behavior.

Deinstitutionalization

A major change affecting the lives of individuals with mental retardation and developmental disabilities is deinstitutionalization. As stated by J. F. Gardner and Chapman (1990, paraphrasing Bachrach, 1985), deinstitutionalization consists of "the transfer of persons with developmental disabilities from institutions to community-based care systems . . . the effort to prevent new admissions to institutions . . . [and] the concerted attempt to improve conditions in the institution" (p. 6). The United States has been experiencing a wave of deinstitutionalization, with a move toward smaller and smaller residences, using the community model of the least restrictive environment. It would seem that this movement would create an environment in which there would be fewer restrictions on overt sexual behavior as long as partners are choosing each other and there is no forced sex. However, it is harder for the advocate, professional, or family member to push for choice of partner and freedom of sexual behavior and activity in the 1990s. In the face of the AIDS epidemic, responsible sexual behavior no longer involves just birth control and "private versus public" issues.

Individuals with mental retardation and developmental disabilities need to learn how to have fun and enjoy each other in many different social environments, including ones in which sexual activity might be acceptable. Various community resources, including public health and mental health, need to develop and provide systems of support for community-based citizens with mental retardation. These systems might include community programs for teaching psychosocial skills and behaviors such as dating, proper behavior in public places, responsible use of alcohol, and appropriate responses to invitations for sexual encounters.

Programs that teach responsible sexual behavior are also a necessity. Given the problem of AIDS, it may be that an emphasis on developing a committed relationship with one life-long partner that involves sexual activity without the exchange of any bodily fluids, until there is testing and assurance that both partners are free of the AIDS virus, is the best counsel to give. This is no more or less than would be expected of any person acting responsibly in the community in the decade of the 1990s. It is unfortunate that the current climate surrounding sexuality issues may hinder the progress of achieving sexual rights for individuals with mental retardation. Full recognition and promotion of these legal rights in the area of sexuality may indeed lag until some means is found to protect all people.

Supported Employment

Supported employment is also a part of deinstitutionalization. The 1984 amendments to the Federal Rehabilitation Act (PL 98-524) defined supported employment as paid employment that encourages the noncompetitive hiring of individuals with disabilities in work settings also employing average individuals, with appropriate in-service training, supervision, and transportation (J. F. Gardner & Chapman, 1990, p. 13). As individuals with mental retardation have more opportunities to interact in the workplace, they will encounter more peer pressure to form social and sexual relationships with their coworkers. Therefore, preparation for supported employment should include teaching the social skills necessary to help the individual cope with these stresses.

One reason for special emphasis on this topic is to ensure that there will not be an increased risk of victimization. In the supported employment workplace, supervisors should be apprised of the guidance a particular individual might require as he or she learns to interact with a variety of fellow employees in the workplace. Adequate sexuality education and counseling should be provided by the appropriate public or private resource before the contract for supported employment is made. The individual with mental retardation or developmental disability should know how to say no to unwanted sexual advances and should be capable of requesting and asking for help if found in a compromising situation. This is particularly important for the individual with communication difficulties, with whom the supported employment personnel must be prepared to interact in the communication mode he or she uses. Only by developing teaching and counseling programs along these guidelines can the rights of employees with mental retardation be protected.

Legal Rights versus Responsibilities

If the individual with mental retardation or developmental disabilities is going to receive full recognition of his or her legal rights, he or she must assume the responsibilities that accompany these rights. Both sides of the issue will have to be addressed by sexuality educators/counselors. The counselor must ensure that the individual understands that, if he or she is given all the rights to free expression of socially acceptable sexual behavior, he or she must be willing, ready, and able to assume the responsibilities that go along with this behavior. This includes assuming responsibility for having committed criminal sexual acts. However, I have repeatedly experienced or been told of situations in which a person with mental retardation has committed a sexual offense, acknowledged it, gone to court, and been told by the judge that since he or she is diagnosed with mental retardation, he or she should be placed in an institution instead of a prison. The problem is that often there is no treatment available in either place. The case histories of Joseph and Neal (presented in Chapter 10) illustrate how the court often interacts with individuals with mental retardation who have been accused of committing sexual offenses.

Issues of Self-Determination

I have been struck by the answers I have gotten over the years when I have asked individuals with mental retardation and developmental disabilities the following question: "Who is responsible for you?" Inevitably, the answer is one of the following: my mother, my father, God, the lady in the group home, my teacher. It is rare to get the answer "Me." Each person is responsible for himself or herself, and this also holds true with regard to sexuality. Promoting a sense of responsibility for the sexual self is one of the most important tasks of the sexuality educator/counselor.

A key element of developing personal responsibility is the ability to make choices. Choice making is an ability that may not be well developed in individuals with mental retardation or developmental disabilities, since so many choices are often made for them. In order to learn how to make choices, opportunities must exist for the process. It might be helpful to give an individual the choice of which educator or counselor to see when that is feasible.

The emphasis on assuming personal responsibility does not deny the need for teaching age-appropriate activities for all individuals with developmental disabilities or mental retardation. Tremendous effort can be put into teaching community-oriented behaviors that relate to the development of interpersonal communication, friendships, and responsible dating. Parents and professionals should take every opportunity to explore these topics and behaviors and their possible ramifications with the individual, being sure to point out all positive and negative consequences of sexual behavior. The responsibility of the educator/counselor or family member is to ascertain the individual's ability to decode, process, and integrate the information in such a way that he or she can utilize it. If the counseling program is individualized, active, and age-appropriate, the individual will stand a better chance of achieving a sense of empowerment and developing the ability to participate in the process of successful self-determination.

Changes in Response to Public Health Concerns

The nature of sexuality education/counseling has been forced to change in response to current public health issues such as unplanned pregnancy, abortion, substance abuse, and sexually transmitted diseases. The latter issue has become critical in the wake of the rapid spread of AIDS through all segments of the population. Counseling for persons with mental retardation or developmental disabilities must now focus on ensuring that these individuals are capable of protecting themselves from the AIDS virus or, if infected, can take the necessary steps to prevent its transmission to others. In examining the problems inherent in such counseling, it might be instructive to look at the availability of the hepatitis vaccine and its impact on the sexual behavior of individuals with mental retardation.

Hepatitis can be transmitted through sexual acts that exchange bodily fluids. I have counseled many individuals with mental retardation who are active hepatitis carriers, and have found it very difficult to equate the pleasurable sex act with the spread of hepatitis. It is possible to communicate information about the mechanical aspects of the situation to the individual, including the necessity of using condoms to afford the partner some protection. It is the conceptual aspect of the issue that is more difficult to impart; the individual often has difficulty integrating and internalizing the seriousness of the connection between sexual behavior and hepatitis. I have also counseled the sexual partners of these individuals and encountered the same difficulties. However, in the case of hepatitis there is hope because a vaccine is available and the uninfected partner can be encouraged to take the vaccine in order to protect himself or herself from the disease. The sexuality educator/counselor can obtain informed consent to talk with the personal physician of the individuals involved in order to accomplish this, or the individual's interdisciplinary team can deal with the issues of the vaccine.

These options are not available for persons infected with the AIDS virus or their partners. At the Evolution of Psychotherapy conference in December, 1990, Helen Singer Kaplan, a prominent sex therapist, stated in a lecture that there should be an awareness that even condoms and "safer sex" are not safe enough to guarantee protection against the AIDS virus. In addition, the rules of confidentiality regarding testing for the AIDS virus or informing a partner of an infected individual make it difficult for a counselor or caregiver to intercede on an individual's behalf. It is difficult to talk of normalization and the right to sexual expression without realistically addressing all of the issues surrounding the AIDS epidemic.

To advocate for free sexual expression in the 1990s is folly for any individual; sexual behavior must be governed by responsibility for oneself and one's own behavior. It must be reemphasized that the goal is to learn to enjoy activities compatible with one's age and abilities without participating in unprotected sexual intercourse or any sexual behavior that involves the exchange of bodily fluids unless one is involved in a committed, faithful, and monogamous, lifelong relationship in which both individuals are free from the AIDS virus. If that is the case, the sexuality educator/counselor can help these individuals develop the relationship skills necessary to maintain a functional and happy sex life with each other.

THE RIGHT TO SEXUALITY

The basic premise underlying all sexuality education and counseling for individuals with mental retardation or developmental disabilities is that these individuals have the right to develop and express their inherent sexuality in a socially appropriate manner. The educator/counselor's role is to assist them in this endeavor in whatever ways are feasible and necessary, including acting as a legal advocate or a go-between with community-based resources. The concept of the right to sexuality must be accepted at all levels of the fields of mental retardation and sexuality counseling.

I have found community agencies dealing with sexuality issues to be receptive to learning about persons with mental retardation and developmental disabilities. My work in this area has entailed becoming an integral part of the process, so that I have had working connections with legal advocates and community-based resources. I have found others very willing to learn and explore when given the opportunity. However, if other counselors are not approached about the issue and shown feasible ways to include persons with mental retardation or developmental disabilities in their programs, these persons are often left out of consideration. Most professionals involved in counseling individuals with mental retardation and developmental disabilities now accept the premise that more openness and resources are needed to provide them with sexuality education and counseling services.

Developing a Workable Program

Dealing with Societal Rules

In developing a counseling program to foster healthy PSS development, there is an urgent need to recognize the social impact of sexual development on a personal level as well as public, community, and familial levels. Professional and societal biases increase the difficulties encountered by a person with mental retardation by isolating the sexual component of the individual's personality.

There are many implied and direct expectations on the part of society regarding the PSS behavior of such individuals. Two of the most basic are:

1. The implication that people with mental retardation or developmental disabilities should not be or inherently are not sexual. This is most evident in the continuing infantilization of the person with mental retardation or developmental disabilities by family members, professionals, and society. Some members of each of these groups have difficulty understanding or accepting that people with adult bodies have adult sexual needs, regardless of their mental and physical abilities, and that sexual desire usually follows.
2. The rules and regulations of society often enforce asexuality directly, as when families or residential facilities do not allow PSS expression of any form, especially sexual intercourse, by persons with mental retardation.

Such expectations and rules are often based on stereotypical thinking or outmoded perceptions; they are not related to present day life-styles. Some are only enforced in specific states or by certain factions. However, because they exist, the rules govern the sexual choices of persons with mental retardation and developmental disabilities living in a specific society.

To the extent that these rules of sexual behavior are enforced, there are usually well-understood consequences if the rules are not followed. The consequences vary from separation and counseling (which would be appropriate in some situations and not others) to punishment (which is rarely appropriate for two consenting adults who have not been adjudicated incompetent). In other cases, privileges may be withheld or rewards given as positive reinforcement if abstinence rules are followed. This atmosphere is the one in which staff members and administrators are most comfortable.

The sexuality educator/counselor can work to effect a change in the attitudes of staff and administration that will benefit the individual with mental retardation or developmental disabilities and will allow him or her the least restriction on sexual expression that develops a healthy PSS attitude. This can be accomplished by active participation in the interdisciplinary team process to ensure that the needs and rights of the individual are identified and communicated to the appropriate staff and administrators. Sexuality education and counseling will be most effective when there is complete administrative and staff support.

When an individual with mental retardation or developmental disabilities who lives at home commits what his or her family deems an infraction of their PSS behavior rules, the consequences may be equally variable. I have found it very beneficial to approach difficult situations from a therapeutic stance rather than an administrative one. When families are resistant to sexuality expression, there are usually accompanying fears and feelings. The sexuality counselor can provide family therapy to help deal with understanding these emergent feelings, fears, and concerns. Just saying to a family "Your son or daughter has the right to sexual expression now that he or she is an adult" will be less effective than making yourself available to hear the feelings and concerns and deal with them one by one, in a reality-based counseling environment that offers support to all members of the family. In cases in which the family responds with consequences that severely restrict the individual's right to sexual expression, there may be little that the sexuality educator/counselor can do to improve the situation. The rights of the parents to raise their son or daughter as they see fit must be respected if the individual is not of an age or functional level at which more independent living in a less restrictive environment is a solution. Family therapy sessions may provide an opportunity to help change the views of family members regarding the sexuality of the individual.

In order to accomplish such a change, I feel it is important for the counselor to help the family to understand the change process, as taught to me in 1987 by Dr. Virginia Satir, which includes starting at a status quo (the way things are), introducing a foreign element (something new), experiencing the chaos (confusion from newness), practicing the new skills required, and arriving at a new status quo. Change requires time and process. Families need to learn how to go through the change process when they are interested in helping their son or daughter develop new skills.

Providing a Coherent Approach

The best hope for a successful outcome of a sexuality education/counseling program is afforded by maximizing the integration of the program into the individual's ongoing educational programs and the many other facets of his or her daily life. I feel that structuring programs for "success" is vital to the development of self-esteem in the individual. This can be most easily achieved by having all family members and program team members work together toward this goal. For this integration to be most effective, the individual program plan (IPP) team should be actively involved from the beginning. All members of the IPP team should accept responsibility for participating in the actualization of this process.

An important factor in developing an integrated sexuality program is ensuring continuity of the counseling effort. In many cases the counseling program, even when well integrated into the individual's daily life, is viewed as a separate resource rather than practical information that can and should be supplied by others in the individual's environment. The tendency is to immediately refer any and all matters pertaining to sexuality to the counselor for resolution. The problem with an approach that relies on a specially trained counselor is that this person is usually only available when time can be scheduled. In contrast, the staff members and caregivers who interact daily with the individual with mental retardation and have the most contact with that person would be equally or more appropriate as resources both when problems occur and for sexuality education in general. This makes intervention at the most "teachable" moments more feasible, and good counseling and intervention can be provided in a relaxed and nontherapeutic atmosphere.

This is why it is important for every individual, from the highest ranking staff member to all family members, to be trained in sexuality education and counseling to the extent possible. The emphasis in such training should be on ensuring that the individual being counseled receives the same information from and is treated with the same degree of respect and encouragement by each person with whom he or she interacts. This assures that the "message" is coherent and prevents confusion resulting from mixed input. In order to achieve this type of integration, the sexuality educator/counselor obviously must work with staff and/or family members almost as closely as with the individual. Only in this way will the most effective sexuality development system exist and the most productive outcome emerge.

Need for Trained Counselors

It should be apparent from the preceding comments that professional training is critical for effective sexuality education/counseling. The job of the sexuality educator/counselor is to use every possible resource to attempt to provide comprehensible information in a meaningful way to the individual with mental retardation. The other professionals in the individual's environment may be able to utilize available materials to communicate basic sexual information, but the ability to conduct interpersonal therapeutic intervention far outweighs the capacity to select and employ curricula or visual materials.

In addition, the professional counselor is better trained for and more comfortable with talking about sexuality and sexual expression. Many staff and parents have difficulty in discussing sexuality beyond the basics of human sexual functions, and are ill-equipped to handle the more subtle aspects—the feelings and thoughts that accompany developing sexuality. An effective sexuality program must also deal with the social aspects of an individual's sexual behavior. For example, the sexuality educator/counselor must ensure that the person understands and is prepared to abide by society's rules and limitations. The individual must be taught acceptable forms of sexual expression for specific environments that will make his or her life less frustrating.

The basis of achieving all of these goals effectively is to develop a workable and meaningful communication system with the individual being educated or counseled. Considerations such as these are the reason I strongly believe that the most important part of sexuality education/ counseling is to have competent professionals providing the training.

CONCLUDING REMARKS

The nation is going through a developmental cycle in learning to deal with and accept individuals with mental retardation and developmental disabilities into living, learning, and working environments. Deinstitutionalization and normalization are now popular concepts that often are promoted by the same people who advocated for the building of large institutions in the 1960s. As the times change, so do theories and laws regarding the rights and needs of individuals with mental retardation and developmental disabilities. Attitudes sometimes take longer to change. The responsibility of the professional is to set the stage, increase the probability of success, prepare the individuals for the change, and encourage the community to grow to accept the change and the challenge.

I hope that we are witnessing the beginning of a catalytic search for meaningful answers to difficult questions in this area. As doors open, professionals enter, trying out new ideas for teaching the necessary skills for the new adventure. The person trained in mental retardation or developmental disabilities and sexuality education who can work as a consultant to train others in the skills needed to effectively provide quality programming will be at a premium. The need will arise for a transdisciplinary sharing of such skills among child development educators, in-service educators, family members, and the individuals themselves. Joint efforts will be developed between community health departments, departments of mental retardation, state organizations that deliver social services to the community, and mental health facilities. Cooperative teams will be formed to assist individuals with mental retardation and developmental disabilities in executing the rights and privileges given them by law. As more individuals with mental retardation and developmental disabilities are placed in supervised and unsupervised living situations in the community, more resources will emerge to deal with the ensuing problems. The goal will be to develop resources that meet the needs of and benefit both individuals with mental retardation or developmental disability and society.

PART I

About Counseling and Counselors

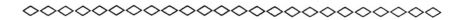

Chapter **2**

Developing an Individualized Education/Counseling Program

NEED FOR SEXUALITY EDUCATION AND COUNSELING

Among persons of average intelligence, much sexuality education is derived from peers, the media, and school. Learning from peers and the media is not the best way to receive this information. Reliance on these information sources can lead to problems because the listener hears things out of context and frequently in pieces. There is no responsible adult present to answer questions and clarify misconceptions.

Kay Frances Schepp (1986) stated:

> An individual's sexual world is made up of ideas, impressions, images, and experiences from countless sources. To call this gestalt a result of a person's "sex education" is a broad definition, but correct. For most people the formal kind of sex education is limited to a small number of classes, texts, or talks. The informal sources of sex education are usually far more significant and the sum of both can be referred to as sexual learning. (p. 34)

Schepp constructed a diagram showing the way in which an individual's concept of sexuality is affected by community, parents, books and magazines, peers, friends of the family, media, relatives, school, church, and experiences, and undoubtedly other sources as well. Schepp further stated that "The ideal sexual learning is positive and informative about sexuality and is appropriately timed for the developing individual. . . . Good sexuality education which is continuous and integrated with other knowledge can be expected to contribute to responsible, comfortable, sexual development" (p. 35). She concluded by saying: Although doing so can be hard to achieve, formal kinds of sex education planned by parents, school, and community are more effective if coordinated with the informal sexual learning coming from peers, media, and culture" (p. 35). The information leads into contexts that fit for the reader as she or he tries to define and develop individualized program plans to deal with sexuality education and counseling issues.

Much of this is applicable to sexuality education/counseling for persons with mental retardation or developmental disabilities. However, there are considerations in developing education/counseling programs for such individuals that involve taking into account the special needs that may exist in this population, and these considerations must be addressed in order for any such program to succeed. All sexuality education processes should be individualized to meet the language and cognitive systems of the individual with mental retardation or developmental disability. The information to be given must not only be specific to the needs of the persons receiving it, but must also be given in a manner that enhances their ability to understand what is being taught. For example, as simplistic as it sounds, if the sexuality educator is working with a nonreader, the program must be individualized to include material that does not require reading skills. It is for simple reasons such as this that sexuality education/counseling that is designed to accommodate retardation or disability is the best approach.

DETERMINATION OF AN INDIVIDUAL'S NEEDS

Desire versus Ability

The fact that an individual desires to participate in adult sexual activity does not mean that he or she is emotionally, educationally, or practically ready to do this. An important first step in enabling the individual to exercise his or her right to sexual self-expression is a thorough assessment of his or her existing knowledge and skills in this area. As an aid in accomplishing this goal, members of the individual's interdisciplinary team might want to review and adopt the simple sexuality assessment provided in Appendix B. It is designed to allow the gathering of basic information and the assessment of basic functional needs and skills that the education/counseling program should address.

It is the responsibility of every team member to incorporate this information into the specific program for the individual. The individual's goals and environment must be ready to support the objectives and service needs that are defined conjointly by the individual and his or her interdisciplinary team, who join together in the process of developing a meaningful Individual Program Plan (IPP) document. As they work to develop this document, interdisciplinary teams need to be aware of all of the responsibilities that accompany sexual rights and of the parameters of social acceptability within which the individual must function. These factors must be considered when developing the program, since they play such an important role in the person's ability to live in the least restrictive environment possible and to achieve a maximally satisfying means of sexual self-expression. They are at least as important as, and perhaps more important than, basic information on anatomy, physiology, and sexual function.

General and Remedial Education/Counseling

There are two basic components to any adequate sexuality education/ counseling program. The first of these is the provision of general education and counseling that addresses knowledge and skills that the individual with mental retardation or developmental disabilities is seen to need as a result of the assessment process. Much of this component of the program consists of teaching the individual what he or she does not already know—a process of "filling in the gaps" and then helping the individual to integrate the information into a functional pattern of appropriate sexual behavior.

There are many available sources for providing this portion of the program. Parents, caregivers, and community resources such as job coaches, teachers, and supported employment counselors can all become competent in providing basic sexuality education as the information relates to living, learning, and working environments. These people can use emergent situations to create teachable moments during which much information can be learned. Interdisciplinary team members can also participate in this process as they prepare their functional assessments. Sexuality counseling should be provided by individuals trained in mental health counseling and sexuality issues.

The second component of the program is the remediation of problem behavior and activities. Many individuals with mental retardation or developmental disabilities, through lack of appropriate sexuality education and counseling, have developed "poor choices"—avoidance of responsibility, lack of self-control, or sexual self-expression based on incorrect information; unavailability of more appropriate alternatives; or physical or intellectual inability to find other means of satisfying physical desires. These poor choices can lead to personal restrictions within the living environment or transfer to a more restrictive environment, may result in civil or criminal penalties, or may endanger the health or life of the individual. In most cases the services of a professional counselor are required to resolve the situation or at least achieve the best possible compromise.

Words of Warning

It has been my experience that three relatively minor factors can have a major negative impact on the success of any sexuality education/counseling program. In developing any such program, a critical component is communication of the program's content. Failure to assess the client's language and cognitive skills before attempting counseling can lead to failure of the program or loss of interest in that or any similar program, as illustrated by the following case study.

Case Study 2-1

A sexuality educator and a physician arranged to meet with a group of teenage male individuals with mental retardation to provide sexuality education. The physician was very open and at ease with the education process. The session began with the physician drawing real-life diagrams on the chalkboard and writing out the proper terminology for the various parts of the anatomy. The sexuality educator sensed that something was wrong because the men did not seem interested and were paying little attention to what was happening in the session. The men were asked to read the words being written on the chalkboard, and not one person in the group was able to do so. The physician and the educator attempted to regroup and erase the terminology, which helped a bit. Unfortunately, the stage had already been set. The men felt inferior and inadequate and were no longer receptive.

The leaders of a sexuality education group should make it their responsibility to know the learning abilities and cognitive levels of the individuals in the group before the sessions begin so that these kind of errors can be avoided.

Another important point to keep in mind is that individuals with mental retardation or developmental disabilities are often shy when they are suddenly confronted with a situation in which it is all right to talk about something that has always been off limits. They will not ask questions or venture forth verbally. When working with this type of group, it is useful to have two adults leading the group. They can take turns assuming the role of student and teacher in role-playing situations and they can ask some of the questions that the individuals may be too afraid or embarrassed to ask. Once the flow of questions and answers begins, the group members will usually join in, relating their own experiences and asking their own questions.

Finally, when developing a sexuality program it is wise never to assume that a client will benefit by the application of a well-designed existing educational tool.

Case Study 2-2

Jane, Susan, and Lori shared a bedroom together in a residential facility for individuals with mental retardation. Staff requested sexuality education for these three adolescents, who were beginning to show an interest in boys. Jane, Susan, and Lori were brought to the office of a sexuality educator, who methodically resorted to materials obtained from various sources.

The educator selected a test designed to determine exactly what information a person already has about sexuality by means of a series of questions. Typical questions were "Do you know what a vagina is?", "What is sexual intercourse?", "What are sperm?" If the individual being tested does not have the ability to read, the test should be given orally. Since none of the girls could read well, the sexuality educator proceeded to individually administer the test orally to the young women.

On the surface these questions sounded very simple. In reality, to persons like Jane, Susan, or Lori who lived in a residential facility and had no background for familiarity with this terminology, the questions meant nothing. Blank stares or "I don't know" were the consistent answers received. It took about 5 minutes per girl for the sexuality educator to realize that the tool she had chosen was totally inappropriate. At this time the educator put all prepared material aside, approached each girl as an individual, tried to find out what they knew, and proceeded from there. These girls had no accurate information but were willing to learn. A simple chalkboard and colored chalk (see Appendix A) were used to help impart information that would be useful and meaningful to the girls in their environment. Had the sexuality educator been rigid and proceeded with the program chosen from the stack of gathered literature, there would have been immediate failure. Neither Jane, Susan, nor Lori would have benefited.

Even with information gleaned from the assessment as to the client's existing knowledge and cognitive/language skills, the educator/counselor must be prepared to adjust the use of various available materials to fit the individual.

DEVELOPING AN INDIVIDUALIZED PROGRAM: A CASE EXAMPLE

When it is determined that an individual with mental retardation or developmental disabilities is in need of sexuality education and/or counseling, an extensive assessment is conducted in order to develop a program for this purpose. In the development of individualized programs, the IPP team process is the most important part of program planning. During this process, functional assessments should address psychosocial-sexual (PSS) needs, objectives, and recommendations for implementation and carryover. This will ensure that the active treatment process will identify the PSS needs of the individual. The IPP should allow necessary inservice training so that everyone on the individual's team, including his or her family, will be comfortable addressing sexuality issues. The team should decide who the most appropriate instructor would be based on the complexity of the individual's needs. If the team does not have a member who is a specialist in sexuality counseling and it is felt that the individual would profit from such a therapeutic intervention program, the appropriate referral should be made to a community resource. The sexuality counselor will be responsible for developing a treatment plan, including discharge criteria, and he or she will be responsible for communicating this information back to the IPP team. Everyone involved in developing the individual's program should communicate with the specialist to ensure carryover to all environments. The program's effectiveness should be monitored on a regular basis. Modifications to the program should be made whenever necessary.

Many of the components of this process can be seen in the following case example, which is presented in some detail in order to illuminate the complexity of sexuality education/counseling.

Case Study 2-3

Ten-year-old Cecily had two hearing aids, but on occasion she did not wear them, and no one, including the audiologist who prescribed them, was exactly sure if Cecily had a hearing impairment or not. Cecily's single mother had great emotional difficulty with the fact that she had placed her daughter in a residential school for children with hearing impairments. Cecily was able to come home only on weekends, during which time her mother was overprotective. Cecily communicated by means of a computer communication device. She had also been diagnosed as having mental retardation and although her mother had been given this information, she had been unable to accept it. She continued to think of Cecily as a child with a hearing loss. Cecily's mother believed that if someone could just teach Cecily to speak then she would be able to care for Cecily herself at home. She had a fantasy that Cecily would grow up to be like everyone else, to have children and take care of herself and her own children independently.

Cecily's mother was bothered by the fact that Cecily often masturbated and refused to accept that this was normal exploratory behavior. In Cecily's case, it was probably self-stimulatory behavior and could be reduced by teaching more appropriate behavior. One weekend during Cecily's visit home she approached her mother's male friend in a sexual way, indicating that she wanted to have oral sex with him. Horrified, Cecily's mother called the local department of social services, accusing teachers at the school of molesting her daughter and teaching her sexual activity. Since Cecily had multiple handicaps, an interview was sought with a sexuality counselor who was also a speech pathologist. The mother and social worker accompanied Cecily to the evaluation, bringing along hopes that everything could be resolved in one session.

It was a long ride from Cecily's home to the interview site. Upon arrival, Cecily needed dry clothes because she had urinated in her pants. Cecily had not indicated her need for a toilet by any means—verbally, manually, with sign language, or with her computer. It was immediately obvious that she could not even meet her own basic needs, which was very hard for her mother to understand or accept. Once Cecily was comfortable in her dry clothes, the interview began.

The sexuality counselor chose to invite another speech pathologist to conduct the session jointly. The speech pathologist attempted to assess Cecily's auditory abilities, working with the hearing aids and the computer system that Cecily had been taught to use. To further complicate matters, Cecily had brought only one hearing aid with her to the session. An auditory trainer was put on her other ear, but she did not seem to respond better with or without the amplification of one or both hearing aids. The social worker said that Cecily needed the hearing aids; her mother said she did not. It was obvious that peripheral hearing loss was not the only factor to be considered. Cecily was perseverative and echolalic and seemed to be in her own little world. She spoke in short phrases, but they were irrelevant most of the time. Cecily did bring along a small augmentative electronic device, but it was useless since she could not use it to communicate any functional language or information.

The sexuality counselor then conducted an interview using anatomically correct dolls and a colored chalk assessment procedure (see Appendix A). Cecily could not respond to any verbal questions posed by the sexuality counselor. She did play with the anatomically correct dolls, demonstrating the female doll kissing the male doll but indicating no contact between the genital areas of the dolls. Furthermore, Cecily did not demonstrate oral-genital contact. The behavior that Cecily did show led the sexuality counselor to believe that she had some knowledge of the male's penis and the position people use when kissing another individual. It is not possible to determine when or how she gained this information or who had shown her this. Cecily behaved in a way that was disconnected from other people in her environment. If any sexual activity had occurred with an older male or an adult, she was not expressing any present concern or distress about it.

Because of Cecily's verbal limitations, it became obvious that a specific perpetrator could not be identified. Cecily was taught to sign "Stop" and say "No" when someone touched her inappropriately. She was taught to distinguish between appropriate and inappropriate sexual responses. Cecily's mother was advised to consult a physician since Cecily had begun her menses. The sexuality counselor considered Cecily to be at high risk for becoming pregnant if further sexual activity occurred and advised that a physician be consulted for consideration for birth control. This was extremely important since no absolute determination of sexual abuse could be substantiated by physical exam or counseling interview. Cecily's mother was advised to keep her under visual supervision at all times.

These guidelines were difficult for Cecily's mother to accept since she was infantilizing her daughter and at the same time was saying that when Cecily turned 18 years old, she could make a decision about having a baby. This seemed totally unrealistic to the sexuality counselor since Cecily wet her pants twice during the morning of the evaluation. Cecily was not capable of meeting her own needs, and it was obvious that her mother had not dealt with the reality of Cecily's limitations and what they would mean for future independent living and life management skills.

As the session continued, it was obvious that Cecily's mother was feeling distressed, and to the sexuality counselor the distress seemed out of proportion to Cecily's behavior. It became clear to the sexuality counselor that Cecily's mother had never dealt emotionally with the limiting conditions with which Cecily was coping. This situation developed in part because no one had helped Cecily's mother deal with her grief in relation to saying "good-bye" to the fantasy of the child with normal skills she had hoped for and accepting Cecily as the child she had now. Cecily's mother believed that if only Cecily could talk, she would grow up to be like everyone else and be able to have a family, work at a regular job, and live independently.

The sexuality counselor advised Cecily's mother that, hard as it was, she was going to have to accept Cecily's limitations in order to recognize Cecily's strengths and try to work with her in a more effective way.

At this point in the interview, Cecily's mother burst into tears. On a hunch the sexuality counselor asked the mother if she had ever been sexually abused as a child. The mother began to sob and related her own sexual abuse as a child, which she had never shared with anyone. Cecily was taken out of the room while the therapist talked with her mother about the mother's abuse and her feelings about it. It was evident that the mother's own childhood experiences had caused her to overreact to Cecily's emerging sexuality and experimentation. No one could be sure whether inappropriate or abusive sexual contact had occurred with Cecily; however, there was no physical evidence of sexual abuse in the physician's report and the behavior that Cecily exhibited in the evaluation session could not substantiate sexual abuse.

The next step was to find support systems for Cecily and her mother. The social worker who attended the session assisted in directing both of them to resources in the community. For Cecily, this included a very intensive speech therapy program to see if someone could break through her emotional barriers and "autistic-like" behaviors to help her build a better communication system. More thorough audiological studies were also arranged to determine whether or not Cecily needed auditory amplification. Cecily's mother was referred for counseling from a professional to help her deal with her own problems and learn to relate better to Cecily. It was recommended that, for the time being, Cecily should attend public school and live at home. This recommendation was made both to protect Cecily sexually and to help ease the separation anxiety her mother was experiencing. Furthermore, the sexuality counselor thought that Cecily's mother might deal with Cecily's future more realistically if she lived and coped with her on a daily basis.

The social worker agreed to follow through with recommendations made for changes in Cecily's circumstances. In a follow-up phone call to the social worker, it was determined that no further reports of suspected abuse had been made. Cecily was living at home and attending school in the community. Her mother was dealing more effectively with Cecily.

This case is a good example of how a consultative model can be effective in helping in the case management of a child who needs support. The social worker was aware that she could call the sexuality counselor back for more help or another counseling session if it were needed in the future.

My experience has shown me that often I can find professionals in the community willing to take on the responsibility of the ongoing sexuality education/counseling once I have done the initial assessment and demonstrated techniques that will be useful to the individual. Using this consultative model allows more professionals in the community to become skilled in areas that are not familiar to them. This opens the door to the enhancement of services in the community for individuals with mental retardation or developmental disability.

SEXUALITY COUNSELING IN
RELATION TO LIVING ENVIRONMENTS

Different living environments require adaptation to the limitations of behavior inherent to the situation. There is probably no single overall factor that has a greater influence on sexuality education and counseling than where the individual lives. The sexuality counselor should be aware of and familiar with the different living environments available to the individual with mental retardation or developmental disabilities. The sexuality counselor should then explore the individual's specific needs for education and counseling with the living environment's limitations in mind.

There is a clear correlation between the degree of restrictiveness of a living environment and the restrictions on sexual expression and behavior in that environment. The main point to consider is whether the restrictiveness is in fact detrimental to the individual. To one individual with mental retardation, a residential facility may be the least restrictive environment and offer the most opportunity for socialization and expression of self, including sexuality. To another individual, the natural home or independent living in the community might be the least restrictive environment.

In this section the relative restrictiveness and limitations of the primary types of living environments are discussed. For each of these environments a case study is provided to illustrate typical problems involved in sexuality education/counseling as it relates to enabling the individual to achieve a satisfactory means of sexual self-expression. In each case it is apparent that the crucial factor in this process is assuring a fit between the person's needs and desires, his or her skills and abilities, and the type of behavior that is considered acceptable in the living environment.

Adolescent Living at Home

The family who wishes their adolescent with mental retardation or developmental disability to have sexually fulfilling experiences may have to assume the responsibility of providing or arranging for sexuality education and counseling to that individual. The family can establish the foundations and rules that will allow or disallow certain types of sexual behavior in the home. This information is provided the same way it is for other siblings. It should be remembered that the individual may not always acquire the small nuances of sexuality and sexual responsibility through the usual channels. Each person must be approached and taught individually. Almost any interested party can learn how to fulfill this role. Family members should feel and be open with the individual about sexual behavior and its benefits and consequences, especially in relationship to birth control. If not, a pregnancy may result when that was not the intent of condoning the expression of sexuality.

For the adolescent living at home, the family members may need to do more than just give permission for sexual activity and provide the normal amount of "birds and bees" teaching. They should be ready to obtain support through community interaction for any of the components of sexuality education or counseling that are needed. In some cases the family members may not be comfortable with or adept at teaching the individual about sex and sexuality. In other cases the child's sexual behavior may become aberrant or result in problems for the individual or family. In such cases a consultation with a professional educator/counselor may lead to a solution.

Case Study 2-4

Ira was a prepubescent boy who was referred to a sexuality counselor by his pediatrician. The physician said that he had diagnosed Ira as having Williams syndrome, a rare syndrome with multiple problems that include heart defects, elfin features, a small penis, kidney dysfunction, very severe hyperactivity, and mild mental retardation. Ira required a large measure of supervision in activities of daily living. Because of Ira's kidney problems, he had to be catheterized frequently. As Ira entered puberty, he started to resist having his mother and school nurse use the catheter. This was a problem since he could not complete this process alone.

The physician referred Ira and his family for counseling, hoping that the sexuality counselor would be able to work with Ira's feelings about his emergent puberty and small penis. A total family approach was used in this counseling situation, involving Ira's mother at all sessions, his sister when appropriate, and his father when he was available. The purpose of the family sexuality counseling was to aid the entire family in supporting Ira as he went through the stages of puberty.

The colored chalk approach (see Appendix A) was used to help Ira understand his body and the changes that were happening to him. Ira was dealing with a lot of ridicule from other children. By building his self-esteem in counseling and in the home situation, Ira began to do better in the school and home environments. However, Ira demanded so much attention from his parents that his sister began to feel neglected. Her grades dropped and she became more despondent and withdrawn. Ira's sister was referred to a child psychiatrist for evaluation for depression. The sexuality counselor began working with the school guidance counselor about the needs of both children. Ira's mother responded to the support and improved her parenting skills and increased her assertiveness in getting help from the available systems.

In family counseling, Ira progressed through his adolescent adjustment problems much more easily than would have happened if the family had not been included. In this situation, the pediatrician was to be commended for recognizing the need for sexuality counseling and total family involvement, which he was very supportive of recommending. The physician's involvement enabled the family to pull together and receive a transdisciplinary approach to health care for their children that better met the needs of everyone in the family.

Ira came from a very cooperative family in which both parents were committed to the idea of educating Ira so that he could function independently as he grew up. Later, when Ira developed some inappropriate sexual behaviors in school, both parents worked in counseling and at the school to help Ira learn the appropriate way to interact in new and different environments. This is a good example of good familial support, from the counseling sessions to the home environment and into the school.

However, not all families are capable of being supportive of their adolescent's emerging sexuality. They may be accepting of the individual's right to sexual self-expression but unwilling to allow sexual behavior in the home. When parents are not able or willing to permit such arrangements, there may be a sibling or other extended family member who can offer this support. Possibly, a small mobile home could be placed on family property or a garage converted into an apartment where the individual could live independently but with as much support and supervision as is required. In other cases the family may seek to actively suppress the individual's sexuality. In such instances transferring the individual to another living environment may be a solution, especially if the person is old enough to seek such a transfer on his or her own. Working with an individual living in his or her home environment requires that the person providing the education and counseling be willing to work with the available support systems, including the courts when it is applicable.

Adolescent Living in a Residential Facility

Adolescence is a time of individuation and the exploration of selfhood, including the development of a healthy PSS attitude. For adolescents, living in a residential facility may result in mixed feelings. The individual might indeed want to be separated from the family; however, he or she may have difficulty adapting to the boundaries and rules in a residential facility. Often, where there is significant family dysfunction, the family court system takes over and determines what is in the best interest of the child.

Case Study 2-5

Shawn was an appealing adolescent, and it was hard to believe he had been on the streets as a child prostitute from early in his young life. At the time of sexuality counseling he was a teenager and very sexualized to males from

his experiences in surviving on the street. Shawn displayed flirtatious behaviors that enticed older men, and had approached boys with severe mental retardation who were unable to speak and involved them in sexual
activity.

Shawn could not live with his family in the community because they
provided very poor and inadequate supervision, which had led to Shawn's
prostitution. The courts had sent Shawn to a residential facility. In the facility Shawn received the supervision he needed, but he begged to go back to
his home. The interdisciplinary team kept trying to honor his requests but
to no avail—each time that Shawn went home there were more troubles,
from his staying out all night to his being sexually promiscuous with the
same-sex partners he sought out.

Shawn was bright and could perform at the top of his special education
class, but his sexual behavior made adults reluctant to work with him. This
behavior was complicated by Shawn's desire for same-sex partners and his
total disregard for his vulnerability to the AIDS virus. Added to this sexual
problem was the fact that Shawn was a pathological liar and seemed to take
joy in getting others in trouble when they had not done anything wrong,
especially staff members. Shawn was placed in an adolescent sex offender
group in which the emphasis was on developing moral behavior, developing an empathic, caring response for younger and more vulnerable boys,
and trying to get Shawn to realize the ramifications of his choice of a homosexual life-style in the community, especially with regard to AIDS. Shawn
was very verbal and able to correctly answer any questions that were asked
of him. However, it was doubted that he had internalized the information
at a level that would allow him to make smart choices for himself if he were
in a situation with limited or no supervision. Sexuality and adjustment-to-
life counseling needed to continue.

As Shawn adjusted to his own maturational process, more became evident about his ability to develop good self-esteem that would allow him to
delay gratification, do good things for others, and not victimize others or
allow himself to be victimized. Shawn responded well to behavior modification techniques that were consistent, and he did well with strict supervision. All attempts will be made to help him move to less restrictive environments when he is ready. He will probably move on to a community
living environment when his impulse control is under better self-monitoring and a community placement can be located that could offer him the
monitoring that he requires.

In this example sexuality education information had been successfully imparted; unfortunately, although Shawn could repeat the information back in a concise, appropriate manner, he could not integrate it or
use it to live his life in a safe, responsible manner. Shawn felt that he was
entitled to behave in any way that he wanted to sexually and, as most
teenagers feel, that he was invincible and would never get AIDS, even
though he knew all of the facts about it. The therapist thought the prognosis for Shawn's adjustment to independent community living was poor
based on these factors.

Adult Living at Home and Working in the Community

I am concerned that, as professionals, we do not reach out adequately to adults who live at home and work in the community. It seems we often only interact with these individuals when there is a problem. I envision the time when community programming will address sexuality issues as part of living, learning, and working on a daily basis and not just at the time of crisis intervention. This would create a healthier atmosphere in which the individual with mental retardation or developmental disabilities could be included in programs to develop positive PSS attitudes, beliefs, and behaviors.

Case Study 2-6

Beau, a man with a significant level of mental retardation, had never been given sexuality education and did not know the rules of society regarding sexual behavior. Beau acted in a naive way and felt very innocent. Beau had been living at home with several young nieces and nephews who liked to play with him because he would squat on the floor and play harmlessly at their level, which many adults would not do. Beau was never warned about not playing with strangers' children.

Beau was attending a work activity center at which he acted daily as a helper to an electrician. The electrician took Beau on a service call to a family with a 6-year-old daughter. While the electrician was repairing a washing machine Beau disappeared for a few minutes. The electrician, busy at his work, did not pay attention to Beau's absence. Suddenly, the electrician heard the mother of the child yelling hysterically, "Leave my daughter alone." The electrician went to find out what had happened. The little girl, responding to Beau's interest in talking to her, had invited him into her bedroom to play with her dolls. The mother found them sitting on the floor playing, and the little girl was sitting in Beau's lap. The mother wanted to press charges for child molestation.

This unfortunate situation is not uncommon. What is the answer to problems like this? Since Beau may not be capable of making the judgment independently that he should not play in strange bedrooms with little girls, he must specifically be taught that this behavior is unacceptable and will get him into trouble with the law. Beau should be made aware of the consequences of his behavior. A competent lawyer intervened in this situation, but the damage to all parties was unnecessary in the first place and should and could have been avoided.

Adult Living in a Residential Facility

Because of the lack of privacy and the encumbrance of rules that are restrictive to personal choice and expression, the individual living in a residential facility will usually be in the most restrictive environment with respect to sexual feeling and sexual expressions. The facility may have recreational staff to provide socialization activities and the most possible fun at a social level. However, the facility probably will also have rigid and restrictive rules and regulations regarding sexual expression, especially concerning sexual intercourse.

The least that the facility can do is offer a good overall sexuality education/counseling program that aims to inform all staff members of the sexual needs and rights of persons with mental retardation. Such a program should also explain administrative rules and regulations of the facility to the residents. There should also be a specially designated person trained in sexuality issues to be an available resource for the staff and residents to ensure that the program is being implemented properly.

Case Study 2-7

A group of young adults, 15 men and 8 women, were living together in a coeducational dormitory. All of these individuals had cerebral palsy and lived in a unit in a residential facility for persons with mental retardation. (*Note:* It is difficult to determine if these individuals were properly diagnosed with mental retardation because testing techniques for this population are so poor.) The social skills of this group were quite high, and sexual feelings and urges were developing rapidly. Yet no one had consistently worked with the members of this group over the years to explain much about sexuality education, why they were going through body changes, feelings, and so forth. One of the women had had a hysterectomy and was never told she was sterile. Although she was completely and irreversibly quadriplegic and nonverbal, she had expectations and fantasies that one day she would have a child.

The nurse in charge of the unit contacted a sexuality educator/counselor, who decided that it was time to provide the group with some aggressive and very open sexuality education. The unit's direct care staff were gathered for a preliminary discussion, along with all parents who desired to attend. It was decided to have the nurse and sexuality educator teach the women and men separately at first and then work with them together in a coeducational setting.

The goal was to give information, develop feelings, teach appropriate coping techniques, and show the group some easy, acceptable ways to deal with some of the frustrations that they were encountering. Because of their physical limitations, their living environment was very restrictive with respect to these individuals' exhibiting any sexuality or developing any permanent love relationship. Helping people accept living environment restrictions that currently cannot be changed is one of the goals of a sexuality education/counseling program.

Since the members of the group had multihandicaps, including the need for augmentative/alternative modes of communication, the skill level of the group leaders was very important. In addition, some very skillful role-playing was required. The group leaders had to serve as catalysts and demonstrate many of the concepts with which these individuals were unfamiliar. This technique was accomplished using the support personnel that normally interacted with the group, including psychologists, nurses, recreational therapists, and direct care staff.

At the end of the counseling sessions the coeducational group decided to plan a holiday party at which they would have the opportunity to demonstrate some of the new social behaviors they had been taught. They all assumed the various responsibilities for preparing the party, the entertainment, and the invitation list. It was very successful, with wheelchair dancing and live music. The party helped prove the point that being in a wheelchair does not have to be antithetical to having a good time.

These types of positive socialization experiences are far too scarce for individuals with physical disabilities, with or without some degree of mental retardation. All efforts should be made to open more doors and avenues for these individuals in all environments. In addition, it should be pointed out that the time is fast approaching when most facilities will serve only persons with severe retardation or disability. All other individuals will be able to reside in a less restrictive, more normalized environment. Such living environments are usually more flexible about sexual expression.

Adult Living in Group Home or Supervised Apartment

Group home and supervised apartment living can be either same-sex or coeducational. In both situations the rules and policies concerning sexual behavior must be developed by the administrators and communicated definitively and appropriately to the residents. These homes or apartments are usually heavily staffed 24 hours a day and are supervised living situations. As such, they do not allow for much sexual expression between residents. These homes or apartments are also usually state operated and the residents must therefore comply with any state laws prohibiting sexual intercourse between unmarried persons.

Although there is usually a lack of privacy in group homes, the need for it must be stressed. Masturbation, when done alone in the privacy of the bedroom or bathroom, should be allowed. The group home or supervised apartment house usually has fewer people assigned to one bedroom, thus making privacy for masturbation a little easier to achieve. If masturbation goes against the beliefs of family members, the professional staff should explain the rights of privacy and sexual self-expression the group home upholds for its residents.

Within the group home or supervised apartment itself, all efforts should be made to engage the individuals in appropriate social activities with minimal supervision. This will help the individuals function at a more independent level in the community at a later date. Most group homes and supervised apartments give their residents the opportunity to sign themselves out for specific amounts of time. It is during these time periods that many of these individuals choose to have sexual encounters. When this occurs, the staff should be sure that the individuals have the appropriate information necessary to deal with the emotional and pragmatic aspects of their behavior. If staff are uncomfortable giving out this information, they should refer the individuals to a sexuality educator/ counselor. Community resources, especially in the area of family planning, should also be used by the staff.

Living in a supervised apartment or group home can be beneficial for the individual with mental retardation or developmental disabilities because in this environment someone is available to troubleshoot when problems arise. In relationship to sexuality, this resource person should be aware of community resources for sexuality education/counseling, birth control, family planning, and diagnosis and treatment of sexually transmitted diseases. Ideally, this resource individual is also open and responsive to discussing sexuality, the emergence of feelings about relationships, and communications that support relationships. This person should be able to act as the giver of information concerning basic experiences and feelings in sexuality so that the individuals living in the apartments will have an adequate support system in force.

In setting up this kind of supervised apartment complex or group home, it is beneficial for the supervisor to have some in-service training in the above areas from someone experienced in sexuality and persons with mental retardation. The professional who provides this training could remain as a resource to the supervisor to help with any developing problems.

Case Study 2-8

Kenny, a young man with mental retardation, was born to a mother who was a heavy consumer of alcohol during the pregnancy and had fetal alcohol syndrome. Kenny had been in foster placement since he was young, and had lost his best foster home placement because he was caught sexually molesting a neighbor's 3-year-old girl. As a teenager, Kenny seemed especially interested in young girls and would spend much time watching groups of them (e.g., Brownie troops). Because of this, Kenny required intense supervision at any time young children were around. Kenny exhibited other unacceptable behaviors such as stealing, lying, and running away. He had trouble with cognitive abstract processing and it was difficult for him to recognize when he had done something that was wrong morally. (*Note:* I find it interesting that I often see similar behavior in other teenagers with fetal alcohol syndrome.) Kenny had a great deal of difficulty with impulse control and a need for instant gratification, which are indicators of low self-esteem.

Sexuality counseling for Kenny included working with his teachers and other significant adults in his environment to effect consistency that would help Kenny deal with life in a practical and concrete way. Kenny was con-fronted with all of his inappropriate behaviors and encouraged to learn to make smart choices instead of poor choices. The concept of choice making and helping Kenny accept responsibility for himself while not blaming others were the two focal points in counseling. Kenny made moderate progress, but the sexuality counselor believed that the therapeutic process was going to be quite lengthy and would have to include adults from Kenny's environment as well as peers since, like many teenagers, Kenny responded to peer pressure and input but was "turned off" by adults.

During his counseling sessions, Kenny was allowed to interact with the counselor's therapy dog (see Chapter 3) and showed a very responsible affect with the dog, holding him, petting him, and taking him for walks. Kenny was taught to treat the dog with kindness and respect, and the sexuality counselor role-played with the dog and Kenny to demonstrate how younger children should be treated with kindness, respect, and protection.

It was the opinion of the sexuality counselor that Kenny would always need some type of protective supervision because of his poor judgment skills. Counseling was recommended to be continued regardless of Kenny's living environment. Kenny moved on to live in a supervised apartment where all of his sexuality education and counseling were carried out by professionals in the community system. Kenny needed ongoing support and guidance in sexuality education and counseling in addition to intense supervision to help guarantee his success in this environment. As Kenny grows, matures, and develops different needs and desires, they will have to be dealt with by those working with him on a daily basis. Kenny's sexual knowledge and sexual preferences must be dealt with in relation to his adaptive living skills and social behavior. He will need to receive as much supervision and intervention as possible to help him adjust to the freer environment in which he currently lives. Any inappropriate sexual behavior on his part would make it difficult for Kenny to remain in this supervised apartment.

Adult in a Boarding Home

Many persons with mental retardation or developmental disabilities have the desire and ability to live alone or with a partner, as long as there is minimal supervision available. A boarding home run by someone who will offer minimal support in the areas of counseling, financial affairs, use of community resources, and compliance with appropriate behavior and social standards for the community will make it easier for certain individuals to live in this situation.

The rules and restrictions that exist in the boarding home should be made clear to all residents so that they can best adjust themselves to comply. Behavior that is often appropriate to one environment and situation will be inappropriate in another situation. This needs to be defined clearly and communicated to the individual in the boarding home.

Many boarding homes will not have curfews stating when the boarders must return at night. Although the boarder may not be able to enter-tain someone of the opposite sex at the boarding home, living in this less restrictive environment does provide the opportunity to choose the time for returning. In turn, this allows visits to other persons' private homes or explorations of community facilities for a sexual experience. By living in a boarding home, there can be supervision for some of the basic daily needs and a great deal of freedom to explore sexuality within the community, even though the boarding home itself might be restrictive.

Many boarding homes are not coeducational; however, this possibility does exist. If it is possible for a couple to live together, the individuals must be properly prepared by family, caregivers, or counselors to live with someone of the opposite sex and to accept the responsibilities that accompany this type of relationship. This situation might also present opportunities for homosexual relationships, but these individuals must be informed of community responses to this type of relationship and the consequences imposed by society when one makes this choice.

Case Study 2-9

Julie, a 30-year-old woman with Down syndrome, was referred for sexuality education by a court order. Staff members and professionals at the boarding home where Julie lived had wrongly assumed that Julie was asexual. The adults close to Julie were shocked when she showed an interest in sex and began soliciting the favors of men in the community and at the boarding home. To complicate matters, Julie often spent time on the weekends with her mother, who was also diagnosed as having mental retardation. Julie's mother had spent a great deal of her life in an institution but now lived in an apartment. She exhibited poor coping skills and had little knowledge of how to parent. Because of problems with these family circumstances, Julie was in family court. The judge was uncertain of what sexual information and protection had been given to Julie so he ordered that she and her mother attend sexuality education classes together.

Once the sexuality educator began the sessions with Julie and her mother, it became obvious that there was something very wrong in the relationship. Julie readily told of her sexual activity with males in the boarding home and in the community. When the sexuality educator was relaying information about developing friendships instead of sexual encounters, safer sex, birth control, masturbation, and so forth, Julie blurted out that her mother "sucked on her titties" and "it felt good." Julie's mother started screaming at Julie that she would never allow Julie to come home again if she did not stop lying. Julie started crying as her mother loudly denied the vivid and realistic descriptions that Julie gave of the sexual activity between her mother and herself. The mother did everything in her power to intimidate Julie so that she would stop talking.

At this point the sexuality educator lost control of the session. A social worker was contacted who returned Julie to her boarding home in a private vehicle. Julie's mother was still so out of control that it required security personnel to transport her home to her apartment. As required by law, adult protective services was notified. A social worker assured the family court that any further visits with the mother would be supervised and guaranteed that Julie would continue to receive treatment at a community facility that dealt with sexual abuse.

The mother's defense was that she was just teaching Julie what not to do with other people. It was clear that Julie's mother had been sexually abused when she was living in the institution; no one had protected her as a child. Julie's mother readily told of her own abuse when given the opportunity. (*Note:* People who have been abused as children often grow up to victimize others. This cycle can and must be broken.) Through community resources, Julie and her mother are continuing to receive counseling. Visits are being supervised by social services and the family court. Julie's mother is learning to parent in a nonabusive way, and Julie is responding without fear of harm. Julie and her mother are learning to communicate in a positive way. It is anticipated that unsupervised visits will soon be approved.

Often, professionals do not believe individuals with mental retardation or developmental disabilities when they talk about sexual abuse. This sexuality educator was in a unique position since both Julie and her mother were attending the sexuality session in the same room. If they had not been together the confrontation would probably not have taken place, and Julie would not have received appropriate treatment or supervision. The intent of the counseling provided subsequently was not to keep Julie away from her mother, because they did have a loving, bonded relationship; rather, the purpose was to teach both of them appropriate and inappropriate sexual conduct and to ensure that Julie would have access to therapeutic systems that could help and support her in dealing with the victimization that she had experienced.

Julie had many of the social skills necessary to live in a boarding home. However, her PSS skills were very underdeveloped and did not generalize to her being able to live a positive and healthy PSS life. Julie needed ongoing sexuality education and counseling and monitoring of her relationships with others to make sure that she ended up in relationships that were helpful to her instead of abusive or harmful. Julie's behavior had confused many people because she seemed so well socialized. Julie is a good example of an individual who has learned good social skills but is doing very poorly in the PSS dimension. With proper teaching and support, Julie can learn much more age-appropriate and safe, nonabusive ways to express herself sexually.

Adult Living Independently in the Community

Many individuals with mental retardation or developmental disabilities consider the least restrictive environment to be living independently in the community. In preparation for this move, parents and caregivers emphasize budgeting, food shopping and preparation, nutritional counseling, dangerous situations, and how to get help when needed. However, few take the time and energy to prepare the young adult with mental retardation or developmental disabilities to live sexually in the community. The community is an environment in which casual sex is accepted and sexually transmitted diseases are prevalent. Individuals with mental retardation or developmental disabilities are prey to prostitutes and pimps, both heterosexual and homosexual.

Appropriate knowledge about birth control, condoms, "safer sex," and family planning clinics is as important as knowing where to go when injured. Someone must address this need for knowledge, introduce the person to the appropriate community facilities, and offer follow-up services. If this information is provided, it is more realistic to expect individuals with mental retardation or developmental disabilities to make the transition successfully to independent living in the community.

The reality is that there are probably thousands of people already living and coping in the community who would score within the range of mental retardation if tested. If this is so, then individuals who have been identified by professionals as being persons with mental retardation, but who have had the benefit of proper preparation, should also be capable of living in the community. Perhaps, once there is recognition of the true abilities of individuals with mental retardation or developmental disabilities to function and to cope in a sexual way, there will be more acceptance for their being able to live independently in the community.

Case Study 2-10

Zachary was living successfully in the community, working at a good job that afforded him enough money to live independently in an apartment. He also had a girlfriend. One night when Zachary's girlfriend said that she did not want sex, Zachary decided that he wanted it anyway and he committed date rape. She reported it to the police and Zachary found himself in a lot of trouble. It was then discovered that Zachary had had a great deal of previous trouble with indecent exposure and public masturbation, as well as some "Peeping Tom" behavior, for which he had not received treatment. In addition, Zachary was resisting the orders of his physician and choosing to drink while taking a medication with which drinking is contraindicated.

A community group of professionals and staff decided that Zachary was in need of residential treatment until he could learn to behave appropriately sexually and follow doctor's orders in relation to taking his medications appropriately. Zachary had all of the necessary skills to live independently but was not choosing to behave in a way that the community would tolerate, so he lost his opportunity to remain in the community until he gained more control over himself.

Counseling focused on helping Zachary develop the skills and behaviors necessary for successful community placement. Zachary was encouraged to masturbate in private and was advised to have sex only with willing adult partners and never to expose his genitals in public. At a cognitive level Zachary was cooperative, but he did have trouble integrating the material at an abstract level, which made him a high risk for independent living at that time. Zachary received ongoing monitoring through a sex offender counseling group. A consultant psychiatrist diagnosed Zachary as having an antisocial personality disorder and needing constant supervision. The prognosis for independent living in the community was poor because of Zachary's aberrant and antisocial behaviors.

It is hoped that Zachary will soon be able to leave institutional placement and go to a group home with a smaller number of people. In the past, Zachary had not liked that placement and had run away. The only arrangement he wanted was to live independently. However, Zachary had shown that he could not handle being without any supervision, so it was a real dilemma with no easy answers or solutions. Therapeutic intervention and counseling were recommended to continue for Zachary regardless of his placement.

Zachary was able to live independently in the community until he broke community rules regarding sexual behavior. When Zachary was returned to a residential facility to get further counseling and learn more self-control, his interdisciplinary team tried to determine whether he could learn to behave in a way that would allow him to go back to living independently in the community. Considering Zachary's success at work and general abilities in living in the community, his team was disappointed that he could not manage the transition in all areas, specifically sexual ones. Zachary has had to make a commitment to follow sexual rules in the community before he is given the chance to live independently again.

ISSUES IN SEXUALITY AND THE LIVING ENVIRONMENT

Making Living Arrangement Choices

Test results and analyses of behavior by professionals and counselors familiar with an individual with mental retardation or developmental disabilities should give a fairly accurate picture of the individual's chances for success in any particular living environment. There are no guarantees, but the acquisition of appropriate adaptive behavior skills will increase the likelihood of success in certain living situations. Permission to make one's own choice of living situation is another matter.

Some individuals with mental retardation or developmental disabilities should certainly be able to actively participate in the choice of a living environment. These individuals also should be able to hire an advocate to help in a fight in the court system if family members and professionals try to take the right of choice away from them. Others with appropriate communication skills should be able to adequately survive in a well-supervised group home or halfway house where there is sufficient teaching and support. These individuals should be given the chance to actively participate in the decision to move to another environment. Possibly, the choice can best be made by giving the individual the opportunity to spend several weekends and vacations in the new environment. These visits will let professionals have a better chance to measure and assess coping skills for dealing with the new environment before the actual move is made.

Each person should be assessed and counseled as individually as possible in a clinical and therapeutic sense. Decisions about living arrangements need to be individualized ones. It should be emphasized that a person can move from one environment to another, finding the place that is most comfortable in which to live and function. Flexibility on the part of the professional ensures protection of the individual's rights.

If the individual has been adjudicated incompetent by the court system or if he or she is not of legal age in that particular state, then he or she does not have the right to make his or her own decisions about living arrangements. The family or staff would have to petition the state through the court system to prove competency before the individual could obtain that right. In addition, new regulations for intermediate care facilities and the federal rights to privacy enable advocates and family members, along with people with mental retardation, to challenge laws restricting living environments as unconstitutional. If the case is taken to court by a competent lawyer, the individual will stand a good chance of achieving his or her goal of being allowed to make the choices that are his or her inherent rights.

The challenge remains with professionals, counselors, and families to help the individual recognize the need to adhere to the rules of a specific society until he or she can change the rules. In the meantime, the individual with mental retardation or developmental disabilities can be helped to develop the adaptive behavior required to live in less restrictive environments. This will enable the person to have more choices about where he or she is going to live and function in the future.

Coeducational Living Environments

Coeducational living environments should be an alternative that is readily available to individuals with mental retardation or developmental disabilities. This will only work with a staff and community that will be able to deal openly with developing sexuality and possible heterosexual and homosexual expressions or relationships among residents of such environments. The staff will have to be willing to channel the energy and sexual interests of the clients in such a way that they exhibit behavior compatible with the societal rules that the residence has adopted regarding such behaviors as masturbation and sexual intercourse. When these efforts are effectively completed, a positive environment can be provided to individuals in a coeducational group home or supervised apartment. It is not necessary for those professionals who feel discomfort with the concept of sexual self-expression to condone overt sexual behavior. There should, however, be a great deal of encouragement for the development of appropriate and meaningful relationships.

There should be no problems in having a coeducational living environment within a society that has rules restricting sexual intercourse. If a couple desired to be sexually active, and this behavior was against the rules of their particular residence, the staff could work toward appropriate movement into a less restrictive environment. The staff members are in a position to make a professional judgment as to whether the couple involved is ready to make a mature and competent decision and able to handle a relationship that includes the emotional and physical aspects of sexual intercourse. It then becomes the responsibility of the staff or others developing the individuals' programs to help the couple find and adjust to an alternate living arrangement that allows this sexual expression. A move to the new residence would occur only after the staff were convinced that the couple could handle the responsibilities.

Double and Triple Standards

Unfortunately, in considering a family home versus a group home versus a residential facility, different standards of allowed and encouraged sexual behavior can be found. This is partly due to puritanical ethics, religious beliefs, and archaic laws that should be challenged or rewritten. A myriad of other factors may also be involved. It is unrealistic to think that the situation will change abruptly. The most effective role to take as an advocate would be to assess whether there is any unconstitutional bias toward individuals with mental retardation or developmental disabilities because of their place of habitat. If there is, the courts should be approached through the advocacy program. Constitutional law and right to privacy should help to eliminate a double or triple standard if one does exist. This will be a slow process but, if never begun, even on the smallest scale, it will surely never be achieved at any level.

Adaptive Behavior and the Living Environment

Are individuals with mental retardation or developmental disabilities able to change their behavior to accommodate rules that change from one environment to another? As has been stated in this book and many others, the area of adaptive behavior is one in which persons with mental retardation have significant difficulty. In fact, such difficulties are one of the reasons for the diagnosis of mental retardation. Therefore, an assessment must be done to determine if the individual has the ability to develop the necessary adaptive behavior required to be successful in a less restrictive living environment. This assessment should involve professionals, counselors, family members, and the individual.

When there is doubt, a trial period of adjustment can be offered with the understanding that, if the person is not successful in the less restrictive environment, he or she should be returned to an environment with more supervision. Specific guidelines in regard to sexual behavior should be presented so that the likelihood of compliance will be enhanced. This experience should aim at being a positive one, even if it is not successful. With more growth and instruction, other attempts to move to a less restrictive environment can be made later.

CONCLUDING REMARKS

Imagination and creativity are the only limitations to exploring, understanding, and developing new and innovative living environments for individuals with mental retardation or developmental disabilities. For responsible choices to be made, responsible options need to be created and be available.

Chapter 3

Fundamentals of Sexuality Education and Counseling

I consider sexuality education as the giving of information and sexuality counseling as the therapeutic process that deals with feelings. Most parents and professionals can easily become comfortable dealing with sexuality education, but it takes special training and experience to participate in sexuality counseling. Usually sexuality education is the first resource to be offered to the individual with mental retardation or developmental disability. Sexuality counseling is called for in cases in which the individual's difficulties in the area of sexuality cause many confusing or unpleasant feelings to surface, resulting in sexual or emotional dysfunction. These feelings may arise as part of the normal developmental process or they may result from a history of abuse. The individual requires the help of a trained counselor to work through these feelings and develop the necessary adaptive or coping mechanisms to remedy his or her situation.

SEXUALITY EDUCATION

I believe that sexuality education begins at birth. As soon as a parent is told "it's a boy" or "it's a girl," he or she begins to project feelings of maleness or femaleness onto the child. Implicit with these feelings is the expectation of certain behaviors. Parents are rarely prepared for the acceptance of their child as a person with mental retardation or developmental disabilities. There is continuous infantilization of the individual, which in itself negates the need for sexuality education in the eyes of the parent or caregiver. Parents need to be helped to understand that all people are sexual and therefore need or are entitled to sexuality education.

If the parent is comfortable with the task, he or she is the best person to begin the sexuality education process, taking it from birth to adulthood. Parents need to be convinced that it is "normal" to ask for help in this process. Assistance can come from many sources, some informal and some formal. Parents and staff can seek out sources of their choice with whom they are comfortable to obtain the assistance they need. They might explore their local churches, synagogues, libraries, departments of education, mental health centers, family planning organizations, and community resources involved in working with persons with mental retardation and developmental disabilities. Again, the most effective approach to take is to use the interdisciplinary team process to ensure that effective programming is accomplished. Formats for providing sexuality education can be as varied as the individuals providing them. This could include the possibility of individual or group work and should explore the use of family therapy. Acceptable locations will vary from a therapist's or counselor's office to a supported work environment, the classroom, and living environments, including homes, community resources, or residential facilities.

The important point to remember is to provide the sexuality education in such a way that it is comprehensible and meaningful to the individual receiving it, regardless of his or her level of intellect. The sexuality education should encompass as much knowledge and information as the individual is able to comprehend and is desirous of receiving.

I feel strongly that sexuality education should be individualized and should attempt to meet the specific needs of the individual receiving it. All professionals and family members should be aware of the content of the program so that they can be part of the carryover process. This will allow an approach to sexuality education as a normal part of life—an entitlement and requirement to be integrated into all living, learning, and working environments as an active treatment mode is used.

When developing sexuality education programs, it is necessary to cover general topics and specific information under each topic. Some basic areas that deserve coverage include:

1. Anatomy and physiology
2. Maturation and body changes
3. Birth control
4. Sexually transmitted diseases and their prevention
5. Masturbation
6. Responsibility for sexual behavior
7. Inappropriate sexual behavior and sex offenses
8. Same-sex and opposite-sex activity
9. Psychosocial-sexual (PSS) aspects of behavior and psychosexual (PS) development
10. Marriage and parenthood

These 10 areas are intertwined, and the sexuality educator should cover those areas that apply to the individual. There is no specific need for approaching the presentation in any set, formal way or in any particular order. The material should be presented to best meet the needs of the individual or group. Sexuality education should be an individualized process, and individual learning styles should be respected.

Individualizing Sexuality Education

Sexuality education programs should be individualized to present the information that the specific person requires to function in his or her living, learning, and working environments. The person providing sexuality education for individuals with mental retardation or developmental disabilities should be aware of the relative level of mental retardation and the learning style of the person receiving the education. This should always be kept in mind as the specific program for an individual is developed. Basic information should be imparted at a level that allows the person to comprehend and process it in a meaningful way. It is important for the sexuality educator to be aware of the communication mode and language abilities of the individual in order to adjust the material as necessary.

The various case studies presented in this book provide useful examples of both the need to individualize sexuality education (and counseling) and the methods by which this may be achieved. If the reader examines some of these case histories, he or she can begin to see how the sexuality educator/counselor individualized the information that needed to be given and the counseling that was provided. Some of the details of the process of individualization are emphasized here, using a few case studies as examples.

Teaching the Fundamentals

Case Study 6-1 presents Suzanne and Wanda, adults living at home and participating in a community program. Concerned about the sexual activity of these women, staff at the community program asked for a one-time consultation for sexuality education for them. Knowing that there would only be one opportunity for input, the sexuality educator had to individualize the session so as to present the most useful information for Suzanne and Wanda in the best possible format. The follow-up recommendations were stated very clearly in a written clinical report so that other professionals could implement them as soon as possible. A main element of the counseling session was the need to prevent any possible victimization. This was done by assessing the situation to determine the most important factors necessary for protection and then locating the appropriate persons in the environment who could ensure that these factors were addressed. Information on community resources for birth control and adult protective services was immediately given to the persons responsible for case management. This example highlights the need for the sexuality educator and counselor to be aware of all of the resources available in the community so that proper recommendations and follow-up can be provided.

Shawn, an adolescent living in a residential facility, presented a difficult case for the sexuality educator (Case Study 2-5). He had been a child prostitute, and was very streetwise and highly sexualized. He had developed a preference for same-sex sexual activity, including anal intercourse, which put him at high risk for contracting AIDS. Shawn could repeat back to the educator all of the important warnings about AIDS, but was not heeding them at all. It was obvious that Shawn would require ongoing supervision and counseling until he began to integrate the information on an internal level and developed a desire for safer behavior. Sexuality education alone would not be sufficient.

Incorporating Aspects of Specific Conditions

Ira (Case Study 2-4) was a prepubescent child living at home, entering adolescence with many questions and problems that his family was not prepared to approach. Ira had been diagnosed as having Williams syndrome, which involves physical abnormalities, including a small penis, as well as retardation. One of the major roles of sexuality education and counseling was to deal with Ira's puberty, and how it might be different for him to go through this process given these added components. The community physicians and school were relying on the sexuality educator/counselor to provide all necessary information and counseling to him. These were provided to Ira and to his entire family using a family therapy approach. The effectiveness of the program was enhanced by the involvement and interactions of his family members. Such supportive therapy helped this family deal with the reality of Ira's emergent sexuality.

To work with Kenny (Case Study 2-8), an adult living in a supervised apartment, in an individualized sexuality program, the sexuality educator had to understand the dynamics of fetal alcohol syndrome and also had to have knowledge about how to work with impulse control problems. In this case the sexuality educator also had to develop a program that could deal with adolescents who molested young children. To extinguish a deviant sexual arousal pattern, the sexuality educator must first be able to identify and understand it. Developing an empathic response for the victim(s) is necessary in the counseling of individuals who commit acts of sexual molestation.

Resolving Situations Involving Harmful Sexual Behavior

Working with Dinah (Case Study 5-8), an adult living in a residential facility, in order to provide sexuality education, was a little different.

Dinah had limited verbal skills and severe mental retardation, and was engaging in masturbatory behavior that was harmful. The job of the sexuality educator was to work with the staff members in Dinah's environment to help them create programs and activities that would offer Dinah the chance to express herself physically and engage in more appropriate sexual behavior. In this case, the staff learned to use their resources, such as an aquatics instructor, to offer Dinah the opportunity to have sensual experiences in the context of water play. Such activities allowed her to have alternative self-stimulatory experiences with adequate supervision. The likelihood of Dinah harming herself was significantly reduced. Dinah responded well to the new activities; her behavior calmed down and the inappropriate masturbation decreased. This case is an example of the creativity that the sexuality educator must use in developing meaningful and helpful programs.

As described in Case Study 2-9, developing an individualized program for Julie, an adult living in a boarding home, was similarly problematic because sexual abuse was involved. The sexuality educator acted as a consultant as the result of a court order. Working under these constraints, recommendations for immediate action and further follow-up become the important parameter. Ongoing, in-depth counseling in the community was recommended for Julie. The sexuality educator made follow-up phone calls to community resources to be sure that Julie had shown up for the appointments that were scheduled for her and that she was responding as needed. In this example a sexuality educator/counselor performed the original intake interview to ascertain where the individual could receive help in the community and then made the appropriate referral. This consultation model is the one I use most often, because it helps a larger number of individuals get the services that they need.

Accommodating Alternative Communication Modes

Case Study 3-9, presented later in this chapter, discusses the sexuality education/counseling provided for Joann, who had specific communication needs because of her nonverbal language system. This sexuality education incorporated knowledge from speech-language pathology and augmentative communication systems to develop techniques to work with Joann. The development of a topic language board was most helpful for sessions dealing with sexuality issues.

For Cindy (Case Study 8-1), the situation was similar in that she communicated by means of a computer. However, Cindy was a victim of incest, and the department of social services and the court system were already involved. The sexuality counseling had to be done by someone who had experience working with court cases and also with the regulations of and laws relating to the department of social services, including working with the foster care system. In this case, sexuality education and counseling involved a good deal of advocacy work and transdisciplinary interaction between agencies to provide Cindy the help that she needed.

The effectiveness of combining speech-language pathology services with the sexuality education ensured better follow-through and opened an avenue for the use of augmentative language systems by these two girls as they worked on their sexuality issues.

The variety of these case histories shows that the approaches taken in sexuality education need to be person-specific and that educators need to be creative in their ability to provide for the individual needs of each different person. In all cases documentation should exist to indicate that needs have been recognized, addressed, and dealt with in an individualized manner.

Content Areas in Sexuality Education

Ten broad topics that may need to be covered in a sexuality education program were listed earlier in this chapter. Each of these categories is discussed here, briefly outlining basic information that should be included in developing an appropriate and meaningful program for individuals with mental retardation and developmental disabilities.

Anatomy and Physiology

It may be necessary for the educator to begin with the fundamentals of the human sexual organs and their function. One method for explaining human anatomy and physiology is to use simple drawings of males and females (see Appendix A). Simple drawings using colored chalk will help the individual comprehend and internalize the information presented, and they are an inexpensive and readily available tool. Anatomically correct dolls may also be used for this purpose (see Bibliography and Related Materials for sources of these dolls). Similarities and differences in males and females should be indicated through these drawings. Often, individuals with mental retardation or developmental disabilities will think both sexes are the same. This is a time to clarify differences. Seeing the differences is important, and understanding them is vital.

It is not enough to just teach a person about his or her own sex. It is also important that males understand female anatomy and that females understand male anatomy. Instruction about anatomy and physiology should also stress that every man and every woman has the same body parts, but they may vary in shape, size, and other characteristics. This helps the individual understand the uniqueness of every person. Furthermore, the instructor should teach that the genitals are private body parts and need to be treated as private. The concept of "public" versus "private" is an important issue, and it is best to deal with this topic pragmatically.

Proper medical terminology for the genitals and their functions should be used when providing instruction about anatomy and physiology. The instructor should respond to current street language being used, if any, by trying to change it to appropriate terminology. Parents, teachers, and professionals are often uncomfortable with street language, but using it when necessary is important. In the process, the proper terminology can be taught.

Maturation and Body Changes

When providing education about maturation and body changes, the instruction should refer to anatomy, showing development of the body from birth to maturity. Using simple, color-coded drawings or dolls as previously discussed is helpful when discussing the maturational process. Each individual should learn to relate to his or her own body as it is today, was before, and will be later in life. Helping the individual accept his or her changing body can reduce fears that might exist without such information.

It is also necessary to teach behavior and self-help skills that are necessary for each gender. For example, teach females about menstruation, elimination of body odor, vaginal discharge, and hair growth in the pubic area, under the arms, and on the legs. Explain about wearing appropriate underclothing, such as bras, and explain proper care of the genitals. For males, teach about grooming techniques (e.g., shaving), elimination of body odor, care of genitals, wet dreams, erections (nocturnal and regular), how to clean themselves after wet dreams or masturbation, and purpose for condoms and how to use them. Open discussion about all of these topics is helpful.

The instructor should provide the appropriate necessary information about the opposite sex so that each individual can understand anything he or she may hear or experience. For instance, males should know about menstruation and females should know about condom use. All individuals profit from learning about the opposite sex.

The feelings that accompany maturation and body changes should also be discussed. Sometimes these changes cause uncomfortable feelings, and understanding this reduces anxiety. The individual's responsibility for dealing with these feelings needs to be emphasized. Feelings are not right or wrong; they exist and should be accepted as a part of life. Being responsible for one's feelings is most important.

At this point, the instructor should discuss outlets for sexual feelings, which include masturbation. Most people are comfortable with masturbation as part of the developmental process; it is a normal release of sexual feelings and tensions. Others, however, oppose masturbation based on religious beliefs. These beliefs should be honored by the educator/counselor. For many people, masturbation is a loaded topic that causes many intense feelings to emerge.

Case Study 3-1

Spencer had been blind since birth. Now, in middle age, he found that he was experiencing feelings about his body that he did not understand. He had been having wet dreams and did not know that this was different from urinating in his bed. He felt embarrassed and did not know who to talk to. Spencer had been masturbating for years and did not understand it when some of his caregivers tried to discourage him, because he did not understand how it could be hurting him or anyone else.

Sexuality education had been provided for the other individuals that Spencer lived with, but because he was diagnosed as having mental retardation in addition to being blind, he was not included. Out of frustration on the part of the staff, an appointment was scheduled with a sexuality educator, who saw Spencer privately. This counselor was the first person Spencer had met who could talk to him about his body and what was happening to him without making him feel embarrassed. He gained a lot of information from the session. Spencer asked for a follow-up session, which was provided for him. His anxiety level decreased significantly, his overall attitude and self-esteem improved, and he was much more social and cooperative in his living, working, and social environments. This is an example of how two short counseling sessions can significantly change a person's daily life.

Birth Control

Individuals with mental retardation and developmental disabilities need to be given basic information about conception and contraception. It is important to make sure up-to-date information is given, including a discussion of "safer sex" and the use of nonoxynol-9 spermicide in condoms. The functions of the ovum and sperm must be explained, using simple drawings and colored chalk (see Appendix A) if appropriate. It is important to communicate these functions in a simple way so that they are easily understood (e.g., explaining how a baby is formed and where it grows and develops in the mother's body).

When explaining contraception, be as explicit as possible in showing different forms of birth control for both males and females. Actual birth control devices that are appropriate for this session include condoms, foams, diaphragms, intrauterine devices, and birth control pills. The same simple drawings and colored chalk can be used to give this information in a way that is easily understood. Simple drawings can also be used to discuss sterilization for both males and females as options for birth control.

When discussing methods of contraception, talk about the responsibility of both partners to practice proper birth control. This is a good time to review and emphasize "responsibility for self." Also, emphasize the necessity of both partners being aware of how to use various birth control devices. It should be explained that no birth control method will be effective unless used properly. Specific information on how and when to use the various types of birth control must be given at a level at which the individual can understand it. The educator should also explain where and how to obtain birth control devices in the community. Information on abortion should be provided, but it is important to determine the opinions of the individual's family on that topic and to respect their wishes.

Further discussion on sexuality education in the area of birth control is provided in Chapter 7.

Sexually Transmitted Diseases and Their Prevention

Sexuality education should include discussion of sexually transmitted diseases (STDs) and means to avoid contracting them. Sexually transmitted venereal diseases need to be defined, and different symptoms of the most common ones (syphilis, gonorrhea, herpes, and AIDS) should be explained. Also, such education should describe symptoms that the individual can identify in a partner before having sexual contact, so that the likelihood of contracting a STD is decreased.

Symptoms and signs that may appear on the individual's own body that indicate the need for medical examination should be discussed. If possible, have a nurse or doctor explain what any lesions would look like. Also, talk about what the physical exam by the nurse or doctor will be like. This will help reduce fear that the individual may experience. The discussion should also include information on where and how to get proper medical attention. Be sure the individual is comfortable telling a family member, staff member, or medical person they need medical evaluation and attention.

Arrange visits to various types of health clinics to meet the staff and walk through certain procedures. Discuss the concept of informed consent. Encourage the individual to ask questions and to say, "I don't understand" if he or she is confused.

Another topic that should be included in this discussion is the use of condoms as protection against STDs. The individual should know where and how to purchase them, use them, and dispose of them. This is also the time to discuss "safer sex" and how to practice it. Explain what this means in terms of abstinence, monogamous relationships, and the use of condoms.

Health problems resulting from STDs should be discussed. Stress the importance of seeking immediate treatment. Also, discuss the permanence of death and how STDs can lead to death. Describe methods of treatment once a sexually transmitted disease is diagnosed, if it is a treatable condition. Methods to avoid transmitting an untreatable STD (herpes, AIDS) should also be explained. The reader will find more information on STDs in Chapter 7.

Masturbation

Masturbation is a form of self-stimulation that is focused on the genitals (for a more detailed discussion see Chapter 5). There are many similarities, as well as differences, in the way males and females masturbate. This is also a sensitive issue and the personal and religious feelings of the individual and his or her family should be honored. The instructor should emphasize that masturbation is a private act. The concept of privacy should be discussed in great detail. Discuss appropriate environmental settings for masturbation and explain the difference between "private" and "public" places in any specific environment.

All aspects of masturbation should be discussed, such as mutual masturbation and masturbation as foreplay to sexual intercourse. The fact that masturbation can result in pregnancy should be emphasized. Explain that sperm can enter the vagina when ejaculate is on the hands or near the vagina even though intercourse has not taken place.

Feelings about masturbation should be discussed openly. This includes how to handle one's own feelings effectively as well as the feelings and responses of people in the environment. The individual with mental retardation or developmental disabilities has to become aware that there will be people in his or her environment who might not approve of masturbation. Both positive and negative feelings need to be explored. Help the person to understand that expressing feelings is a "smart choice."

It should be explained how individuals can masturbate in nonharmful ways. Specific and detailed explanations should be provided. Also, examine harmful ways to masturbate. Talk about not using pointed or sharp objects, and discuss the lethal dangers of autoerotic asphyxiation.

Responsibility for Sexual Behavior

Each individual is responsible for his or her own sexuality. This topic in sexuality education can be introduced by asking, "Is everybody sexual?" Explain the meanings of the words "heterosexual," "homosexual," and "asexual." Encourage the individual to recognize that he or she is responsible for himself or herself, and discuss ways that the individual can develop responsibility for his or her sexuality and sexual behavior. Role-playing various situations in which responsibility for the self must be assumed may be helpful.

Appropriate and inappropriate sexual behavior, problem solving regarding sexual encounters, and how to respond to certain feelings in a responsible way should be covered. Emphasize that it is all right to say "no," and demonstrate how to do this verbally, with sign language, or using any other alternative means of communication.

Explain to the individual that he or she must assume the responsibilities that accompany being sexual (e.g., birth control, family planning). Each individual must understand the specific restrictions of his or her living environment and must learn to live within these restrictions. Each individual must also learn responsibility for following society's rules and laws governing sexual behavior in certain environments. Explain how different environments have their own sets of rules. Individuals should be taught to use advocacy programs to challenge and/ or change rules and laws that they believe are unfair or unconstitutional. Individuals with mental retardation or developmental disabilities should be encouraged to use the protection and advocacy programs in their areas.

Inappropriate Sexual Behavior and Sex Offenses

Individuals with mental retardation or developmental disabilities should be provided with specific information about inappropriate sexual behavior and sex offenses. For example, explain the concept of age of consent and how it varies from state to state. (Sexuality educators need to be aware of the laws of the state in which they are practicing and should provide the necessary specific information to their clients.) Appropriate versus inappropriate sexual behavior should be discussed here also, including "public" versus "private" behavior and the specific rules for that individual's living environment.

Behaviors that are considered to be sexual offenses should be explained. Be explicit about child sexual abuse, molestation, incest, rape, and so forth. Explain why such acts are wrong and how they hurt the victims. Describe deviant sexual arousal patterns and explain that sexual offenders commit sex crimes because of them. Present information on moral development and the empathic response to the extent that it can be internalized. The stages of moral development should be explained to certain individuals. Review how an individual moves from a "law and order" stage of moral development to a "spiritual" stage. Try to develop the empathic response that inappropriate sexual behavior and acts of molestation are wrong because they hurt the other person. Work in this area requires the therapist to be very concrete.

The response of the legal system to sexual offenses should be discussed, along with information on the statutes specific to the state in which the individual lives. Describe the consequences of such offenses, including jail and probation. Explain what will happen in jail and review the restrictions an individual lives under when he or she is on probation. Talk about sex offenders and treatment for them (see Chapter 10 for further information on specialized treatment programs involving group counseling using confrontive techniques to work on the deviant sexual arousal pattern).

Taking the opposite perspective, explore how someone becomes a victim. Describe victim behavior and discuss how it can be changed. Teach individuals to avoid victimization by saying "no," pushing away an offender, or getting help. Role-play these situations until it is clear the individual understands and can take protective action.

Case Study 3-2

Henry was a teenager with very overprotective parents who had infantilized him. Since Henry was an individual with severe mental retardation and no language skills, his mother could not see how any sexuality education would be beneficial to him. However, since other males in his living environment were approaching Henry sexually, the sexuality educator thought it was worth a try to attempt to work with Henry. She asked Henry's mother to be present at the session as she role-played with Henry to teach him to push away people who were trying to touch him and to sign "stop" when he was touched inappropriately. The role-play was re-enacted over and over again in many different variations. No one knew if the attempt to teach Henry to avoid victimization had truly worked until one day when the mother called the sexuality educator with good news. She had taken Henry home the past weekend and, during the drive, she had casually touched Henry on the thigh while talking with him. He immediately pushed her hand away and signed "stop," which made her feel that Henry had indeed learned this protective behavior. She now felt much more secure about Henry's safety. Sexuality educators should never assume that any person is incapable of learning to protect himself or herself until all efforts have been made to teach the protective response in the most concrete and positive way.

Same-Sex and Opposite-Sex Activity

The sexuality educator must discuss same-sex and opposite-sex activity with individuals with mental retardation or developmental disabilities. The educator should first differentiate between heterosexual and homosexual behavior and explain how during adolescence this might better be referred to as same-sex or opposite-sex behavior. It should also be explained that in most cases such behavior does not mean that definitive gender preferences and life choices have been made. The individual with mental retardation or developmental disabilities should be encouraged to discover his or her sexual self. This usually involves exploration of same-sex and/or opposite-sex activities, each of which involves different reponsibilities and response patterns. This is a good place to discuss the development of the healthy psychosexual (PS) self and the development of appropriate PSS behavior.

A discussion of same-sex and opposite-sex activities should include the benefits and problems often encountered in such sexual experiences. Be specific about what reactions the individual can expect from community, friends, and family. More importantly, talk about inherent risks from such behavior, especially the risk of contracting AIDS during same-sex activities. Explain how a disease like AIDS can lead to death. Make sure that the individual understands the concept of dying from AIDS and discuss the permanency of death.

The ability of the person to understand and work within existing rules and structures of society should be evaluated. The individual with mental retardation or developmental disabilities needs to understand society's rules in order to be successful in the community.

Aspects of Psychosocial-Sexual (PSS) Behavior and Psychosexual (PS) Development

The PSS aspects of behavior may be a little more difficult for individuals with mental retardation or developmental disabilities to understand. One starting place is a discussion of appropriate and inappropriate behaviors, particularly regarding issues about maturation. Distinguishing between "private" and "public," privacy, and the rights to privacy should be reviewed. For example, the issue of indecent exposure should be explained to the individual. Discuss such things as learning to look for a bathroom in a public place.

The discussion can then shift to topics such as developing good communication, friendships, and nonsexual behavior. Individuals with mental retardation or developmental disabilities need to learn to be a part of the entire community. Explore with them the opportunities for using community resources for recreation. Teach them techniques to ensure productive and meaningful use of leisure time. The individual should be encouraged to develop skills in areas of interest with the resources available in the community.

It should also be explained that relationships should be expressed differently in various environments. Emphasize the importance of determining when sexual behavior should be exhibited and where it is acceptable. Appropriate PSS behavior needs to be explained for different situations, such as parties, dances, or dates. Individuals with mental retardation or developmental disabilities must learn to generalize appropriate behavior to different environments. The entire scope of dating and courtship should be explored. Teach and practice skills in various social situations, including developing friendships and recognizing danger. Role-playing exercises are one way to teach individuals to generalize appropriate behavior. The "dating game" is exciting for young adults, but it can be dangerous. The pros and cons should be outlined and discussed. Explore difficulties encountered in this process.

Individuals with mental retardation or developmental disabilities may have a difficult time understanding the laws about sexual behavior between consenting adults. The counselor should make certain that the individual understands the consequences of involvement with someone who is under the age of legal consent. The different aspects of these consequences, such as police involvement, trials, probation, and jail, should be discussed. Review the laws of the state in which the individual lives, and point out that, in addition to state laws and regulations, communities have different standards of behavior. Discuss the way society controls inappropriate PSS behavior in the community (i.e., consequences of inappropriate behavior).

Societal rules, laws, and expectations should be explained in detail. Explain where and how one can get counseling and help in adjusting to societal demands. More importantly, teach the individual how to recognize the need for help. The use of available community resources should be discussed, and visits to community mental health clinics should be arranged. Teach individuals how to obtain an appointment and how to state their needs.

As the individual with mental retardation or developmental disabilities learns to deal with PSS behavior, he or she will develop a healthier PS self, learning to make responsible and smart choices in all situations.

Finally, individuals with mental retardation often feel ashamed of being labeled "mentally retarded." These feelings should be discussed in order to alleviate them. These individuals should be taught how to respond properly to labeling. I feel it is important to help the person feel like "a person with a disability" instead of "a disabled person."

Marriage and Parenthood

In the 1990s individuals with mental retardation and developmental disabilities are getting married and having families. Unfortunately, many states have laws prohibiting marriages. Discuss the laws concerning marriage with individuals, as well as ways to accept or fight these laws through the courts and advocacy programs. The responsibilities and pragmatics of entering into marriage and/or parenthood (i.e., coping skills, technical skills, financial skills, and resources) should be discussed at length. Many support systems now exist in the community and within families to help the person with the prospect of marriage and/or parenthood. These support systems should be identified and explained to the individuals.

Specific topics that should be discussed include consideration of marriage without parenthood (i.e., sterilization and how/where to have it done). Medical and social agency contacts should be provided when needed. For couples thinking of marrying and starting families, the counselor could suggest experiences in babysitting and living independently for the couple to get an idea of what family life might be like. The couple should also receive teaching to develop the necessary communication skills, skills for running a household, and budgeting skills before marriage. A reality-oriented support structure should be established to help the couple assess what aspects of parenthood and marriage they are ready for and what aspects they need help with, and to set goals for learning about the latter. The individuals should also be made aware that one can be fulfilled (including sexually) and happy without either marriage or parenthood.

SEXUALITY COUNSELING

Sexuality counseling is different from sexuality education in that, in counseling, there is a desire for the development of insight and integration of the material so that the individual's thoughts and feelings are congruent with his or her desire to behave appropriately. When feelings match behavior, there is a higher rate of success in sexual self-expression. The main purpose of providing sexuality counseling for individuals with mental retardation or developmental disabilities is to help them achieve such congruence and thereby assume responsibility for their own sexuality.

    Parents and professionals, on the whole, underestimate the abilities of individuals with mental retardation and developmental disabilities to enter into and profit from this type of counseling session. Sexuality counseling should be explored more frequently to determine if it has something to offer the individual. For example, community mental health centers could incorporate a sexuality counseling program and make it available for individuals with mental retardation or other disabilities living in the community. The reality, however, is that in most communities, if an individual is not living in a residential facility where there are qualified staff to help with sexual problems, there might be difficulty obtaining such counseling in the community because of a lack of resources.

Goals of Sexuality Counseling

A basic assumption of all sexuality counseling is that individuals with mental retardation or developmental disabilities are capable of being responsible for their own bodies, emerging sexuality, and sexual selves. Historically, society has generally not considered individuals with mental retardation as responsible persons and has not expected or demanded responsible sexual behavior from them. However, society has also taken away rights of such individuals to marriage, privacy, and so forth, thereby preventing them from assuming certain roles in which they could demonstrate their capacity to be responsible. It is up to the individual to prove through responsible sexual behavior that he or she is not only entitled to the same rights as others in society but can handle the responsibility inherent in those roles. Therefore, the sexuality counselor can be a most influential person in the lives of individuals with mental retardation or developmental disabilities who are achieving personal sexual responsibility. The sexuality counselor has the perfect opportunity to reinforce the information given in sexuality education and should use this to the best advantage to help the individual achieve maximum growth and understanding of human sexuality.

As with sexuality education, sexuality counseling can be provided either in individual or in group sessions. Group counseling provides the advantages of peer pressure and interaction, which can be powerful forces in helping the individual achieve standards of behavior appropriate for his or her living environment. A successful sexuality counseling group for individuals with mental retardation and developmental disabilities will become a vehicle for developing pleasant and positive, fun-oriented, nonsexual encounters. It is also an open forum where men and women are able to talk freely about their feelings about themselves, each other, their expectations, and how they can help each other achieve these or modify behavior when it is needed. There is no better pressure than peer pressure. The sexuality counselor leading these types of sessions is only a facilitator and giver of information. Role-playing and reenacting the experiences that have been negative help turn them into positive feelings and productive learning experiences.

Whenever possible, the sexuality counselor should help the individual with mental retardation or developmental disabilities live in the least restrictive environment possible. Obviously, this would be an environment in which sexual expression is under fewer restrictions and is better tolerated. Anyone capable of living independently should be encouraged to do so; however, each individual must be responsible for his or her behavior and performance. The sexuality counselor can be an important person in the preparation process for the individual to move into the community on an independent basis and can continue to provide a support program for the individual.

Specifics of Counseling Individuals with Mental Retardation

The sexuality counseling experience is more than just giving information and assuring comprehension. The person providing the sexuality counseling should be experienced both in counseling and in human sexuality, as well as being experienced in counseling individuals with mental retardation or developmental disabilities. The ideal person to provide sexuality counseling is a sex counselor certified by the American Association of Sex Educators, Counselors and Therapists (AASECT). If a certified sex counselor is not available, a licensed social worker, psychiatrist, psychologist, or licensed professional counselor should be able to provide the necessary counseling.

The sexuality counselor should apply personal counseling experience with individuals with average intelligence and can adapt those techniques and procedures used in general counseling in such a way that they are meaningful and comprehensible to the individual with mental retardation. The qualified sexuality counselor need only increase his or her knowledge and understanding of the needs of individuals with mental retardation or developmental disabilities. Once this competency level in the field of mental retardation is obtained, the sexuality counseling program will be well on the way to becoming meaningful and enriching.

The sexuality counselor should also be aware of the procedures and policies of the state and federal government regarding rights to privacy and the interpretation of these rights for specific environments. The sexuality counselor can be effective by involving advocacy programs to ensure that the rights of the individual are not being abused.

Sexuality counseling with individuals with mental retardation usually is done in a verbal mode. However, some individuals are nonverbal or use alternative/augmentative modes of communication, such as sign language, language boards, or prosthetic speech devices. The sexuality counselor should be familiar with the communicative processes needed to provide the sexuality counseling. Speech pathologists on transdisciplinary teams are capable of teaching these modes to other professionals. The assurance that all efforts will be made to receive and interpret his or her message increases the desire of the person to communicate. He or she feels the counselor is trying hard to understand his or her needs.

At this time, all responsible sexuality counseling with the individual should be done in a verbal (or appropriate augmentative/alternative communication) mode using acceptable psychotherapeutic techniques. Any hands-on teaching is taboo and probably will remain so for quite some time. The counselor must always maintain the integrity of professionalism. It is against the ethics of all professional organizations for a counselor or therapist to inappropriately touch any individual. Licensure boards will not tolerate this behavior, and if it occurs and is reported, legal action will be initiated.

Emphasis of Sexuality Counseling Sessions

The sexuality counseling sessions should emphasize bringing feelings to the surface and responding to them as feelings rather than just expanding on information or knowledge that has been acquired. For PSS growth and resolution of sexuality problems to occur, the person must be able to express his or her feelings and function at an emotional level. This can best be achieved once sexuality information is received and processed on a concrete and meaningful level.

An excellent text for the professional who wants to develop his or her skills, or improve proficiency, in sexuality counseling is *Sexuality Counseling: A Training Program* (Schepp, 1986). Although this book is written for use with a population with average intelligence, it provides a good foundation for understanding the sexuality counseling process. In discussing counseling techniques, Schepp emphasized an important point: "The counselor can raise developmental questions directly, may bring up possible consequences of behavior, but must not try to make decisions for the client" (p. 263).

Schepp recommended the following sexuality counseling techniques (p. 263):

1. Assess when and where obstacles to comfortable sexuality occurred.
2. Facilitate reality-based self worth, rather than idealized body images, hypersex, or stereotypes.
3. Pinpoint cultural, sexist, religious, ethnic, or other social pressure which lead to feelings of failure, guilt, or inadequacy and thus difficulties with sexual development.
4. Assist the client to verbalize real motives and fears about his/her changing body or some new aspect of sexuality.
5. Help the client develop perspective and own the pressures which interfere (now or in the past) with comfortable sexual development.
6. Recognize that reasons for developmental sexual problems are important to acknowledge, but are not excuses for discouragement. The counselor can help the client understand the obstacles and then obtain needed information and experiences.
7. In the action phase, develop a clear plan to remedy past developmental lag and deal with present attitudes and behavior.

Schepp warned that:

[T]he major pitfall when a counselor looks at a client from a sexual development viewpoint is the possibility of jumping to unwarranted conclusions. . . . One can think of the needs and concerns usually associated with various life stages as a broad stencil, and use this knowledge to illuminate possible reasons for a client's sexual problems. (p. 264)

Furthermore, Schepp pointed out that:

If a client's cognitive development and learning style are within the usual expectations for chronological age, the counselor has an easier task. But the sexual development of a learning disabled, mentally retarded, or gifted client is likely to be affected by these aspects of development. Here again stereotypes need to be avoided. (p. 260)

She added that "the task for the counselor is to be aware that other aspects of human development may affect sexual development, and to look closely for clues in related areas" (p. 261).

With regard to making progress in counseling, Schepp stated that:

[T]he treatment phase may be fairly condensed if a specific problem is located, clarified, and new behavior shaped which leads to increased pleasure. . . . When many related issues are present, progress obviously must be slower, because behavioral, attitudinal or situational contributing factors, and/or sexual problems rooted in relationship issues can require time to modify. (pp. 329–330)

She concluded that:

Sexual expression can become a problem in so many possible ways that no index or laundry list of symptoms and cures is adequate. . . . Occasionally problems of sexual expression occur which are so deeply rooted in a client's history or self that even the famous clinics and specialists cannot effect a cure. The general counselor needs humility to accept failure or partial improvement on occasion, and to have effective procedures for referral. (p. 330)

Schepp also specifically addressed individuals with disabilities:

Counselors can demystify sexuality for the disabled by encouraging clients to call on strengths which they have used successfully to compensate for loss in other areas of functioning. Exceptions to the usual way of doing things are often required, so the counselor may have to counter rigid sexual rules imposed on the sick or handicapped by others. One of the hardest things is knowing that the disabled have a far higher rate of sexual victimization, and finding ways to communicate that without scaring or over protecting the client. Finally, continuous work needs to be done with the ill/disabled client's self image. As the counselor becomes familiar with the client, the disability can be accepted easily and the unfounded assumption made that the client is confident about himself/herself, too. (p. 368)

Schepp pointed out that successful counseling will stress similarities between people rather than disabilities.

At this point, I would like to present some of my own feelings and premises about sexuality counseling for individuals with mental retardation and developmental disabilities. I perceive sexuality counseling as a more in-depth, ongoing process than sexuality education. The counselor must establish a relationship of rapport with the individual in which growth toward congruence can occur. I define congruence as a cognitive-emotional status in which feelings fit behavior—the individual expresses his or her emotions, has feelings that match his or her statements, and behaves in a manner that corresponds with those feelings and statements. In other words, congruence is when you mean what you say, say what you mean, and do what you say. Achieving this status requires a therapeutic environment and a person (the counselor) to act as the guide.

Counseling is a process of working along a continuum toward congruency. The goals and objectives of counseling are discussed and agreed upon by the counselor and individual entering the counseling process. The discharge criteria are set in much the same way. The counselor discusses with the individual what expectations for behavior are desired before the therapeutic relationship is terminated. This is a fluid system, involving a give-and-take relationship among all of the participants. The clinical notes taken in counseling assist in the setting up and implementation of new goals at any time that the individual and/or the counselor feel a need to make a modification. If a family therapy approach is used, the same tasks are undertaken, but with changes in the family's dynamic system to achieve healthy family functioning being the goal. The measure of the effectiveness of counseling is the degree to which the individual or family feels that new tools have been gained to use in everyday living that increase the likelihood of congruency and comfort with the self in relationship to life.

Counseling the Sex Offender and the Victim

In acts of sexual offense, ongoing sexuality counseling is needed for both the victim and the perpetrator. Several case studies presented in this book are examples of the need for ongoing sexuality counseling. Counseling for the victim of a sexual offense is well illustrated by Case Study 2-9 (Julie) and Case Study 8-1 (Cindy).

When working with the sex offender, long-term intensive counseling is often a necessity, as shown in the history of Timothy later in this chapter (Case Study 3-5). Timothy entered into individual, group, and family sexuality counseling for a period of several years. With the support of his family, his residential facility, and the community, his adjustment to returning to the community seemed realistic. The use of family therapy, as illustrated in Timothy's case history, can greatly improve the chances of success. This is also evident in Case Study 10-2. Neal, who had been charged with child molestation, would have been in jail had the judge not remanded him to a sexuality counseling program. The sexuality counselor involved Neal's elderly parents in the therapeutic process, which helped with supervision and reinforcement of the counseling goals until Neal gained the insight and skills to live independently in the community again.

As illustrated in Case Studies 9-2 (Carl) and 9-3 (Jacob), trying to change fetish behavior is very hard. Using a pure sexuality education approach would not be effective. Such an approach must be joined with a program in sexuality counseling that helps the individual deal with the feelings accompanying the fetish, with the understanding that internal change is necessary for the individual to be able to modify some of the unacceptable behavior.

Final Comments

Communities and many professionals do not seem to be prepared to handle problems of sexual dysfunction among individuals with mental retardation or developmental disabilities because the public has not yet admitted that these individuals are sexual. This is a situation that will be extremely difficult to resolve because of the courts' and parents' tendencies to perpetually infantilize persons with these labels. In addition, some morality groups do not agree with the concept of sexuality counseling for individuals with mental retardation or developmental disabilities. The topic of sexuality is difficult for many people to deal with, and admitting that sexuality counseling should also be provided for individuals with mental retardation or developmental disabilities may be still more difficult.

Historically, these individuals have been thought of as nonsexual or thought to need at most only enough information to understand maturational changes in their bodies. Everyone has ignored the feelings that accompany these changes, whether the individual can verbalize them or not. It will take time to develop the concept of sexuality counseling as a viable tool and effective avenue for individuals with mental retardation and developmental disabilities. The end goal is to help the individual achieve a fuller and more complete life in general, while becoming more responsible sexually at the specific level appropriate for the individual.

FAMILY THERAPY

Family therapy can be a wonderful experience for anyone entering the process. It opens the door to the possibility of growth for all members of the family. It generates a sense of cohesiveness enabling healthy dependency between family members to evolve. Members of the family group easily move to new positions of empowerment and strength. Relationship wounds can be healed. Family members learn to ask for new information and clarification without jumping to conclusions. Appreciations are voiced instead of just complaints. Hopes and wishes are honored and recognized. The puzzles of confusion in communication are unraveled.

Communication is a big issue. Dysfunctional communication is most often exemplified by the individual blaming other members of the family group. It is often easier to blame instead of accept responsibility for one's own feelings. When someone blames, it is easy for the other person to accept the blame or seek to placate the blamer. Such a stance only serves to reinforce the blamer, and the communication becomes circular. Talking in circles is not productive. The role of the therapist is to help redirect family communication so that it is straightforward, ensuring that what each member says is heard and understood by the others. Family members need to learn to listen and speak to each other in "I statements" that are nonblaming.

It is so easy to intellectualize about what is right and wrong and who is right and wrong. However, the reality is that no one has a crystal ball that allows him or her to see into another person's head or heart. To find out what someone else is thinking or feeling, one must ask, not jump to conclusions. It is better for family members to learn to respond to each other with respect and dignity without guessing at or pretending to know what the others are feeling. It is amazing to see how much better a family can function once they learn some of these basic skills.

Family therapy is an excellent tool to use in sexuality counseling with individuals with mental retardation or developmental disabilities. Many relationships and families disintegrate when a child is born with mental retardation or developmental disabilities. All relationships will have stressors; it is important to learn how to deal with the problem. People develop coping strategies and are capable of developing new, innovative, more functional ways to deal with situations if given the proper guidance. This is where family therapy can be beneficial. The role of the counselor is to be the guide to help the group progress toward more functional and loving interactions through which everyone's needs can be recognized and dealt with in a positive way. Family therapy is a process in which there are no easy answers. Hard work usually brings success in developing a better coping mechanism within the family system.

Benefits of Involving Family Members

In family therapy all members of the family are present, including the individual with mental retardation or developmental disabilities. It is also good to involve grandparents or other family members who participate in caring for the individual with mental retardation or developmental disabilities. Often these extended family members have feelings of sadness and grief that they have not been able to deal with and, therefore, they have developed very superficial relationships with each other. Sometimes the therapist is hesitant to invite the whole family because a high level of intense feelings may be generated that might be overwhelming to the therapist and/or individual. It is true that the sessions might be filled with intense feelings, but the opportunity for growth will also be evident.

Case Study 3-3

Steven, a teenager with mental retardation, was the oldest son of a single mother. Steven's mother and grandparents were having trouble controlling him. He was cutting school and acting out in the neighborhood and had been kicked off the school bus. Steven's mother was able to deal with most of this effectively, but as he acted out more, she became further distressed. One day she caught Steven forcing his 8-year-old brother to perform oral sex on him. This sexual act and Steven's general defiance pushed Steven's mother to seek help and to ask for placement in a residential facility. She stated that if she could not get him placed, she would just leave him somewhere because she could not control him and was very scared of where his behavior might lead.

The sexuality counselor entered Steven in an adolescent sex offender group and requested that his mother be present also. The mother did not drive, so Steven's grandfather was recruited to drive them both to the group sessions. The sexuality counselor then decided to include Steven's grandfather in the group also, creating a three-generational support system. His grandfather, his mother, group members, and the sexuality counselor all joined forces to confront Steven and help him learn to be responsible for his choices and his behavior.

Gradually, Steven's denial decreased, he became more compliant, and he learned to respect authority and rules. Steven was placed in a residential facility, and gradually was allowed to make visits home, where he behaved appropriately with his brother and other children. As soon as he was ready, Steven moved to a community group home for school-age individuals, where he made a good adjustment. Steven's mother remarried, so the sexuality counselor worked with Steven's mother and stepfather to make sure they could present a united and consistent front as they parented Steven together. Steven has begun to express himself sexually in a way that is appropriate for a teenager, and no one fears that he will continue to seek out younger children as sources of sexual gratification. It is anticipated that Steven will be able to return to his home to live until he is an adult and is ready for independent living, with minimum supervision.

This case study is a good example of residential living services supporting home placement when it is appropriate. Steven started therapy while living at home. He later entered residential living, participated in group and family therapy, and was moved to a group home with frequent home visits. Steven was no longer able to coerce his younger brother or others into sexual acts as the consequences of these acts became more defined for him.

Family therapy can help the family learn more about parenting and being effective and consistent with discipline, something every child needs regardless of the level of ability or disability. Often when a child is born with a disability the parents feel so much guilt that they overcompensate and the child becomes incorrigible and difficult to handle. Parents need to learn that setting limits and expectations is an important step in helping their child reach his or her fullest potential.

Family therapy can also assist family members in grieving for the loss of the "perfect child" that they had fantasized about. Once this occurs, they can open their hearts to accept and love the child who does exist as a part of the family. Only then are family members able to begin enjoying and appreciating the unique beauty and individuality of the family member who was born with a handicap.

Avoiding "Identified Patients"

The approach taken in family therapy is to look at all family members and their interactions with the individual with mental retardation or developmental disabilities in addition to looking at the interactions between other members of the family. In this way, instead of feeling "sick" and like the "identified patient," the individual can see himself or herself as connected to others who care and are willing to be part of the healing process. This support and inclusion in the family is a powerful therapeutic tool.

Case Study 3-4

Marcelle, a teenager with mental retardation, was adopted when she was a young child. Her adoptive parents felt they were capable of dealing with any issue that might be presented, but they were not prepared for the difficult problems that Marcelle developed regarding sexual issues.

Marcelle had poor hygiene skills and was self-destructive, often picking at her skin until there were sores and showing symptoms of trichotillomania. Marcelle's parents tried placing her in a psychiatric hospital, but that did not help. Of most concern was Marcelle's refusal to defecate, causing severe fecal impaction and leakage of bowel waste onto her clothes. Marcelle refused to wash and care for her clothes, and hid soiled underwear and jeans under her bed.

In the family system, Marcelle had definitely become the identified patient. Her parents were near the end of their ropes and had reconciled themselves to placing Marcelle in an institution, deciding that they had done their best. But, like many parents, Marcelle's parents thought that if they could "just love Marcelle enough," everything would be OK. In a last effort, they contacted a sexuality counselor for help.

The first issue the sexuality counselor discussed was the issue that "love is not enough." By enabling Marcelle to remain the identified patient, her parents were taking away her need to become an active participant and member of the family. Marcelle needed to assume her share of the responsibility, regardless of the fact that she was an individual with mental retardation. A recommendation was made for skilled educators to go into the home on a daily basis to work with Marcelle, teaching her to take care of her body, her clothes, her room, and her elimination problem. The sexuality counselor contacted community resources to help line up the supportive help. The sexuality counselor felt that once Marcelle began to assume some responsibility for her own choices, the family system would change and institutional placement might be avoided.

It was strongly recommended that the family continue in family therapy with a therapist who knows how to work with the issues arising from adoption of a child with mental retardation. Further medical evaluation was recommended to investigate Marcelle's self-abusive behavior in order to determine if she does have trichotillomania and, if so, whether it can be treated. Also, on learning that Marcelle's biological mother was a heavy drinker, the sexuality counselor thought it would be beneficial to evaluate Marcelle for fetal alcohol syndrome, since some of the behaviors Marcelle exhibited might be attributed to that syndrome.

In a family therapy setting, the parents learn better parenting skills relevant to setting boundaries and realistic limits. They are connected to local community resources that can provide follow-up interviews and intervention. The therapist is instrumental in engaging administrative support for the family. However, regardless of the ultimate diagnosis the fact remains that in order for the family to stay intact, further family therapy may be required.

So often a family therapist is reluctant to include the child with mental retardation in the process. It is hoped that this practice will diminish as more trained family therapists realize the value of including the child in the sessions. Giving a parent instructions to take home is not nearly as effective as role-playing actual situations in the therapy session.

Family Therapy with Sex Offenders

Family therapy can be an especially helpful technique with individuals who have committed sex offenses. By bringing in family members, including siblings, parents, and grandparents, an environment of systemic health can be created. The person can be aided in confronting his or her problems within the family support group. This will increase the possibility that there will be acceptance of reality in all environments. Even in a group therapy format, using family members as adjuncts to the base group is also helpful. Family members reach out to others in the group, giving a better sense of balance.

Family members often feel responsibility or guilt when a sexual offense has occurred. By working in the family therapy mode, it is easier to help the total family place blame and responsibility where it belongs, which is with the individual who committed the sexual offense. With the therapist as a guide, the family can help break through the perpetrator's denial. Since they become part of the process, family members are more willing to follow through once they are out of the therapeutic environment. In the case of incest, the perpetrator and the victim should not attend the same therapy sessions until a "clarification" process has occurred with a therapist skilled in this type of intervention with families in which incest has occurred.

Case Study 3-5

Timothy had been accused of molesting young male children who were his relatives. Because Timothy was a teenager with mental retardation, the solicitor's office thought it would be better to send him for counseling rather than to prosecute him. This was a difficult situation because, without the court system to provide leverage, counseling is often not effective. (Among sex offenders, motivation to change is often low and denial is very intense. Leverage from a court is most helpful in breaking through the denial and moving forward in treatment.) An interview with Timothy and his father was set up with a sexuality counselor who was experienced in this area.

Timothy arrived for the appointment with a very belligerent attitude and in total denial that he had done anything wrong to any child. Breaking through the denial required a very direct, confrontive, therapeutic approach. Since there was no judicial leverage in this situation, Timothy's father was engaged in the therapeutic process and in essence became the judge, court, and probation officer. He set the limits for Timothy, telling him he must cooperate or he would have no freedom and that, if necessary, the father would arrange to bring charges and have Timothy sent to jail. Timothy took his father seriously. Timothy's mother was not initially involved because it was very hard for her to acknowledge Timothy's behavior, even when he told her exactly what he did. However, Timothy admitted that he had also sexually molested his younger sister. When Timothy's mother confirmed this with her daughter, she became very angry at Timothy and joined forces with Timothy's father to give a unified front that created even more leverage in the counseling process.

After working with Timothy and his parents in family counseling, it was decided that Timothy would respond well to therapy in a group of adolescent sex offenders. The process used in the group involved integrating the family members into the group so that there would be consistency and follow-through outside the therapy sessions. Timothy's father became a very active participant, acting as a positive and effective role model for all of the young men in the group. Timothy's father supported Timothy in the group for 2½ years, at which time it was felt that Timothy was ready to be discharged from the group.

Timothy had worked on his deviant sexual arousal pattern by using the Relapse Prevention Chart (see Appendix C) and seemed to have developed an understanding of why it was wrong to molest children. Timothy had used force when he molested the male children and he had threatened to hurt his sister when he molested her. During the group sessions, Timothy began to understand that the reason his behavior was wrong was because it hurt his victims, and that he did not have the right to hurt another human being. The development of this empathic response was the first indicator that Timothy's prognosis was improving. This, in addition to Timothy's recognition of authority and willingness to comply with the rules of society, helped him function more independently in society. He began to move toward independent living and gainful employment.

A year after being discharged from the adolescent offender group, Timothy displayed inappropriate sexual behavior with an adult staff member in his living environment. Timothy showed very poor judgment in this situation, indicating that he needed more therapeutic intervention. A counseling session was held with Timothy and his father at which it was decided that Timothy would enter another sex offender group to help give him the support he needed to maintain his ability to make appropriate and positive choices in relationship to his sexual behavior. This time Timothy's father was not required to come. Timothy moved through the denial stage much faster, and he came willingly to the group, working on his behaviors as he strove to move toward more trust from adults and staff. Some of the issues that Timothy dealt with in counseling included the following:

1. Increasing self-esteem
2. Developing positive skills for future independent living
3. Reducing depression and feelings of hopelessness and helplessness
4. Reducing anxiety by increasing coping skills in difficult situations
5. Increasing self-direction and responsibility for self
6. Improving decision-making ability
7. Learning to make appropriate choices in relationship to sexual behavior
8. Continuation of development of accepting moral responsibility for his behavior
9. Solidifying the empathic response so that internal integration can continue to emerge
10. Developing an appropriate sexual arousal pattern to adult females
11. Acknowledgment of necessity of appropriate sexual behavior on the job site

Timothy met most of his goals and made great strides during his participation in this group. He no longer needed his father's presence as an impetus or for leverage. Since Timothy's father and mother had participated so actively in the previous group, the sexuality counselor felt comfortable with the support they were giving Timothy in this situation. Timothy chose to stay in the group longer than required because he felt he was receiving support that enabled him to stay more positively engaged in his job. Timothy got much better at handling minor problems before they became major infractions. Timothy also learned how to reach out to other men in the group, offering them support that came from his own internal growth and success.

As Timothy moves on to other challenges in life, he may want to reenter a sexuality group for booster sessions if he feels he needs the support. Timothy's judgments were still poor at times but he no longer seemed to get sexually aroused by children, and he had become sexually interested in women his own age. As he gains more experience in this appropriate expression of sexuality, Timothy will be even less of a risk to society.

Construction of a Substitute Family

When a biological family is not available for the family therapy process, a therapist can explore developing a "substitute" family from persons in the environment who are meaningful to the individual. This group could include caregivers, professionals, friends, coworkers, or volunteers who interact with the individual on a regular basis. The purpose of this therapeutic group is to create communication routes and bonding that will go with the individual as he or she leaves the therapy environment. These people can help create an environment for growth and exploration that becomes the basis for change and improved functioning. Family therapy usually occurs once a week, and each session is just the catalyst for other relationships to develop and expand at other times. Family therapy, even with a substitute family therapy group, encourages the building and solidifying of other relationships.

Integrating the Interdisciplinary Team

The interdisciplinary team process can be well integrated with family therapy sessions. Clinical reports can be written by the therapist and distributed to all team members so that goals and progress are communicated and follow-through is assured. Team members can report back to the therapist with useful information from the living environment. Support persons from all environments can help the individual generalize his or her learnings in the family therapy sessions, improving his or her chances at becoming integrated within himself or herself and in his or her environment. This interdisciplinary process leads to transdisciplinary action. The family therapist acts as a facilitator in communication, healing, and the forming of new, functional relationships.

Final Comments

There is a lot of literature on the market concerning family therapy and its application to intervention procedures. Books written by Dr. Virginia Satir, one of the founders of family therapy in America, would be valuable for both families and professionals to read. In *Peoplemaking* (1972), Satir discussed the family process and the ability to have a family member learn self-esteem through work within the family system. I encourage the reader who is interested in developing family therapy skills to read this book and any others by Dr. Satir to get a complete understanding of the positive interactions that can occur in family therapy.

In *Peoplemaking*, Satir explained her own personal learning:

> I did not come to this formulation via religion or through the study of philosophy. I
> came to it through a tough, trial-and-error way, trying to help people who had se-

rious life problems. I found that what healed people was getting them to find their hearts, their feeling, their bodies, their brains, which once more brought them to their souls and thus to their humanity. They could then express themselves as whole people, which, in turn, helped them to greater feelings of self-worth, to nurturing relationships and satisfying outcomes. (p. 78)

Dr. Satir was a giant in her field and certainly one of a kind. I studied intensively with her for a month in 1987, and it is my hope that the wonderful principles Dr. Satir taught me will be passed on in the humanistic family therapy that I now provide.

CREATIVITY IN COUNSELING

Developing the Empathic Response in Sex Offenders

In working with people who sexually abused children or adolescent sex offenders, it is important to focus on the development of the empathic response. Some therapists are exploring the use of therapy animals with persons who are receiving mental health counseling. Sometimes, the person has had traumatic life experiences and does not relate well to other people. When this occurs, the person often will be more comfortable with expressing feelings to an animal.

People of all ages are attracted to animals. An animal freely gives nonthreatening and affectionate responses that are truly healing in the therapeutic process. The therapy session becomes a place for an individual to safely practice emotional responses with the therapy animal. Relating to a therapy dog is a good way to express emotion. An animal is accepting and eager to be played with and nurtured and will easily give back the attention that is given to it.

As I developed my skills as a counselor, I decided to explore the use of a therapy dog in my counseling sessions. A Maltese was chosen because of the breed's warm, affectionate personality and because they are content to sit for hours on a person's lap. I agree with great clinicians like Dr. Virginia Satir and Dr. Bernard Segal, who believe that the longest trip anyone ever makes is from their head to their heart. I named the therapy dog "Magic" because, according to Dr. Segal, one of his patients said "When you live in your heart, magic happens." I started using Magic when he was just 6 weeks old and weighed 1½ pounds. I took him everywhere to expose him to many different kinds of people and environments. He adapted well and began adding a dimension to my counseling programs that I had not seen before.

It is fascinating to watch the development of relationships between Magic and the participants in a counseling group. In the beginning, the group participants are not sure how they feel about having this little white puppy running around in their therapy session. However, one by one, the individuals begin to pick Magic up, talk to him, pet him, and interact with him. It is obvious that needs for affection are being met in an appropriate fashion. All individuals in the group eventually warm up to Magic and interact with him. Magic will go from one to the other, relating and bringing smiles and a positive affect that has a positive spin-off for the individuals.

In groups for sex offenders, many members have committed child molestation. These individuals need to learn to accept responsibility for their behavior and their actions. Use of a therapy animal can be especially valuable for such individuals. I have used Magic in sex offender groups for this purpose. For example, a sense of responsibility for others can be built by allowing the group members to take turns taking Magic outside for walks. At times, Magic can be mischievous, and the group partici-pants learn to be tolerant of Magic's behavior and begin to develop a feel-ing for protecting someone who is smaller and relatively fragile. The hope is that learning this protective response can help the individuals learn to behave appropriately with other people in the future. This is im-portant since many of the individuals in therapy are there because of acts of child molestation.

Case Study 3-6

Claude was a young adult man with mental retardation who was par-ticipating in sexuality counseling because he had been demonstrating in-appropriate sexual behavior. He was expressing a great deal of denial of his behavior and was having trouble relating honestly to the therapist. Magic acted like a distractor that helped Claude focus on the topics that he felt were very unpleasant for him to discuss in therapy. He developed his own way of playing with Magic. Claude enjoyed throwing a toy to Magic and having Magic fetch it. When Claude came to therapy sessions, Magic would go over to Claude to let him know that he wanted to play fetch. He was the only person Magic would play fetch with.

It was interesting to watch the relationship develop between Claude and Magic. Claude was not showing good empathic responses for the therapist or members of his living or home environments. With Magic, he had the opportunity to practice caring responses that he could then learn to gener-alize to other persons in his environment.

If a therapy animal is not available, the use of good-quality large animal puppets can be explored. People of all ages respond to puppet play in the therapeutic environment, and this technique can be most suc-cessful. The puppets can be used in much the same way that sexually explicit dolls are used to help an individual act out the experience that he or she is trying to communicate. This is especially useful in working with an individual with mental retardation. Often children can demonstrate what has happened when they do not have the words or skill to tell the adult what has happened. When using puppets in family therapy, all family members participating in the therapy session should have puppets and accept a role. When working with children who have been abused or with adolescents who have abused others, it is good to incorporate any and all techniques to make the child feel comfortable in the environment. This will help break through the denial and enable therapy to be more effective.

Alternative Therapy Modes

Creative therapists use a variety of play therapy techniques to reach the inner feelings of the individual. Using drawings to incorporate art therapy techniques is also valuable. Therapists should keep a supply of tools available for the individual to use in the session. By helping the individual to move from one resource to another, the appropriate therapeutic medium is eventually found.

Therapy rooms need to be inviting, welcoming atmospheres—safe places to explore and process feelings. The use of a therapy animal, puppets, doll families, art supplies, and toys all help create an environment where personal growth can occur. The therapist should be skilled in interacting with the individual in such a way as to employ any of these techniques that are available. Therapists need to be flexible, moving from one medium to another as the need arises. Perhaps an individual will want to role-play with a puppet or draw a picture of feelings. Therapy is a creative process, and there is no limit to creativity. Being creative merely involves using the gifts of knowledge and insight to invite an individual, family, or group into the therapeutic process. Limits of imagination can always be challenged. Therapy is an exciting process—it leads to growth!

DEVELOPING HEALTHY PSS ATTITUDES IN INDIVIDUALS WITH MENTAL RETARDATION

How can healthy PSS attitudes be developed? The first step in this process is making the decision that it is a necessary and appropriate area to approach programmatically. If this basic premise is lacking in the attitude of those counseling and teaching the person to function and live within society, a healthy PSS attitude can never be communicated to the individual.

In the policies and procedures that are established to provide sexuality education/counseling to individuals with mental retardation or developmental disabilities, it ought to be an accepted premise that these individuals, as sexual beings, go through a process of developing a PSS self as part of their ego structure and in response to their social milieu.

Operating from this premise, it is possible to structure the learning process in such a way that the end result is a healthy PSS self. This is an achievable goal, and one that requires community, administrative, and family support.

One might ask at this point, "Why be concerned about PSS attitudes in the first place?" The answer is simple: When an effort is made to establish and develop healthy PSS attitudes, there is a decreased possibility of negative and undesirable sexual behavior developing. Self-esteem will be improved and general ego development will be enhanced. The individual will have a much better opportunity to respond appropriately when encountering community pressures and developing relationships.

PSS attitude development should be the natural outgrowth of any competent sexuality education/counseling program that deals with feelings and development of one's self. Such a program should also teach the basics of body anatomy, birth control, and so forth, because these are survival skills. However, developing positive PSS feelings and attitudes will help in the enrichment of life experiences.

Who is responsible for developing these attitudes? Every person who comes in contact with the individual from birth will influence that person's PSS feelings. Therefore, teaching should be done cooperatively by parents, counselor, and staff. Consistency in philosophy is critical to achieving a positive outcome. If a staff member is enhancing one type of ego development in the PSS area while the family is doing the opposite, the confusion will cause anxiety, will be unproductive, and, in the end, will produce an unhealthy outcome.

Case Study 3-7

In a residential facility, staff were encouraging Arnie to masturbate in order to feel good sexually and to develop positive PSS self-concepts. During a visit home, Arnie's mother found Arnie masturbating and told him that masturbation was bad and wrong and to stop doing it. The result was confusion and a poor self-concept. Arnie was made to feel failure again, along with the inability to please anyone, including himself.

ADAPTING PRINCIPLES AND TECHNIQUES TO ALL INDIVIDUALS

The tenets and principles set forth in this chapter demonstrate an approach to sexuality education and counseling that works for all individuals with mental retardation and developmental disabilities. The language systems employed emphasize clarity, simplicity, and concreteness. These concepts are therefore applicable to all individuals, both children and adults. To be successful, a sexuality education program must see the person as an individual with unique strengths and weaknesses. This person is entitled to appropriate education and counseling regardless of his or her level of disability.

Case Study 3-8

Seth, an adolescent with severe mental retardation and autism, twirled and spun around continuously; he seemed to be in constant motion. Seth was easily overstimulated and had trouble processing verbal information. The staff in his residential facility called a sexuality counselor for assistance in developing a program for Seth, who had begun taking his penis out and putting it in the mouth of any other child he could find, male or female. The staff was most upset and wanted an immediate solution. The solution offered began to take effect within 36 hours, the length of time necessary to extinguish the undesired behavior. Since sign language and total communication (talking while signing) were being used in Seth's living environment, staff members were instructed to do the following. Every time that Seth attempted to have fellatio with another individual with mental retardation, a staff person was to approach the situation and say and sign "Seth, stop; penis in pants." Simultaneously, Seth was to be gently led by the arm into a toilet stall, where he could be alone to do whatever he chose.

This redirection was done to show Seth that the toilet area was an acceptable private place to have his penis out of his pants. When Seth left the toilet stall, the staff person was instructed to say while signing, "Seth, penis in pants; zip your pants," and then lead Seth back to the group. Every time the behavior was exhibited, the staff was to follow-through with the above actions. Keeping the communication simple and restricted to the above phrases, all presented in a total communication mode, and having the staff members always use the same response of removing Seth from the situation and taking him into the bathroom, helped extinguish the oral sex behavior.

The success of this simple technique within the short time period of 36 hours is indicative of how easy it can be to extinguish behavior or to condition incompatible responses, if the staff is well trained in these techniques. Therefore, it is well worth the administrative time to teach these techniques to the staff as extensively as possible, until they are comfortable using them in all areas of the residents' programs.

Children and adults with learning disabilities will need to have information presented to them in a manner that is consistent with their unique way of decoding, processing, and encoding information. This would also hold true for an individual with cerebral palsy or any other physical disability. The individual needs a means to communicate so that the sexuality educator can ensure that the information was received and understood.

Case Study 3-9

Because of a lack of oxygen to her brain at birth, Joann had severe quadriplegia and cerebral palsy. She had limited ability to even sit up in a wheelchair without straps supporting her and she could not speak, which caused her a great deal of frustration. Joann seemed to have so much inside of her that she wanted to say and no way to say it. Thus, her speech pathologist made a lap tray language board for her using a set of Blissymbols, part of the Blissymbolics program.

As Joann reached puberty, she indicated on her board that she wanted to talk about her body. A sexuality educator worked with the speech pathologist to develop a special language board that would help in providing sexuality education. After the board was made, the sexuality educator sat in on the first session with the speech pathologist to assist in communicating the material. When it became evident that Joann was very comfortable with her speech pathologist, who was able to conduct the sexuality education, the sexuality educator quietly left the session. The sexuality educator felt confident that the necessary information was being communicated to and received by Joann.

It was suggested that this special topic language board be used with Joann at any time she indicated that she wished to discuss her body, her developing self, or any questions that she might have about relationships. Because of the lessons the speech pathologist provided, the sexuality educator also felt that Joann was better protected from abusive situations. Joann would not only know how to tell someone if something happened but, by use of the special language board, she could tell another adult exactly *what* had happened. Providing sexuality education to Joann was a means to prevent an abusive situation from developing.

This case study shows why interdisciplinary and transdisciplinary work is so important. The speech pathologist or other professional becomes a great asset to the sexuality educator when information is being given in a system that is unique to each person. If the person is not receiving the information, it usually is the fault of the instructor, not the individual. It must be remembered and emphasized that each child is an individual and, as such, must be approached in his or her own special and meaningful way. The most meaningful sexuality education will be that which is individualized to the needs of the person and which addresses his or her needs in a comprehensible manner. It must also be acceptable to the individual's family and living environment. Therefore, it is good to begin with a general curriculum, but if that curriculum is not individualized, it will be of little use to many individuals and may be rejected.

CONCLUDING REMARKS

Sexuality education and counseling should always emphasize the positive things or skills that individuals with mental retardation or developmental disabilities have that make them feel good about themselves. The feelings of maleness or femaleness and the roles that sexuality usually plays in the development of self should be explored. Many individuals with mental retardation or developmental disabilities see themselves as nonsexual because they have been viewed as nonsexual by their family and by caregivers. People tend to respond as they are treated. If the desired end result is for the person to feel good about his or her emerging sexuality, then all of the technical aspects of sexuality education plus the areas of understanding of feelings that accompany these topics should be taught.

The emphasis in developing a sexuality counseling program should be focused on the fact that, because a person is labeled "mentally retarded," much of society will consider that individual as having no PSS feelings or problems. These individuals need to be helped to understand that they do indeed have these feelings and problems. They should be encouraged to accept them within the scope of their environments, families, and society. Counseling should be provided to help the individuals handle those aspects of their PSS makeup that are poorly developed or causing inner feelings of conflict.

A sexuality educator/counselor should always be willing to explore comfort levels with individual families. By doing so, the family will not reject education and counseling for sexuality issues creating discomfort. The risk involved in giving up one's own dogma is rewarded by the ability to touch more people in a positive way. For example, if a family is strongly opposed to masturbation as a sexual release and does not want to give the individual any information about masturbation, the sexuality educator/counselor must follow the family's wishes. The sexuality educator must assure the family that their belief system will be upheld. In situations like this, it is advisable that the sexuality educator be present to assist the parents when they are imparting to the individual their views about sexuality. During the session, opportunities will arise to help the family discover comfortable ways of discussing uncomfortable information with their family member. A family therapy approach can be used in this type of situation.

Even when working against strong family opposition to any sexuality education, the counselor has some options. For example, the sexuality educator/counselor might note that giving the individual information about sexuality will help protect him or her against unwanted sexual advances and possible sexual abuse. This principle is one all families will want to respond to in counseling. It is often hard for the parents of an individual with a developmental disability to let go and allow the person to grow up. Every child grows up and discovers his or her sexual self, despite the parents' desires to always think of the individual as young and in need of constant protection. Hormones do not seem to realize that they too are expected to be mentally retarded or developmentally disabled. They blossom on schedule in most human beings, regardless of the level of cognitive ability.

The sexuality educator/counselor can help guide the family as well as the individual with mental retardation or developmental disabilities on his or her journey to self-actualization. Every child and adult should be recognized as an individual with an unlimited amount of growth potential. Parents and family members will learn that the individual with a disability is sexual, too, and there is nothing to be feared in providing him or her with sexual knowledge. It is the lack of knowledge that is frightening and that puts individuals at risk. Society needs to realize and acknowledge this sexuality in a positive way. This will enable all individuals to become more fully human.

Chapter 4

Pragmatics for the Educator/Counselor

All people are born sexual, including those individuals classified as having mental retardation and developmental disabilities. They do not learn things as subtly as the person with average intelligence; therefore, education and counseling strategies must sometimes be more specific and different to meet the needs of this population. Although the sexuality education strategy must be different, this does not negate the definite need for the strategy to exist and be developed. The strategy also needs to be effective and meaningful. In this way, the individuals who receive sexuality education and counseling may live their lives to their fullest capacity, regardless of their disability.

ARRANGING TO PROVIDE SEXUALITY EDUCATION/COUNSELING

Who is the most appropriate person or persons to provide sexuality education and counseling to individuals with mental retardation and developmental disabilities? As is true of any child, the most appropriate and easiest learning will take place in the natural environment, usually directed by the caregiving adult in that environment. It therefore stands to reason that the most appropriate person to talk to someone about growing up, body changes, maturation, and sexual feelings is the person closest to the daily life of the individual.

The most effective sexuality education is not done in a classroom or therapy room but rather occurs in the daily interactions between adults and children. Before removing sexuality education to the classroom and a clinical setting, all efforts should be made to explore emerging sexuality within the natural living environment of the individual. Professional counselors can lend support to caregivers and parents so they will be more comfortable with their interactions, information giving, and permission giving to be sexual. If a classroom setting is used—for example, in a residential facility—the caregivers must teach generalization techniques so the knowledge obtained can be useful to the individual in other environments.

Orientation for Caregivers

In discussing with caregivers how to conduct sexuality education with individuals with mental retardation and developmental disabilities, emphasis is placed on the need to start with very basic tenets and move gradually to the more complicated aspects. One way to fail in a sexuality education program for individuals with mental retardation or developmental disabilities is to begin at a level that is cognitively too high for the individual. The programs that are developed should reflect the cognitive, adaptive, learning, and communicative abilities of the individual who is receiving the sexuality education.

Each individual should be assessed for existing knowledge, desire for more knowledge, ability to integrate the desired knowledge, and appropriate ways to present the material that will be meaningful and transferable to real life. For example, a female with severe mental retardation does not need verbal information on tubal ligation. However, this individual and the caregivers in her environment may well need information and techniques to help this adult handle her menses in a nonharmful and sanitary manner. In such a case sexuality education is achieved through a process of program development to meet specific needs.

In contrast, an individual with a milder degree of mental retardation or developmental disabilities, whether male or female, needs specific information about anatomy and physiology, conception, contraception, use of available community resources, sexually transmitted diseases, and marriage and parenthood. The educational process for teaching sexuality to this group will not differ widely from that used with a population with average intelligence. The primary differences are that the process will take longer, will need to be more concrete, and will require a repetitive system of delivery of information.

Who Provides the Education/Counseling?

It is difficult to have just one person who is available and competent to provide the sexuality education/counseling within a particular living environment. Therefore, the experienced sexuality educator/counselor should always attempt to include someone from the individual's daily environment in the sessions. In that way this person can learn how to follow-through on what is being taught. This will also heighten the ability of the other significant people in the individual's environment who will deal with sexuality education on a daily basis.

It has been found that once one or two other significant adults are included in several sexuality education/counseling sessions, two things will happen:

1. These other adults will assume more responsibility for completing the programming without calling the "expert" every time there is a question or a problem.
2. The individual with mental retardation or developmental disabilities will be able to identify another person in the living environment with whom it is all right to discuss problems concerning sexuality and will begin to use this person as a resource.

Sexuality education for individuals with mental retardation and developmental disabilities takes a great deal of creativity and flexibility. Each individual deserves to be treated as an individual with his or her own merits, needs, and abilities. A good educator/counselor will be able to identify an individual's particular traits and work within their context. It should be recognized that there will always be someone in the individual's daily milieu who has more skill at providing the actual sexuality education/counseling than others. This person should be used wisely and effectively. However, the providing of information and counseling about feelings should be consistent within the individual's living environment, no matter who is acting as the provider at any given moment.

The Need for Consistency

The actual instruction in sexuality education can be done by a myriad of people. The instructor can be school faculty, staff, parents, or a combination of any significant adults in the individual's environment. Whether one individual or several provide instruction, an important point to remember is that the same material must be delivered and the same language or communication system used so that the information is consistent and meaningful to the individual receiving it.

An individual with mental retardation or developmental disabilities may go to the person with whom he or she feels most comfortable to glean desired information about sex. This may not always be the person who has been designated to provide sexuality education. Therefore, everyone involved in the individual's daily life ought to be willing and prepared with the proper information if the program is to be successful. Everyone should be aware of the constraints and rules of that individual's living environment and the consequences when rules are not followed, so that consistency will be evident and meaningful.

Consistency is a main ingredient of a good, successful, and productive program. Everyone involved does not have to believe the same way, but everyone has to react the same way about sex and sexual behavior or the program's effectiveness will suffer. Without consistency and support of all responsible adults in the individual's living environment, it will be difficult to develop these concepts and behaviors. Teaching the ethic of responsibility in relationship to sexuality to individuals with mental retardation or developmental disabilities would then be just a fantasy of the caregivers involved.

Promoting Age-Appropriate Behavior

Well-trained sexuality educators/counselors need to establish programs and provide situations in which individuals with mental retardation and developmental disabilities can practice the skills that have been taught and thus develop some age-appropriate socialization behavior that is fun-oriented and interactive, but nonsexual in nature. It is then that a decrease in sexual behavior that is unacceptable in the individuals' living environment may be noticed.

Social behavior and all of its interactive processes, from learning to greet people and developing conversational skills to sharing social experiences, must be discussed and developed. Time should be spent on teaching the individual to have a good time with others in a social milieu that is not sexual in nature. The individual needs to learn how to enjoy same-sex or opposite-sex experiences that are affectionate in nature but do not culminate in sexual intercourse.

As sexuality education is provided, an important factor to communicate to individuals with mental retardation and developmental disabilities is that they have the right to express themselves sexually. There is a need to inform the person of societal biases and any existing laws or rules in the environment in which he or she lives. All of this should be done within the perspective of how to respond to these laws or rules. If there are feelings that these rules are unfair or infringe on the individual's right to express his or her sexuality, there will be a problem. Advocacy services should be made available to these individuals if necessary.

Ensuring Comprehension

Regardless of the content or the focus of sexuality education/counseling, the responsible adult should always use repetition and get feedback from the individual to make sure he or she understands the content and meaning of what has been discussed. The individual with mental retardation or developmental disabilities must be able to apply the material he or she learns to daily living situations or it will be useless.

Individuals with mental retardation and developmental disabilities have been found to respond very positively to role-playing techniques. At first the males and females can role-play separately; then joint role-playing can be utilized, beginning with familiar situations and the behavior observed and generated by those situations, and then moving to role-playing of appropriate versus inappropriate behavior. Such an approach has proven extremely effective in helping the person establish and maintain the concepts of who is responsible and what is appropriate and inappropriate. It is important not to label behaviors as either "good" or "bad," but rather as "appropriate" or "inappropriate" in relationship to the environment in which the individual lives.

Working in an Interdisciplinary Team Context

If an individual is living in a residential facility, the interdisciplinary team will have a meeting each year to develop the Individual Program Plan (IPP) for the following year. It will be the responsibility of this team to perform a functional assessment, identifying whether or not sexuality education and/or counseling would be beneficial. The individual and his or her family should be part of this process. At this time, it is important to ask the individual or the family members if they have a preference as to who provides the sexuality education and counseling.

If the staff or family have access to a certified sex educator/counselor, the appropriate referral should be made. When families are willing to participate, a family therapy approach is meaningful and beneficial. As a family therapist, I prefer working with the family unit of the individual. Sometimes, this means creating a family from those significant people who live in the environment of the individual. The main thing is to involve others in the process so that the sexuality education and counseling continues beyond the sessions provided.

At this point, it is important to stress the difference between sexuality education and sexuality counseling. The education process deals with the giving of information and the counseling process deals with the feelings surrounding the information, integration of information and feelings into the self, and ability to express feelings. Most team and family members can participate in the instruction process, but trained professionals should be the ones handling the counseling.

The interdisciplinary team may not have a person on it who is qualified to deal with either sexuality education or sexuality counseling. If this is the case, the function of the team is to find a consultant to either train one or more team members or to work with the individual himself or herself with or without his or her family. The person providing the sexuality education and counseling needs to be familiar with more than one realm. It is critical that this person be qualified in sexuality education/counseling as well as be knowledgeable in the field of mental retardation. This person can determine what needs to be taught and the most meaningful way to explore the topics with an individual with mental retardation. He or she needs to know how to meet individual needs in the area of

sexuality education and counseling in an up-front, honest way. Unfortunately, there are many who are experts in one or the other of the fields,
but do not know how to combine the two. Also, if the instruction is being
given as part of an organization's program offering, the sexuality education and counseling will have to be congruent with the organizational
procedures, goals, and policies. However, it is important for the provider
to promote rights concurrent with responsibility for self, inclusive of sexual behavior.

For example, promoting the individual's rights is especially important if the individual wants to pursue marriage, which is still illegal in
many states for individuals with mental retardation. (The reader who is
interested in studying this area in depth should refer to Haavik, 1986.) I
believe that the responsibility of the sexuality educator/counselor is to
help the individual decide whether he or she is ready to manage his or
her adult life independently and within the constraints of marriage. If the
answer is yes, then all efforts should be made to assist the individual and
couple in gaining the necessary skills to be successful in this endeavor.

Within the interdisciplinary team process, it is the responsibility of
the team members to advocate for marriage if the individual requests it
and can handle it. The counseling necessary for this process to be successful should include all appropriate support members of the team. Licensed social workers, psychologists, and professional counselors should
be able to join forces with the chaplain and sexuality educator/counselor
to provide the necessary information and guidance. Parents and extended family members should be involved when appropriate and
feasible.

With regard to competency-based evaluation techniques, I believe
that there is a problem in verification. The limitations of these techniques
in relation to sexuality seem to be quite diverse. For example, it is one
thing to know that an individual understands what a condom is, where
to purchase it, and how to use it. It is another thing, indeed, to try to
verify if and when and how consistently the individual uses the condom.
I believe it might be more realistic to assume that there will be inconsis-
tencies in personal reports from individuals with mental retardation and
developmental disabilities regarding their personal sexual practices.
Therefore, I find it personally difficult to sign off on an evaluation form
saying that a certain individual "will now practice 'safer sex' " at a certain level of success. I have found this particular process to have too many
loopholes, leaving a large window of professional responsibility. Instead,
I rely on my own experience of 25 years as a therapist to make clinical
judgments on a very individualized basis as to whether criteria for discharge from counseling have been met.

As a trained therapist, I work from a subjective, clinical perspective, evaluating the psychosocial-sexual (PSS) needs of the individual and providing counseling that is communication based and reality oriented to help the individual reach his or her own human potential in the area of sexuality. I provide clinical, subjective evaluations after counseling in which I describe what was said in the counseling session and delineate further needs for counseling sessions. I seek information from other significant people in the individual's life to see if generalization and carry-over are occurring.

TRAINING PROGRAMS IN SEXUALITY EDUCATION/COUNSELING

Goals of Training Staff and Family Members

The main goal of an in-service training program like the one described in this chapter is not to make sexuality educators or counselors of everyone. It is intended to heighten the level of sensitivity and awareness of sexuality in individuals with mental retardation and developmental disabilities. These individuals will then stand a better chance of being accepted as sexual beings. They will be allowed to explore themselves sexually in acceptable and nonharmful ways. Such training is also given in an effort to establish consistency in the environment so that all adults are communicating with and behaving in a similar way toward the person, providing reinforcement of the information and a sense of security. A big step in training programs is developing a comfort level among staff and family members so that individuals with mental retardation or developmental disabilities will be given proper information, be allowed to explore appropriately, and not be punished for being sexual.

A great deal of desensitization and general awareness of one's own sexuality will be developed during the training sessions. It is only when persons become comfortable with their own sexuality that they can be most effective in helping individuals with mental retardation, developmental disabilities, or anyone else. This fact should be emphasized to the trainees so that they will be more receptive to the training content and profit from the information given during the in-service training sessions. Some participants have difficulty with sexual content of the material because of strong religious or cultural training. For example, opposition to masturbation on such grounds can cause conflicts within the staff members or between staff and family members if the individual they will educate or counsel is living in an environment where masturbation is encouraged as a sexual outlet.

Desensitization to street language is an important part of training. The person providing the in-service program must help the trainees detach such words as "fuck," "screw," "cunt," and "prick" from personal meanings and connotations. The trainees must become comfortable with hearing such language because this language is often used by individuals with mental retardation without awareness of its "shock value" or offensiveness.

In training workshops, it is also important for the participants to realize that their own knowledge of sexuality is influenced by their personal biases, past education, and experiences. For example, in providing sexuality education, it is important to explain the possibility that a woman can become pregnant through heavy petting without having sexual intercourse. If a man is masturbating and ejaculates and gets the semen on his hand and then touches the woman's vagina, the sperm can enter the woman's body. It is amazing how many adults believe that if you do not have sexual intercourse, you cannot get pregnant. Does this sound like basic information? It is surprising how ignorant of the facts some adults are and how much fantasy, myth, and imagination exist about the topic of human sexuality.

Most people did not have the good fortune to learn about themselves sexually through a responsible adult providing appropriate information and counseling. Most people at some time in their lives are given accurate information concerning such things as the trip of the egg down the Fallopian tubes. However, feelings are not often discussed. In-service training sessions can help accomplish some of this sexual development and shaping of attitudes that make people more capable and desirous of dealing with sexuality in individuals with mental retardation and developmental disabilities.

If given the proper guidance and information, many adults can put aside their own prejudices and feelings to help individuals with mental retardation or developmental disabilities cope with their sexuality. However, in an institutional setting, success will only come when the facility director and administration are directly involved and supportive, even participating in the in-service training sessions. The most important support that can come from the administration is requiring every person, from the groundskeeper to the physician, to attend and participate in the sessions.

The person providing training should be very aware of the policies and procedures of the administration of a facility whose staff members are receiving training. Providing sexuality education/counseling without administrative support can make a staff member's life very difficult. If a person is functioning under certain policies and does not agree with them, this should be resolved at an administrative level before proceeding. It is difficult for a program to succeed without administrative support. With it, the sky is the limit.

Use of Videotaped Training Sessions

An effective method for utilizing a consultant for staff training is to have that person's training program put on videotapes. In this way, the material presented in the training sessions is always available for reference and in discussion afterward, with the added benefit of having the material presented consistently when repeated. In my early work in sexuality education in the 1970s I was part of a team that developed a videotape training program that I have used in the past in training staff and parents of individuals in a residential setting. I also currently provide in-service training workshops that include the exploration of multimedia resources that can be used to meet the specific needs of the environment (see Appendix F).

If videotapes are to be used, four training sessions are proposed. It is suggested that the training sessions be 1 hour long, but the videotape should be a maximum of 30 minutes long. The remaining 30 minutes of each session should be left for discussion, role-playing, or other activities. A pre- and post- attitudinal test on sexuality and individuals with mental retardation can be developed and administered to determine if there is effective communication and growth in personal awareness during the training sessions.

In the ideal situation, every staff person in a residential facility is required to go through the 4 hours of training. (This total staff participation requirement is based on the premise that sexuality issues may be encountered on a daily basis by everyone who comes into contact with individuals with mental retardation.) If it is a 24-hour residential facility, the program is presented to all three shifts of workers. The training session can run 4 hours consecutively. This is a very heavy dose of sexuality training but sometimes it is the most efficient way to deliver the material, especially if the lecturer is from out of town. One or two hours per day is preferable since the trainees then have at least a day in between sessions to assimilate the information presented.

Suggested topics for the tapes are as follows:

Tape 1:   Overview of sexuality with individuals with mental retardation or developmental disabilities, anatomy and physiology.

Tape 2:   Birth control for individuals with mental retardation or developmental disabilities.

Tape 3A: Masturbation, wet dreams, fantasies, sexually transmitted diseases, dating procedures, use of condoms and safer sex, heterosexuality and homosexuality.

Tape 3B: Sex crimes, treatment for sex offenders who are individuals with mental retardation or developmental disabilities, incest.

Tape 4:   Marriage and parenthood for individuals with mental retardation or developmental disabilities.

The ingredient to success in this type of audiovisual training program is to have a dynamic and qualified trainer who can initiate group
discussions and include the audience in role-playing at the conclusion of
the tapes. Even if the tape material appears sterile or too low-key to
some, the trainees can be involved through a group interactive process in
the discussions following the tapes. The tapes can be effectively used with
small or large groups as long as there is at least one television set for every
30 people in the audience.

Ways to Obtain Training

There are many ways to obtain training in sexuality education and counseling. I believe that attending workshops with individual and group
training is the best and most pragmatic way. When that is not possible,
reading and studying different theories and programs is very helpful.
There are many recognized experts and programs available on the national and local level. The person wanting to learn this information
should begin with local resources, including libraries and bibliographies
such as the one in this book. Sometimes, a new professional entering the
field of sexuality education and counseling will want to read as many
different viewpoints and thoughts as possible before formulating his or
her own set of perceptions from which to begin functioning.

Training methods will vary with the person providing the training.
This is to be expected. Especially in the area of sexuality, providers tend to
find a method that is comfortable for and congruent with their personal
style and the material they will be presenting. Some providers, myself
included, will only present their original work, modifying it to meet the
needs of the group or individual as the training develops. One of the specific skills that I bring to training is my intuitiveness and ability to problem solve and come up with creative solutions. In my workshops, individuals coming for training are encouraged to bring their difficult cases
and problems to present them for group analysis and suggestions for
remediation during the workshop. This is a process that is often helpful
in unsticking a professional who feels he or she cannot move on at that
time.

I believe that the ability to be open and knowledgeable about sexuality far outweighs having a specific curriculum that covers topics in a
step-by-step approach. Other types of training will present the information as the most important part and will have specific steps to do at specific times, and so forth. The Bibliography and Related Materials found at

the end of this book list many such resources. If this is the style that better suits the reader, this author would encourage in-depth study of these programs so that the reader can find one that feels right for him or her.

Toward the goal of instructor competency, I provide workshops throughout the world in which I take large groups of parents and professionals through a full day of lecture, videotapes, and role-playing, all based on the premise that instructing someone to do sexuality work is a process, not a question-and-answer session. By going through the process, the participants become more comfortable with their own sexuality, and the sexuality needs of persons with mental retardation and developmental disabilities. They come to recognize the need for learning to go through the process of giving information and dealing with feelings in a realistic, reality oriented, pragmatic way that deals specifically with the parameters of the environment in which the individual resides, works, or learns. Appendix E has a full outline of what is covered in an all-day workshop with this author.

Important Considerations in Sexuality Education/Counseling

Whether videotapes are used as a vehicle for in-service training or not, there are four important considerations when providing sexuality education with individuals with mental retardation and developmental disabilities. These considerations must be covered in the staff, faculty, or parent training sessions before the material is presented in the actual sexuality education program with individuals with mental retardation and developmental disabilities. Kempton (1979) described these considerations as follows:

1. Sex education involves relationships: how we feel about ourselves in relationship to family, friends, lovers, spouses, etc., and how we act according to these feelings.
2. Sexuality education means learning the physiology of the human body, the respective male and female roles in human reproduction, and the activity involved.
3. Sexuality education consists of the understanding of (erotic) sexual impulses or body feelings and how they are aroused and controlled.
4. Feelings must be differentiated from information.

In her many publications, Winifred Kempton, one of the forerunners of sexuality issues for individuals with mental retardation and developmental disabilities, developed many techniques and procedures that are effective in sexuality education/counseling. Interested readers may refer to the Bibliography and Related Materials found at the end of this book for citations of other of Kempton's works.

MATERIALS, RESOURCES, AND TECHNIQUES

Materials and Resources

People who are trained in sexuality education/counseling with populations with average intelligence, but have limited experience with individuals with mental retardation, must recognize the need for extreme concreteness of language when working with the latter individuals. Abstraction in language ability develops slowly and sometimes not at all. Materials developed and used should emphasize low-level language and augmentative/alternative communication modes where applicable (e.g., sign language, language boards, picture boards, Blissymbols, prosthetic speech devices). If pictures are used, they should be clear, concise drawings, easily explained and color coded for explicitness (see Appendix A).

I believe it is the job of the therapist to create materials that are concrete, specific, and capable of enabling the individual to visualize, conceptualize, and internalize behaviors in the therapeutic process. In the appendices, the reader will find examples of an Anger Ladder (Appendix D), Happy Steps (Appendix D), and Relapse Prevention Chart (Appendix C). These are examples of tools that I have developed in therapy that work for me as I take individuals and families through the process of change and growth. The ultimate goal of using these tools is to assist the individual in gaining more self-control, self-actualization, and congruency. Therapeutic materials need to be developed in such a way that they can meet the individualized needs of the person in therapy. The reader should explore ways that he or she can adapt such tools as the Anger Ladder and Happy Steps and create new ones to meet the needs of the individuals with whom he or she works. With creative energy, solutions can be found to most problems.

An area often neglected in working with persons with mental retardation and developmental disabilities is that of "choice making." The therapeutic environment is a perfect situation for offering opportunities in this area. I belive the job of the therapist is to help the individuals realize they are in charge of the choices they make. With children and adults, I work with the concepts of "smart choices" and "poor choices" and the responsibility for one's own actions in making choices. The materials that I develop rely heavily on "choice making" and "personal responsibility."

Many different texts, assessments, and programs on sexuality education/counseling for individuals with or without mental retardation and developmental disabilities are currently available in printed form (see Bibliography and Related Materials found at the end of this book). Anyone developing a sexuality program for individuals with mental retardation or developmental disabilities should look carefully at the available resources to see what is usable for their situation. Also, knowing what has succeeded and what has failed for others is often helpful in designing and developing meaningful programs. Therefore, consultation with other professionals in sexuality education/counseling for individuals with mental retardation and developmental disabilities is advisable.

Sample Dialogue

Parents and staff members often ask, "Exactly what do I say and how do I say it?" The following is a sample dialogue about sexuality that can be used with young adults with mental retardation. This style can also be used for individuals with other developmental or physical disabilities, such as cerebral palsy. The important thing to remember is to use language that is comprehensible to the individuals involved, adapting vocabulary, visual aids, and other materials to meet the specific needs of the clients.

The following dialogue might take place in a sexuality counseling group for four young adult males with mental ages of approximately 10 years. All have good verbal skills but have little or no knowledge of the correct terminology for sexuality, genitalia, and so forth. The sexuality counselor is providing basic sexuality education.

Counselor:	Today we are going to talk about our bodies and ourselves and how we change as we grow and mature. I guess that is something that happens to all of us. Don't you agree? Can anyone in the group tell me something about yourself that is different from when you were a little boy?
Johnny:	I got hair on my face.
Counselor:	That's right. As you grow up, you grow hair on different parts of your body. When you grow the hair on your face, you will begin to shave. Has this started happening to all of you?
Group:	Yes.
Counselor:	Where else do you have hair that is different from when you were a little boy?
Bennet:	On my thing.
Counselor:	By your thing, do you mean your private part, which is called your penis?
Bennet:	Yes.
Counselor:	You are right. As you grow up, you will begin to grow hair around your penis. This is part of becoming a grown man. You will also grow hair under your arms and on your chest. Has this happened to all of you yet?

Group: No.

Counselor: Well, it will soon. You might notice that your muscles are getting stronger too. As your body changes and matures, you will have to do different things that we can talk about.

Ken: You mean like using deodorant?

Counselor: Right. As an adult, different parts of your body will begin to perspire, such as under your arms. In order not to have a body odor, you will want to be sure to use deodorant after each shower. Learning to keep your body clean and appearing nice is your responsibility and part of the responsibility you develop as you mature. So, let's see. We've said that everybody's body is changing some. You're growing hair around your penis, under your arms, and on your chest, and face. You are beginning to shave and use deodorant, and learning the responsibilities that come with being an adult man. Do you think that it is the same for the girls that you know?

Bennet: I don't know. Is it?

Counselor: We are going to talk about how the girls change too as they grow up to become women, but let's finish talking about some of the other changes that you men are having first.

Ken: OK.

Counselor: Along with your body changing, some of you may have started having some new and different feelings. I think that some of you have told me that you like girls better now and that you like kissing and touching them. So we want to do some talking about those feelings. We should also talk about appropriate and inappropriate behavior and how you are responsible for your behavior.

Jack: I have a problem.

Counselor: OK, Jack, let's talk about it.

Jack: I wake up at night and it is like I have peed all over the bed. I have been scared to tell my mother, so I try to hide it, but I did not even wet the bed when I was a little boy.

Counselor: You are not wetting the bed now. Most men have something called "wet dreams." This means that while you are asleep, something happens to your body called erection and ejaculation. Some of you men call that "getting hard" and "shooting off." When you "shoot off" this sticky stuff comes out of your penis. It is called semen. It is not urine or "pee," as you may call it. It is important for us to understand what semen is because it contains the sperm that can make a girl pregnant. Even though we haven't discussed that yet, we can say right now that is very important for all of you to understand what this semen is. It is just as important for you to understand what an erection and ejaculation is so that when this happens to you it will not be a frightening or unpleasant thing. When you have an erection and ejaculation in the middle of the night, while you are asleep, this is called a "wet dream." It is OK and normal, and it happens to most men at one time or another.

Bennet:	What do I do when I have that kind of dream and the bed is messed up? I don't want anyone to see it.
Counselor:	Can anyone give Bennet a good suggestion on how to handle that situation himself?
Jack:	He could get a new sheet.
Counselor:	Good answer. Without making a fuss about it, Bennet can just go get a fresh sheet from the closet and put the messed-up one in the dirty clothes hamper. He will have taken care of the problem himself.
Ken:	Won't his mother get mad?
Counselor:	I don't think so. Mothers understand what it is like when you become a man. It may be hard for her to talk about, but you can help the situation by letting her know that you have learned something about it here. Let her know that you are comfortable talking about your body.

As your mother and father see that you are willing to accept adult responsibilities for your body and the way it functions, they will give you more understanding and it will be easier for them to talk to you, too. Remember, not everyone is comfortable talking about sex. However, you know that I am comfortable. I will always be glad to answer any questions that you might have, as long as you come to ask me.

Well, let's move on. We just talked a little about wet dreams, which brought up the words erection and ejaculation. I want to make sure that you understand what these words mean. Can anyone explain the word "erection" to me?

Ken:	Getting hard?
Counselor:	OK. Can you tell me more?
Ken:	It gets hard.
Counselor:	What does "it" mean? Remember, just like others who are around you, I will never know exactly what you are talking about and what you want to know if you don't explain exactly.

Ken: I mean my private thing. I can't remember the word you used.

Counselor: That is fine. It may take a while for you to learn the proper words. The word is "penis." You may hear other words such as "prick," "dick," "peter," "weiner," or "cock," but the appropriate word is "penis."

Ken: Yea, I knew some of those words. But I heard those were dirty. I thought you would get mad at me.

Counselor: I would not get mad at you. I think that you have to realize that some of the other adults in your enviroment might be uncomfortable with words like those, but if you and I are better able to understand each other by using these words, then it is fine for you to use the words in here. I would like to have all of you try to remember the proper or appropriate words too. We will work on it together. Why doesn't everyone say the word "penis"?

Group: Penis.

Counselor: Good. Now let's get back to Ken trying to find out more about erection. What he was trying to tell us was that an erection was when the penis gets hard.

Jack: The bone in it straightens up, huh?

Counselor: No, Jack, there is not a bone in the penis. There are blood vessels. The blood flows in a certain way that makes your penis get hard when your penis receives certain stimulation. That stimulation may come from a thought you have, which could be called "fantasy," which is something we will discuss later. This may also happen from your touching yourself. This is called "masturbation," which we will soon talk about. This may also happen in "sexual intercourse," which is what two people do when they are making love. For right now, I just want to make sure that everyone understands when I say "erection" that what I am describing is your penis getting hard.

               Everybody understand? OK. Now let's move on. When your penis has an erection, there is a chance that the white sticky stuff, which is called "semen," will come out before your penis loses its erection or gets soft again. This is called an "ejaculation." Have some of you heard other words for this process?

Jack: I heard "come."

Bennet: How about "finish"?

Counselor: OK. I can tell that you have heard about some of these things before. I hope that as we talk together, you will be sure to tell me anything that you don't understand. Then we can clear it up. It is your body and you are the only one who can be responsible for it. However, you can't learn how to take care of your body until you understand how it works.

Let's review for a moment. We have now talked about the fact that you each know that the word for your private part is "penis." We have talked about your wet dreams. When your penis gets hard, this is called an erection, and if semen comes out, that will be an ejaculation. Ready to move on?

Bennet: OK.

Counselor: Everybody else? We can go over it again.

Ken: No. Go on.

Counselor: OK! Let's take a minute to talk about "masturbation." What are some other words for masturbation.

Ken: I don't know. I have never heard that word.

Counselor: Have you heard "playing with yourself," "jerking off," or "beating off"?

Jack: Oh, yea, we know all that!

Counselor: Well, those are just other words for "masturbation." I'm sure that all of you have masturbated at some time.

Bennet: Do you masturbate?

Counselor: Masturbation is normal and OK. Most people masturbate at some time in their lives. There are some important things to know and realize about masturbation. It is your body. You are responsible for your body and you don't want to do anything to hurt your body. You want to be sure and not masturbate with any object that will hurt you. We usually think of masturbation as something you are doing to yourself that makes you feel good. We want to think of masturbation as something that is private. Usually, it is done alone.

However, when and if you are ever in a sexual relationship with another person, masturbation is something that you may do with or for another person as part of making love. Nevertheless, right now, we are talking about self-stimulation or masturbation by yourself. It is very important to understand and remember that it is OK and normal. Most people masturbate or play with themselves because it feels good. But it is a private thing. Masturbation should be done in private. People masturbate in different ways. Can some of you tell me some of the ways you have masturbated?

Bennet: I like to look at pictures of naked women while I play with myself and jerk off.

Counselor: What you are saying is that you use "fantasy" or use a picture to help you think of something sexual, such as a naked woman, in order to get some good positive sexual feelings as you touch yourself. When you masturbate, do you have an erection and ejaculate?

Bennet: Yes. I get that sticky stuff all over me.

Counselor: Do you remember the name of the white sticky stuff?

Bennet: No, but it makes babies.

Counselor: You are right. It is called "semen" and it has sperm, which helps make babies. If you are masturbating alone, there is no problem about the sperm getting in the girl and making her pregnant. However, when we talk about pregnancy and how girls get pregnant, I want you to remember what we are saying about the sperm. Remember that any way the sperm gets near the girl's egg, it can cause a baby.

Babies are not just made when people have sexual intercourse. They can also be made when a boy and girl are just "playing around" and doing some things such as "masturbation." Because if there is an ejaculation, then the semen and sperm will be on your hands, and if you put your hand near or in the girl's vagina, then the sperm may be able to get to the egg.

Ken: What is a vagina?

Counselor: Do you men feel comfortable enough about your own bodies to do some talking about the female's body now?

Group: Yes.

Counselor: OK. Let us look at some of the things that are similar in boys and girls. We both start as babies and then we both grow up. As we grow and change, our bodies change. Different things happen to us, because our bodies are made differently. We have different private areas or private parts, which we called "genitals" in an earlier session. As we mature, our genitals change, becoming different as we grow. Girls do not have a penis, do they?

Jack: No.

Counselor: Girls have an opening to their body called a vagina. Can everybody say the word "vagina"?

Group: Vagina.

Counselor: The outside part of the girl's private parts is called a "vulva." Can everyone say "vulva"?

Group: Vulva.

Counselor: Good. That is a hard word for some of us to remember. It is the appropriate word. We are going to use it here. What are some other words you have heard a girl's vagina or vulva called?

Bennet:	"Pussy."
Ken:	"Cunt."
Jack:	"Box."
Counselor:	Right. Those may be some of the words you have heard other men or boys call a girl's private area. The proper or appropriate words are "vagina" and "vulva" and we are going to use those words here. We can look at our drawing on the board and see that, whereas the boy's private part, or penis, mainly is outside his body, the girl's vagina leads inside her body to where she has a very special area called a uterus or womb. That is where the baby grows and develops when she is pregnant. Under normal conditions, the baby is delivered through the vagina.
	The girl also has some tubes leading from the womb to the ovaries, where the eggs are kept. Every month an egg drops into the womb through the tubes, which are called the Fallopian tubes. If some of the man's sperm gets into the womb, the egg and sperm will join together and make a baby. The baby will continue to grow inside of the womb. That is why we don't want to let sperm get into the vagina, unless we want to make a baby. Does everybody know how the baby is made?
Ken:	No.
Counselor:	Let's review that. The sperm has to get inside the womb to meet the egg. This can happen more than one way. The man can put his penis in the vagina, which is called sexual intercourse. If the couple has been masturbating and there is sperm on the man's hand, and if he puts his hand in the woman's vagina, the sperm might travel up to the womb and find an egg.
	If you don't want to have a baby, then you have to use some kind of birth control. With birth control, the girl will not take a chance of getting pregnant. We should always realize that we are responsible for our own bodies. It is our responsibility to find out about and use birth control effectively—especially if we choose to be sexually active but are not ready to have a baby. Birth control could be a later discussion for us as a group.
	Right now, I would like to mention a few things that you may have heard before. For the woman, there is the birth control pill, IUD, diaphragm, foam, or in some cases a shot that can be used. For you men, there is the condom, or rubber. The condom is a good form of birth control. Another thing important to know about the condom is that it will

help protect the man and woman against sexually transmitted diseases like AIDS, which is a disease you can get from having sex with someone who has the AIDS virus. You may not know if the other person has AIDS or not. It is very serious because if you get the disease, there is no cure and you will die.

You know, we just can't talk too much about your responsibility to know about your own body and how you need to be responsible if you decided to become active sexually. You do not want to make a baby when you are not in a position to take care of it.

We have gotten off the topic of how we are different as men and women. As girls grow they develop breasts. The breasts are where the milk is made that can feed the baby. As you look at our diagram, you will see that women develop breasts and men do not. Men do have nipples, which can be sensitive to touch. Both men and women get sexual feelings from touching certain parts of their bodies that are sensitive and respond to sexual thoughts and touches. Men masturbate by rubbing their penises. Girls masturbate too. They touch a sensitive area near their vagina called the clitoris and sometimes they rub their breasts or nipples.

Men and women who are making love touch each other in these sensitive areas also. This brings about good and positive sexual feelings. Learning how to respond to them in acceptable ways for the environment in which you live is important. Knowing the rules and limitations on your behavior in that environment helps make everything easier for you.

Jack: I have a problem. I want to make friends with girls, but I don't want to touch them yet or screw around or anything.

Counselor: That is a really important point. How can we learn to be friends and enjoy each other's company without making everything a sexual encounter? Can some of you think of fun things to do with girls that do not involve sex?

Bennet: Going to the show.

Jack: Taking a walk and maybe holding hands. Would that be OK?

Counselor: Sure, that's a good idea, especially if the girl likes to go for walks and hold hands, too.

Ken: How do I know when I can do more with a girl—you know —make love and all that?

Counselor: Well, you both have to be ready to have the experience, accept the responsibility for your actions, and live in an environment where this kind of behavior will be allowed. If you decide to make love, you have to make a decision about birth control first, unless you are in a position to take care of a baby.

Ken: What does "abortion" mean and why can't we do that?

Counselor: "Abortion" is when a woman has a doctor terminate, or end, a pregnancy because she has decided that she does not want to have the baby. There may be many other reasons involved in the decision for abortion. Rather than discuss that here, which I think is a very personal decision between you, your families, and your doctors, I would like to repeat what your responsibilities are as you begin to act in a sexual way and discover your sexual feelings. I want to discuss again with you that it is OK to have sexual feelings and thoughts. We all have them. They are natural and good. We just have to be responsible for our actions. I feel that we are discussing those things together today.

A similar dialogue with females could go in reverse order, presenting the information about the female body first.

Whenever a parent, educator, or group leader feels uncomfortable with a topic area, it can be helpful to present the material from a prepared outline. This will ensure a proper flow of the material and information. Dialogues about sexuality become easier to participate in and lead once the leader has had some practice doing it. It is often helpful to use an experienced co-counselor in the beginning.

DEVELOPING COMMUNITY SUPPORT

To provide adequate sexuality education/counseling programs for individuals with mental retardation and developmental disabilities, the often adverse reactions of parents, staff, and community need to be countered with positive and effective public relations. There should be a concerted effort to have public relations information presented by someone knowledgeable and experienced in the field of mental retardation or developmental disabilities and sexuality education/counseling. There will be many questions asked, and the more experience and confidence the speaker has the more effective the program will be.

Methods of Presentation

Professionals capable of presenting information about such programs can choose among different ways of making an impact on society and its views. The method of presentations can be lectures, question-and-answer sessions, interviews in the mass media, or dissemination of printed material that is meaningful to audiences. When possible, workshops should be held in which the participants have the time and opportunity to work through their feelings and thoughts regarding sexuality in individuals with mental retardation or developmental disabilities.

Videotapes showing specific examples, visual graphic displays, and, when appropriate, individuals with mental retardation or developmental disabilities participating on a panel to express their feelings and views can be very useful. It is also good practice to involve an advocacy office or legal counselor in these presentations so that the rights of individuals with mental retardation and developmental disabilities, as granted by the Constitution, can be presented. Having a medical person available to discuss family planning clinics and their roles, sterilization and its ramifications, birth control, and related topics is beneficial in a group presentation. Often members of a group will only acknowledge and accept information that is given directly by a medical person.

The main goal of any public relations program would be to build comprehension of the needs, problems, and approaches to possible solutions that can be incorporated into existing programs. Information on how to begin a new program will be beneficial to the participants.

Targeting the Audience

If the audience is specific (e.g., all parents or extended families of individuals with mental retardation), then an approach that emphasizes that group's role in healthy PSS development is also important. However, if the target audience is the community, the topics and subject matter should be more general. Emphasis should center basically around recognition that individuals with mental retardation or developmental disabilities are sexual beings and behave as such, which is their innate right. In speaking with advocacy groups, current knowledge of the laws affecting sexual expression and rights to privacy become vital information.

Using the Mass Media

The mass media, including television or radio talk shows (local or national), newspaper and magazine articles, and other written material that can be dispensed readily to the public, should be explored as avenues for dissemination. Simple, concrete terms and language should be used to explain the basic premises of sexuality education/counseling. Informing the public of the need for awareness of and recognition of the sexuality needs of individuals with mental retardation and developmental disabilities is the responsibility of those professionals working in the fields of sexuality education/counseling.

Sexuality education/counseling programs for individuals with mental retardation and developmental disabilities should be presented in such a way that they are not offensive to the target audience. They should also be as implicit or as specific as needed to communicate the information that is required. The person providing the lecture or answering the interview questions must know the audience. For one audience, using street language for its shock value and for desensitization might be of a great value. However, when speaking to a very conservative group, this would be a counterproductive approach to use. It would stop the communication and nothing would be accomplished. The target audience needs to be accepted at its present level of sophistication and then encouraged and guided to move to another level when it is ready.

CONCLUDING REMARKS

In planning a sexuality training program for staff or family members to provide individuals with mental retardation or developmental disabilities with sexuality education and sexuality counseling, several things are imperative:

1. Policies need to be developed and supported by the administration and communicated to the parents as well as to all caregivers and professionals working within the system.
2. Everyone involved with the individual must assume some responsibility for at least feeling comfortable enough with their own sexuality so that they can deal with the sexuality of others.
3. Any rules or standards expected for appropriate sexual behavior in a particular environment should be clearly communicated to all and enforced by everyone involved.
4. Using videotapes as an in-service training device that keeps material consistent is an excellent tool. This techique allows for review and for personal interchange and role-playing regarding feelings that arise in response to the material or the tapes.
5. It is imperative that the sexuality training be provided by someone experienced both in sexuality education/counseling and in the field of mental retardation and developmental disabilities. This ensures that there is good comprehension of both fields.
6. Without good administrative support, well-informed staff, faculty, and parents, and a qualified trainer, there will be no adequate sexuality program for persons with mental retardation or developmental disabilities. All of these components must exist to make the significant impact that is needed.

PART II

Education and Counseling Principles

Chapter 5

Self-Stimulation

Self-stimulation encompasses the five different senses of vision, hearing, touch, taste, and smell. Thus, self-stimulation may encompass all aspects of adaptive behavior in a social context. This includes eating, dancing, singing, games, recreation, movies, religious nurture, and all types of interpersonal relations. Other self-stimulation activities are sexual in nature. Genitally oriented self-stimulation, or masturbation, provides psychosexual (PS) release and fulfillment for the individual(s) involved. Engaging in any of these activities appears to be motivated by pleasure seeking on the part of the individual.

Most people masturbate at some point in their lives. Many people choose to masturbate throughout their entire lives, regardless of whether they have a sexual partner or not. Some partners masturbate in front of each other as part of sexual play and some partners participate in mutually satisfying masturbation of each other. When illness or disability interferes with a person's ability to have sexual intercourse, masturbation is often the sexual activity of choice for two partners to share as they enjoy their sexual lives together.

It is the innate right of every individual to masturbate if he or she desires to do so and if it is done in a private and nonharmful way. However, all persons have their own sets of values and moral beliefs, and many individuals will feel their personal value systems do not honor the concept that masturbation is appropriate, acceptable, or normal. I feel that masturbation is a normal part of the developmental process of growing up, as well as a normal part of adult life, for all persons. It is possible that some care providers and some family members will have difficulty with this concept as it relates to individuals with mental retardation and developmental disabilities. Administrators, supervisors, and therapists should make every effort to help such people deal with their personal views, while advocating for the rights of individuals with mental retardation and developmental disabilities to discover and enjoy the masturbatory response. As professionals, it is not our job or responsibility to infringe upon the opinions of care providers to try to change those opinions outside of the workplace. It is our job and responsibility to set parameters of acceptable and appropriate self-stimulatory behavior that will be honored by all care providers in the living environment.

For individuals with mental retardation or developmental disabilities, family feelings and beliefs, constraints of the living environment, and societal mores and opinions are often factors in the discussion and expression of genitally oriented self-stimulation. A sense of "permission giving" on the part of family members, care providers, and society adds tension to the issue. However, these individuals have an inherent sexuality and are going to explore pleasurable sexual behavior. Why not help them express such behavior in a purposeful and non–guilt-ridden manner? Attitudes and sexuality policies that allow for masturbation that is nonharmful, is done in private, is done during leisure hours, and is done alone (as opposed to mutual masturbation) seem appropriate. In cases in which objects are used that are harmful, or when a couple is engaging in mutual masturbation against the will of one of the participants, staff and family education is needed in addition to working with the individuals to help them understand appropriate versus inappropriate methods.

RIGHTS OF INDIVIDUALS TO SEXUAL EXPRESSION

The rights of individuals with mental retardation and developmental disabilities with regard to masturbation must be accompanied by a willingness and ability to be responsible in the practiced behavior. This would hold true for any masturbatory practices, especially those that involve mutual masturbation and the potential exchange of any bodily fluids. The issue of responsibility is examined more closely in Case Study 5-1.

Case Study 5-1

Ernest, an adult with mental retardation and a severe physical disability, was having a difficult time adjusting to the idea of becoming an adult and accepting adult responsibilities. Ernest often engaged in infantile behavior, exemplified by frequent temper tantrums, quickness to anger at minor teasing (especially about his expressions of sexuality), an obsessional desire to be parented as a young child, overdependency with frequent refusal to perform self-help skills that had been mastered (such as feeding himself), and deliberate urinary incontinence. These infantile behaviors caused Ernest to be ridiculed by other men in his living environment. Ernest had requested that he be given a doll with which to masturbate. However, the staff ascertained that Ernest was not physically capable of keeping the doll clean or appropriately storing it in or retrieving it from a private place. For these reasons, use of the doll as a masturbatory aid was not encouraged.

After consultation with members of Ernest's interdisciplinary team, who knew his physical limitations and abilities, the following suggestion was made by the counselor. Since Ernest could reach his penis with his hands and could masturbate, but was not able to clean himself afterward, he should be placed in a shower with a privacy curtain where he could sit either in a chair or on a mat on the shower floor. He would then be left alone to masturbate. Afterward, an attendant could help turn on the shower so that Ernest could clean himself.

Both the staff and Ernest were provided the information needed to develop this more appropriate, alternative behavior that would allow Ernest to function within the limitations of his disability. Ridicule from other individuals diminished because Ernest was given the opportunity to explore his own sexuality in a private place. Staff felt more comfortable about the way in which they were helping Ernest express his sexuality—all adults involved felt uncomfortable about Ernest, a grown man, using a small female doll, but had a much more positive response to the idea of private masturbation in the shower.

The caregivers in the environment of an individual with mental retardation or developmental disability should be the permission-giving force that says, "As long as you are in a private place, relating to your body in a nonharmful, self-stimulatory, and positive way, masturbation is all right." It must be emphasized that one cannot abuse or take advantage of another person, especially if that person is younger or has a disability. Respect must be given to other people as well as to oneself. Also, it must be taught that sexual activity is a private and personal act. Sexual expression in a public place is a violation of the privacy of others and is unacceptable behavior.

Individuals with mental retardation who function at a higher level of intelligence and adaptive behavior will have minimal difficulty in learning to express themselves sexually in an appropriate manner. However, as the level of functioning decreases, more behavior modification programs and analysis of environmental factors will be required to help the person develop appropriate behaviors. It should be recognized that some individuals with more significant mental retardation may never achieve the development of inner controls. This is not a problem as long as the self-stimulatory behavior they exhibit—whether genitally or nongenitally oriented—is acceptable within their living environment and is nonharmful to the individuals or to others.

How can caregivers and professionals be helpful to individuals with mental retardation and developmental disabilities so that their sexual expressions can be more meaningful and more acceptable to the environments in which they live? Whenever masturbation is explored, there are factors that should be acknowledged and understood. These include the cognitive, adaptive, and environmental restrictions surrounding the individual. These factors can act as either aids or restraints to the individual.

Value Judgments of Others

Not all people find masturbation an acceptable sexual activity. The religious and moral persuasions of many members of society oppose masturbation as a meaningful form of sexual expression. Other individuals are uncomfortable with the idea of sexual behavior in persons with mental retardation or developmental disabilities, some because of long-held myths about the nature of such persons and others because of a belief that such impairments precludes the development of the necessary restraint and consideration for others that society demands in any form of sexual expression.

Again, I believe that it is important to recognize that all individuals have the innate right to experience the masturbatory response and that it is within the realm of normal behavior to participate in this self-stimulatory activity or to choose not to participate. I feel strongly about advocating for the rights of individuals with mental retardation and developmental disabilities to explore the feelings and actions of masturbation in a non-harmful and private way, if they so choose.

For those persons who are able to accept masturbation by individuals with mental retardation and developmental disabilities, other value judgments enter into consideration; most of these are related to appropriateness and level of involvement. For example, if masturbation exists to the point that it is distracting from any other activity, it is seen as being too egocentric. Masturbation will never be accepted as the only purposeful activity in which the individual engages, hour after hour, day after day. Perseveration of masturbatory behavior, to the exclusion of all other meaningful activities, often is seen as undesirable by society and non-contributory to the well-being of the individual. In addition, masturbation that disturbs others or involves other individuals in a harmful way or against their will is seen as a violation of the other person's rights and would be subject to legal action. To be accepted by society, conditions must exist so that an individual who chooses to masturbate cannot take advantage of other people.

I understand that no one person or one program can change society, but each of us must accept the responsibility of advocating for the rights of the individual with mental retardation and developmental disabilities so that he or she can participate in society to the best of his or her ability, exhibiting healthy psychosocial-sexual (PSS) attitudes and behaviors. It is imperative that society recognize that individuals with mental retardation and developmental disabilities do indeed have the right to masturbate, if done in an acceptable way and in the proper setting, without violating the rights of others.

Rules and Regulations of the Living Environment

Living environments for individuals with mental retardation and developmental disabilities often have restrictions on sexual behavior. Before beginning a sexuality counseling session, the counselor should be aware of the limitations that the structure of a given person's environment and the staff or others in that environment have put on individual sexual expression, specifically concerning masturbation. Different residences and staff or caregivers have different rules. Counselors should focus on discussing acceptable rules for that individual's particular environment. The avenue of education about masturbation should encourage the development of healthy PSS development and good overall ego development within the constraints of the individual's environment.

One primary problem encountered is the situation in which not all caregivers, staff, or family agree that masturbation is not only an acceptable form of sexual expression, but that it is desirable and should be encouraged. Counselors may have to deal with caregivers, staff members, or family members who believe that masturbation is not acceptable. It may go against their religious beliefs, or perhaps they just cannot tolerate seeing the individual expose, touch, rub, or play with his or her genitals. When this attitude occurs in a group residential situation, it may be necessary to acknowledge these personal feelings, but point out that within this residence these behaviors are acceptable and will be handled nonjudgmentally. When dealing with such a person, the counselor must accept this person's attitude and help him or her to function within the broad scope of the residence's policies and the resident's program. This staff member or caregiver must learn to work and interact with the particular resident and to respond to this individual's sexual behavior according to the established program, not his or her personal feelings.

The situation is slightly different if the individual is living at home and the parents find masturbation unacceptable. In sexuality counseling sessions with the parents, it should be stressed that this is an appropriate form of sexual self-expression for the individual. The parents should be taught to guide the masturbatory behavior so that it is exhibited in a socially acceptable way. For example, masturbation should occur in private, not in public, and within reasonable time frames instead of nonstop marathons that require seclusion from the remainder of the family for an extended period.

Attitudes and Desires of Parents

Most parents want their children to have the fullest life possible, regardless of their level of ability. Nevertheless, it is difficult for most parents of individuals with mental retardation or developmental disabilities to admit to or cope with the emerging sexuality of their offspring. Parents see this development as the beginning of endless frustration. They often cannot conceptualize any situation in which their child will be able to feel and participate in those sexual experiences that the parents have found to be meaningful to them.

In these situations, it is important to try to help the parents see the positive aspects of sexual behavior instead of focusing on the negative ones. The parents can be helped to see that there are many different types of sexual expression. The fact that their child may never experience traditional marriage and parenthood does not make that person an asexual being. Instead, the individual may come to discover, explore, and use his or her sexuality in different ways to achieve good, positive feelings and self-images.

Once the parents accept these limitations and stop seeing their child as an extension of their own egos, they are in a better position to recognize the important and valuable place that sexual expression in general, and masturbation in particular, can have in the life of their offspring. They will begin to realize that masturbation is not just a method of personal sexual fulfillment or a part of foreplay, as they may have experienced it, or a developmental sequence in the discovery of the self, as their other children may have experienced it. For the individual who lives in a restricted environment, it may become the best and most satisfying sexual release mechanism that exists.

RELATIVE SEXUALITY OF SELF-STIMULATION

Persons with milder mental retardation are capable of engaging in many kinds of purposeful self-stimulatory behavior as they develop their PSS selves, and of deriving fulfillment from such activities. A sexuality educator/counselor working with these individuals can therapeutically assess their genitally oriented self-stimulating behavior in a straightforward manner, since their language skills are often concrete and functional and their sexual behavior patterns are similar to those of individuals without mental retardation. Antisocial and problematic areas of sexual expression can be dealt with through fairly traditional and available modes.

However, problems are inherent in this approach. These individuals have lowered adaptive and discrimination skills. They may not know how to choose a masturbatory method that is nonharmful, and in fact may be totally unaware that there are different ways in which to masturbate. Therefore, the development of positive sexual feelings about themselves and an emphasis on appropriate masturbatory techniques should be the most important points to communicate to those individuals with milder mental retardation.

In contrast, individuals with more significant levels of mental retardation often engage in perseverative self-stimulatory activities, such as rocking, head banging, thumb sucking, or twirling—behavior that is generally considered nonpurposeful and sometimes detrimental. An observational and behavioral evaluation is necessary to determine whether the sexual behavior of such individuals is voluntary and purposeful behavior directed toward sexual release, or merely perseverative pleasure-seeking behavior with no ultimate sexual goal. As the level of mental retardation increases, language, cognitive, and adaptive skill levels dictate that professional interaction must change. The counselor must decide whether the person is deriving satisfaction and pleasure from masturbation or whether this is just becoming a conditioned self-stimulatory activity. Questions that must be addressed include: "What sexual behaviors are acceptable in the individual's living environment?" and "How can that person best be helped to exhibit the necessary adaptive behavior to live within that environment?" These individuals should be allowed to develop appropriate methods of self-stimulation that are more purposeful and nonharmful.

Perseverative Self-Stimulation

The sexual behavior of individuals with more significant levels of mental retardation is sometimes perseverative to the point of being detrimental to their ability to achieve their maximum potential in the least restrictive environment possible. Staff members may find excessive masturbation by these individuals to be annoying or counterproductive, especially when it is not seen to lead to sexual release. Many state that, "If I could only help them masturbate to climax, they would stop and move on to a purposeful activity, and next time they would know how to do it themselves." However, this may not be the case. If the individual generally engages in many types of self-stimulatory behavior, whether genitally oriented or not, it may be difficult to inhibit or develop incompatible responses to the behavior. In such situations, behavioral observation, program analysis, and other techniques must be used to help assess exactly what the individual appears to desire from this behavior. Does the individual want to achieve sexual release, or is his or her goal merely generalized self-stimulation? If the behavior is harmful or socially unacceptable, substitute behavior and/or activities need to be established, conditioned, and reinforced.

Case Study 5-2

Chester was an adult with severe mental retardation who was deaf and blind. Chester seemed to have no awareness of anyone around him or of his environment in general. He communicated by rocking and did not know how to get others to help him meet his needs. He masturbated for hours on end, regardless of attempts by the staff to engage him in some activity related to his program, and regardless of whether he was clothed in overalls that he could not unzip or in pajamas that he could remove while in bed. Chester masturbated in bed to such an extent that the bed shook and made a great deal of noise.

The other residents, most of whom had visual and hearing impairments, were not much affected by this behavior, but the staff were upset and wanted the behavior to stop. Most staff members thought the problem was that Chester was never able to climax and therefore was always sexually frustrated. To some extent that might have been true, but it was more likely that masturbation had become a perseverative self-stimulating behavior because no other efforts to bring external stimuli into Chester's personal world were working.

The sexuality counselor worked with the staff to establish that the act of masturbation was acceptable in general but that in this case it was becoming nonpurposeful. Because no "hands-on" techniques of teaching and/or assisting in the masturbatory process are allowed, the only solutions available were to look intensively at available techniques to condition an incompatible response, such as having Chester do something with both of his hands that is perseverative but nonmasturbatory. A very direct and forceful approach was taken during activity hours to try to condition incompatible responses to the excessive masturbation that Chester was exhibiting.

This was a very difficult case. The staff were minimally successful in getting Chester involved in behaviors that were incompatible with masturbation because they were unable to gain access to his self-stimulating world to the extent necessary. Chester was able to shift to another activity temporarily, but the ideal goal of reducing the excessive masturbation to a point where it occurred only in instances in which it was purposefully directed toward a climax was never achieved. It finally had to be accepted that there was little that the staff can do regarding Chester's excessive masturbation in bed during sleeping hours. They had to readjust their thinking, realizing that it was not harmful and negative for the masturbation to be excessive at times.

Staff members involved with individuals with more significant levels of mental retardation have an added responsibility to study the programs set up for these individuals and ensure that any excessive self-stimulation is not occurring because of a lack of activities or simply boredom. With these individuals, more fundamental techniques might be required to change dysfunctional sexual behavior. If the individual is masturbating in an inappropriate environment, it might be necessary to physically remove the individual to a more appropriate environment or provide an alternative activity that involves the use of both hands. This latter procedure will help to condition a type of self-stimulatory behavior that is incompatible with masturbatory activity.

Case Study 5-3

Darrell was a young man with severe mental retardation who continuously unzipped his pants, removed his penis, and rubbed and stroked it in public. Darrell's caregivers had two options. The first was to consistently remove Darrell from the public place to a bathroom or bedroom and make him remain there until he had completed masturbating and was redressed. However, if this was self-pleasuring behavior that was perseverative in nature, it would be more beneficial to condition a behavior that was incompatible with Darrell's masturbatory behavior, such as involving him in an activity that required the use of both hands to manipulate a toy or other item. This shifted Darrell's perseverative behavior to a more appropriate and acceptable activity.

Individuals with mental retardation and other handicaps, such as hearing and visual impairments or autism, exhibit a great deal of perseverative and self-stimulating behavior. Thus, a higher incidence of prolonged masturbation might be observed because these individuals do not have the opportunity to receive many stimuli from the outside world.

Self-Stimulation that Becomes Harmful

There are many methods of self-stimulation or masturbation that are unacceptable because they are harmful to the individual. What is the solution for a young man who frequently has a red, raw penis from rubbing it continuously without any lubrication? It is the responsibility of the staff or caregivers to teach the individual that it is not appropriate to walk around with his penis hanging out of his clothing so that he can rub it whenever he wants. The individual should also be taught an appropriate means of self-stimulation to use when in a private place. It is also the responsibility of the staff or caregiver to impart the necessary information in a way that can be understood.

Case Study 5-4

Steven frequently rubbed his penis until it was raw. In this case, it was decided to teach Steven to use a readily available lubricant such as body lotion or soap while in the shower when masturbating so that his penis would not be injured. The counselor was careful to give this information in a clear and comprehensible manner:

"Steven, you are hurting your penis by rubbing it a lot and making it dry and raw. If you put some lotion on your hand first or rub your penis with soap while you shower, it will feel better and you will not make your penis red and raw. Why don't you try this the next time you feel like rubbing your penis? Just remember, you should not be playing with your penis in front of anybody else. Let me know if it hurts when you masturbate with the soap or lotion and we will try to find something else. OK?"

This teaching method should not be uncomfortable to the counselor or caregiver. However, if the level of mental retardation is such that language skills and cognitive comprehension and processing are insufficient to use the information as presented in the above case study, what is the responsibility of the caregiver?

To help the individual with more significant mental retardation engage in masturbation and self-stimulatory behavior appropriately without causing himself or herself harm, the caregiver must emphasize nonharmful techniques, especially use of the individual's own hands while masturbating. The likelihood of the individual choosing an inappropriate object with which to masturbate is then decreased. Masturbation with inappropriate objects can be most harmful if the individual does not have the ability to discriminate what will or will not be harmful.

Case Study 5-5

Blair was a very sociable and pleasant person with a milder level of mental retardation who lived in a residential facility. After a recent visit home, Blair told the facility's nurse that he had pain is his rectal area. He explained that he had inserted four sewing machine needles into the area between his rectum and his scrotum, and the needles had begun to hurt. Because Blair's discriminatory responses were poor, he did not know how to handle the situation. He had inserted the needles whole but during the course of normal activity the needles fragmented internally. It was only later, with the intense pain caused by the needles breaking into fragments, that Blair realized he had to go to the nurse and seek medical attention. At first no one believed Blair, but he was taken to a physician, who examined him and ordered x-rays that confirmed the problem. Surgery was then performed to remove the needle fragments.

At this point, the staff physician, staff psychologist, and clinical counselor all decided that Blair's harmful behavior needed to be changed. The sexuality counselor noted that Blair probably did not mean to engage in dangerous behavior, but rather was masturbating inappropriately with objects that were harmful. During the sexuality counseling sessions, it surfaced that Blair did actually think that he was doing something pleasurable. Blair said that inserting the needles, even though painful, was exciting. He did not realize that he would have so much trouble as a result of what he did. He revealed that, in the past, he had inserted Q-tips into his penis so far that they infiltrated the bladder.

Here was a young man who wanted to take care of his sexual needs by masturbation, but no one had talked to him about the process. Blair did not know how to properly stimulate himself and was using inappropriate and harmful objects. The sexuality counselor discussed the development of appropriate and nonharmful masturbation techniques that would make him feel good sexually without injuring himself. It was explained to Blair that once he understood and learned appropriate behavior, a recommendation for transfer to the group home where he wished to live could be made.

Emphasis was placed on helping Blair assume responsibility for learning how to masturbate harmlessly so that he could express his sexual feelings and achieve sexual release. This was done in a visual and verbal mode. Pictures were drawn of a flaccid and an erect penis, and the methods by which a man can stimulate his penis through rubbing and stroking (including the use of lubricants that might be available to him), eventually leading to ejaculation, were discussed. The positive sexual feelings that Blair desired surfaced. He easily understood the techniques described and went on to experiment in the privacy of his bedroom.

In further sexuality counseling sessions, Blair indicated that he was now able to masturbate without harming himself. A good prognosis for his adjustment in a less restrictive living environment seemed more probable and reasonable. However, this dangerous situation could have been avoided if, in a sexuality education program, Blair had had a discussion with someone about appropriate and inappropriate ways to masturbate.

Women with more significant levels of mental retardation often use pointed or dangerous objects to insert into the vagina for stimulation and, in the process, damage tissue. Because these individuals have poor language and cognitive skills, there is a need for increased staff supervision to see that no harmful objects are available for masturbatory use.

Case Study 5-6

Rachel, a woman with a moderate level of mental retardation, was often very bored and it was difficult to keep her interested in an activity. Rachel had discovered the pleasure of masturbation, and was found using a coke bottle to masturbate. She was told that this bottle could break and cut her vagina, causing her pain and requiring her to see the doctor. She was encouraged to use her hand, especially while bathing, because the soap would provide some lubrication and keep her from rubbing herself raw or dry. Rachel was encouraged to use a soft toy or other object to masturbate. If the caregiver had just said, "Rachel, you are doing something bad. Stop it," and had not given Rachel alternate solutions on how to stimulate herself, negative feelings about masturbation might have developed and the use of harmful objects might have continued.

In addition to masturbating with harmful objects, women often explore their genitals with their own fingernails, using a digging motion that can tear and injure tissues in the genital area. This problem can be mitigated by clipping the fingernails short and by engaging the individual in an incompatible behavior, such as interacting with objects that requires the use of both hands. If a woman is engaged in tabletop activities that require manipulation of objects or toys with both of her hands, she will not have a free hand to dig at her genitals in a perseverative and self-stimulating way.

An added problem occurs during menstrual cycles, when blood is smeared during masturbation. This is especially true for women with a level of mental retardation that makes it difficult for them to understand the conditions for not masturbating. An additional problem involves the female destroying the sanitary pad and possibly ingesting it. Unfortunately, these behaviors have led parents to request private physicians to do a hysterectomy for sanitary reasons.

TEACHING SELF-STIMULATION

For many individuals masturbation is often a part of foreplay and/or sexual performance. For individuals with mental retardation, masturbation can also be presented as an acceptable nonharmful sexual behavior. This being the case, it should be taught in depth. At the very minimum, family, caregivers, or staff should be fully aware of the extent of knowledge the individual has about his or her body and about masturbatory techniques. This information will make it easier to redirect sexual activity that appears to be perseverative and nonpurposeful in nature. The implication here is that the caregiver or staff member must become aware of the various self-stimulating activities of the individual in question. When these self-stimulating activities are sexual in nature, they are to be accepted as such and the individual directed to appropriate and nonharmful ways of masturbating. The caregiver should help the individual to feel good sexually in a way that is compatible with the constraints of the living environment. However, assumptions cannot be made that the individual knows how to do what will feel good in terms of masturbation.

Masturbation as a Private Act

I believe that masturbation takes two forms in sexual development. One is the individual exploration of the self in a self-stimulatory way that produces a PS feeling. The other is the use of mutual masturbation, which couples often engage in as they develop their PSS feelings and behaviors. Like all forms of sexual expression, different individuals are incapable of progressing to certain levels of sexual interaction. For a couple engaged in a faithful, monogamous relationship, nonharmful mutual masturbation would be seen as appropriate and acceptable by most individuals. Again, this is an individual issue. Professionals on interdisciplinary teams and family members should make an effort to help the individuals deal with their own special sets of circumstances, feelings, and beliefs.

In working to develop feelings, attitudes, and techniques of appropriate masturbation, the emphasis should be on communicating a sense of privacy and responsibility. Masturbation should be presented as a private self-stimulatory activity that should be done only in a private place. Both inclusion of others in masturbatory activities without their consent and performing such activities in public violates the privacy of others, and is inappropriate. Also, each individual is responsible for his or her own body, and nothing harmful should be done to the body in the process of self-stimulation. There are appropriate, nonharmful ways to masturbate. Teaching the appropriate actions and attitudes that accompany sexual self-expression involves teaching the ethic of responsibility to persons with mental retardation or developmental disabilities.

As long as these tenets are upheld, there will be less resistance from family, caregivers, or staff, who may be having difficulty dealing with their own feelings about masturbation or may be faced with problems arising from an individual's public display of a private sexual act, from the involvement of others in that act, or from the use of harmful techniques.

Appropriate Time and Place

There are many times and places in which masturbation is considered socially unacceptable, the most prominent being in a public setting. "Public" can be defined in many different ways. In addition to parks or public facilities, places within a specific living environment where other people walk freely or are allowed to enter without knocking are also considered public. This significantly limits the meaning of "private" to a place where the individual can either close or lock a door or partition, such as a bathroom or bedroom, and where no one should enter without first knocking or making their presence known. To masturbate in front of others or anywhere other than in a private place should be considered inappropriate and unacceptable.

The ability of any individual with mental retardation or developmental disabilities to comprehend the concept of private versus public is relative to that individual's level of mental retardation. Individuals with less significant levels of mental retardation can be educated and counseled to use private places, whereas those with more significant levels of mental retardation may have to be removed from a public place to a more private place. This removal may have to be repeated until it becomes a conditioned and learned response. The analysis of the individual's ability to act appropriately and the implementation of procedures to enable positive sexual self-expression are the responsibility of the caregivers or staff in the living environment.

Individuals with more significant levels of mental retardation frequently engage in perseverative genitally oriented self-stimulation. It may seem that the individual's sole purpose in life is to publicly expose and play with his or her genitals. No form of intervention or interaction on the part of the caregivers seems to have any effect on changing or modifying the individual's behavior to a more acceptable form. When staff or caregivers begin to feel helpless in changing sexual behavior, the individual may be isolated so that others will not be involved directly or indirectly. The problem is that the situation then becomes self-perpetuating and self-fulfilling. The normal routine in a residential facility may be severely disrupted both by the individual's behavior and by the increased need for staff involvement. Certainly it is difficult, if not impossible, for normal family life to continue when one family member continuously demonstrates unacceptable sexual behavior. It should be an accepted premise that the individual can learn to control and inhibit responses that are unacceptable, but it may take much longer and it may be necessary to try many different techniques before one is found that will develop necessary coping skills.

Constraints of the Living Environment

The reality is that living environments provide different restraints for all persons in society. College students living in a dormitory must abide by the rules and regulations set forth by the college or university. The same principle applies to individuals with mental retardation and developmental disabilities, whether they live at home, in supervised apartments, in community residences, or in residential facilities. All societies have rules and, most often, the rules are based on the laws of the state of residence.

   In order to participate in a certain living environment, the individual will be required to follow the rules. If the individual and/or his or her family are not comfortable with the rules of that environment, I would encourage them to seek another living environment. Relating this back to the college student, if the college student desired to have a friend of the opposite sex in the dorm for overnight visits and it was against the rules of the college dormitory, the student and family would have to make a decision about accepting placement in the dormitory or seeking out another place for the student to live, such as an apartment where those specific rules did not exist or apply.

   If an interdisciplinary team and family, along with the individual with mental retardation or developmental disabilities, make the decision that he or she is capable of and desires to participate in certain PSS behaviors, it is the responsibility of this team to find appropriate housing that will allow the behavior.

Case Study 5-7

Tonya, a woman with milder mental retardation, had been very sexually active with male partners in the past. She had also experienced some same-sex foreplay and mutual masturbation. However, Tonya had to accept that she was in a living environment that had rules prohibiting sexual intercourse between two people of either the same or the opposite sex. It was explained to Tonya that masturbation might help her receive some of the same positive sexual feelings she had experienced previously with partners.

Verbal sexuality counseling was used to provide the information about masturbation and to help Tonya explore her sexual feelings. It was suggested that Tonya explore ways to use her own hands to stimulate her genitals and breasts. Also, by using a soft teddy bear as a rubbing aid, she explored her own breasts and genitals in a stimulatory way. This helped Tonya develop erotic feelings about her own pleasurable sexual needs. Masturbation became a more satisfying and acceptable form of sexual expression to her, and she soon learned to masturbate to climax. At this point in sexuality counseling, information about cleanliness and the use of the teddy bear was discussed. Tonya learned to wash the teddy bear to avoid infection and irritation of her genitals. Tonya was also able to generalize this sexual behavior to other soft objects, such as pillows.

Incidences of sexual intercourse and same-sex foreplay in the living environment decreased. Tonya now had a more appropriate way to express her sexuality and to feel good within the constraints of her environment.

Use of Nonharmful Techniques

Masturbation must be done in a nonharmful way, and the use of dangerous objects must be prohibited. Family members and staff should counsel individuals about nonharmful techniques when masturbating. It is not unusual, for example, to find that individuals who have been sexually abused will insert unusual and dangerous objects into their bodies. There is no simple answer to a problem like this. One of the secrets to success in developing a program to solve such situations is to be as creative as possible and to use whatever resources are at hand, being very sure to acknowledge and accept the preferences, needs, and desires of the individual, as the following case study illustrates.

Case Study 5-8

Dinah, a young woman living in a residential facility, had limited verbal skills and engaged in a great deal of self-stimulatory behavior. She had frequent outbursts of bad temper as a result of poor impulse control. Dinah was very sexualized and had been openly masturbating for a long time. She also engaged in sexual intercourse with someone the staff thought was not an appropriate partner, raising concerns about the potential of sexual exploitation. As a result, Dinah was given more supervision. As the supervision increased, the staff became aware of more masturbatory behavior, including the use of harmful objects such as coat hangers. Dinah had also pulled out the metal stopper in the bathtub and inserted it into her vagina.

The staff invited a sexuality counselor to come to a meeting to discuss possible solutions to the problem. In discussing what kinds of things were pleasurable to Dinah, the sexuality counselor discovered that Dinah found water relaxing and soothing, whether in a bathtub or swimming pool. The sexuality counselor suggested that a maintenance person be hired to make a nondetachable stopper for the tub so that during "down time" or times when Dinah was observed self-stimulating, she could be offered the option of taking a bath without the need for supervision. Dinah was also referred to an aquatics instructor for a swimming program. Swimming was age-appropriate and facilitated an activity in which Dinah both would be using her arms and hands in a meaningful and purposeful way and would be engaged in an activity incompatible with inappropriate masturbation.

In Dinah's situation, it was also important to make every effort to involve her in situations in which she had the opportunity to learn to socialize appropriately with men without such socializing being sexual in nature. In this way, she was more protected from potential abusive situations or possible victimization. Masturbation was a good sexual release for Dinah, but she needed to learn how to masturbate in nonharmful and pleasurable ways. Staff were encouraged to give Dinah a washcloth when she was in the bath and to tell her it was OK to rub herself with the washcloth because it would not hurt her. Staff were also advised to then give Dinah private time in the bathtub if she chose to masturbate.

Using these suggestions, the staff were very successful with Dinah. There were no reports of inappropriate masturbation during her aquatics program, and she was being offered the opportunity for more baths. She had become less abusive in her masturbatory behavior.

Self-Stimulation versus Mutual Masturbation

Another consideration in teaching self-stimulation is self-stimulation versus mutual masturbation, especially in situations in which certain types of sexual behavior are against the rules of a residential facility or against state laws. The question is often asked, "Isn't it all right to allow mutual masturbation?" Basically, the answer lies in the specific laws of the individual's residence. Some laws do not allow any type of sexual intercourse on state property or between unmarried adults but do not address mutual masturbation between consenting adults.

There are additional concerns regarding mutual masturbation that must be addressed. The first of these involves the notion of privacy. Whereas self-stimulation does not violate another person's right to privacy, mutual masturbation may violate this right if there is one willing and one unwilling partner. Also, with self-stimulation there is no fear of pregnancy. However, mutual masturbation between opposite sexes raises the possibility of pregnancy as well as that of sexually transmitted diseases. Individuals with mental retardation or developmental disabilities must be informed that pregnancy and sexually transmitted diseases can result from mutual masturbation. Emphasis should be placed on the fact that if the sperm enters the vagina, and birth control is not used, pregnancy can result. If couples make the decision to engage in mutual masturbation, they need to be aware of and capable of using birth control.

Another serious problem that needs to be addressed concerns mutual masturbation and oral sex. In the process of exploration and sexual maturing, many young adults engage in oral sex. This can be a dangerous activity if the active partner has grand mal seizures: a passive male partner could suffer serious penile injury. This is a difficult concept to communicate both to individuals with mental retardation or developmental disabilities and to staff and caregivers. The situation may seem unlikely, but the possibility exists and should be considered before it becomes a reality.

In residential facilities for individuals with mental retardation it is not uncommon to find mutual masturbation between two people of the same sex. This is mainly due to availability of partners. One of the primary ways to discourage same-sex activity is to encourage opposite-sex activity. However, because both behaviors are considered unacceptable in many living environments, it then becomes the job of the sexuality counselor to help the individuals establish sexual release mechanisms that are acceptable in their specific environment. Couples engaging in mutual same-sex masturbation can easily be counseled to use self-stimulation as a private act, involving no one else.

Case Study 5-9

Elise and Cassandra, two young women with milder levels of mental retardation living in the same residential facility, were the best of friends. They shared all of their possessions and loved to watch TV together. The two were engaging in mutual masturbation, often sneaking off together and climbing into each other's beds. Since such behavior violated the rules of their residence, Elise and Cassandra were encouraged individually to privately stimulate themselves in appropriate ways. The sexuality counselor explained how women masturbate by rubbing their breasts and clitoral area. This was hard for Elise and Cassandra to accept at first, but eventually they learned to have a friendship without sexual activity with each other.

As the level of mental retardation of the individuals involved becomes more significant, the need increases for more environmental controls and program planning. Traditional verbal sexuality counseling, as used with Elise and Cassandra above, will not be effective. For individuals with lower levels of intelligence, staff or caregivers must ensure that the rights of privacy of all concerned, including the individuals themselves, their family members, visitors, and other residents, are protected.

Such concerns are also important in a residential facility for individuals with less significant levels of mental retardation when mutual masturbation between two or more individuals of the same sex leads to anal intercourse. A frequent misinterpretation is that the individuals involved are not sophisticated in their sexual experimentation. The following case study demonstrates that the level of sophistication and experimentation is greater than that imagined by most people.

Case Study 5-10

Simon, an inquisitive and curious young adult with milder mental retardation, often approached other males and asked them to participate in mutual masturbation. This activity usually ended in anal intercourse with Simon being the aggressive partner. Simon was experienced in this behavior and was able to coerce other males into being his passive partner. The staff considered this behavior unacceptable because it violated the privacy of Simon's partners, and a sexuality counselor was asked to help.

Once Simon was given the suggestion of self-masturbation with his hands, he began to experiment on his own. Since Simon was used to having a male partner, his heterosexual mental imagery was not sufficient to make him successful in his attempts to masturbate alone, using fantasy. Therefore, it was suggested that Simon purchase a magazine from the drugstore that had erotic female pictures in it. He was then advised to use the magazine in private, while stimulating his penis with his hands, to see if a fantasy level could be developed. This did indeed work. Instead of participating in same-sex activity, Simon began to use his magazines in private. He stopped involving others in his masturbatory activity.

Concurrently, Simon began to exhibit more appropriate social behavior in general. He gained more control over his behavior around both males and females. More importantly, Simon developed a much healthier and self-satisfied PSS personality. This gradual increase in appropriate behavior appeared after 9 months of weekly group sexuality counseling sessions, during which time there were regressions and a great deal of ambivalence shown by Simon, both in what he said and in his behavior. As Simon began to adapt and generalize his behavior in a self-satisfying way, his ego development increased and improved.

There also appears to be a fairly high incidence of opposite-sex mutual masturbation in residential facilities. This often involves more than two individuals at a time. Depending on the circumstances, there may be two or three people participating, with one individual stationed as a look-out person. Many of these opposite-sex encounters end in vaginal intercourse, and some involve an individual having intercourse with two or three people consecutively. Such situations involve a high risk of acquiring sexually transmitted diseases, including AIDS.

There are numerous solutions to the problems associated with mutual masturbation, and the responsibility for solving them lies with many different people. Supervision must be increased, especially when it is known that an individual has a history of being sexually active. Birth control must be prescribed for people who are active sexually. Careful medical inspection for sexually transmitted diseases should be available. All sexuality education and counseling efforts should impart information that develops inner knowledge and inner concepts that increase the probability of more appropriate and socially acceptable behavior. In addition, self-stimulation when alone and in a private location should be encouraged. This will better ensure that sexual needs are met. It is not the responsibility of the counselor to be judgmental about the behavior. Rather, the counselor should help the individual adjust to the restrictions of his or her living environment while achieving personal sexual fulfillment.

Teaching Techniques

In developing proper attitudes and behavior with regard to masturbation, emphasis is placed on the fact that masturbation is a private act, done by one person, in a private place. However, generally accepted learning avenues, such as books, erotic movies, peer learning, and extended family interactions, are often not available to individuals with mental retardation or developmental disabilities. If available, the individual might not possess the skills needed to interpret and process the information into meaningful and useful material. To be useful, this information should be incorporated into a daily living schema.

The young adult who has good cognitive skills can be encouraged to use fantasy, especially with the aid of erotic pictures, to help in developing the desire and techniques to carry out successful masturbation without harm or involvement of others. Clear definitions of any terminology should be communicated in whatever way is necessary and appropriate. For individuals with more significant levels of mental retardation, simple pictures, slides, prosthetic aids, and so forth, may be more useful. Other commercially available materials, such as anatomically correct dolls, can also be effective (see Bibliography and Related Materials).

The question is often asked, "What about the individual with mental retardation or developmental disabilities who masturbates but does not know how to climax? Look at how frustrating that is. How can we help? Do we have to go as far as some propose and teach the individual to masturbate by using a 'hands-on' technique?" Hands-on teaching of masturbation is not an accepted practice at a pragmatic level, nor is it ethically, morally, or legally acceptable. A physician, within the restraints of the profession, may want to take the risk of touching the person with mental retardation or developmental disabilities in a sexually instructive way. However, the issues of ethics, malpractice, pragmatics, and appropriateness must be decided beforehand by the particular physician. I personally feel it opens the door to potential abuse. I strongly advise against any hands-on teaching by anyone.

For anyone interested in this topic, the child abuse laws of the individual's place of residence must be studied to determine at what age an individual with mental retardation or developmental disabilities is still considered a minor in that state. Further study of state statutes constituting a sexual offense, whether it be fondling, masturbation, assault (rape), or intercourse, in addition to the laws regarding the ability of an individual to give consent, must also be undertaken.

In many states, one will find that a sexual offense against someone under the age of 21 is subject to punishment in court according to the child abuse laws. It is possible that even a physician could be charged if hands-on attempts were made to teach masturbation and the parents of the individual with mental retardation or developmental disabilities considered it child abuse. In the area of hands-on teaching of masturbation, it seems that being overly cautious is judicious. Why not instead develop programs and situations in which the individuals can have privacy, explore their own bodies, learn what feels good, and learn when and where it is appropriate?

Professionals can use training techniques to teach the responses and desired behavior. This is also the perfect opportunity to teach the concepts of respect of self and others, privacy, and appropriate and inappropriate behavior. However, it is important to realize that, for individuals with mental retardation or developmental disabilities, the counselor may be teaching masturbation as the desired and ultimate sexual release mechanism for a specific person in a specific living environment. This is different from saying, "Everyone masturbates because it feels good. As you grow up, you will learn to have other sexual interactions with another person, and you will feel more sexually complete." An open PS communication with the self through masturbation may be the only available lifelong avenue for the person who is not living in an environment that permits choice of partners with whom to share sexual expression. If masturbation is to be the end goal for an individual, then it is our responsibility to help that end goal become obtainable and reachable.

An important, but difficult, task of the sexuality educator/counselor is to communicate the fact that self-pleasure and positive sexual feelings can be felt with masturbation. It is fairly easy to talk about feelings with individuals with milder mental retardation, and to instill good self-monitoring techniques for deciding what feels good at an emotional level. This becomes more difficult if not impossible as the level of mental retardation increases. There is no final test of being able to maintain appropriate and meaningful behavior; only the passing of time is an indicator of success and a judge of whether a sufficiently sophisticated internal monitoring system has developed during the sexuality counseling sessions. At necessary intervals, follow-up sessions should provide the support that will help sustain internal control for external behavior.

I believe it is important to remember and accept the basic premise that masturbation is a normal sexual behavior and that most people masturbate at some point in their lives. If staff, caregivers, or family members choose not to masturbate, then that is their right. However, when an individual with mental retardation or a developmental disability wants to masturbate and does it appropriately, in private, using no harmful objects, during leisure hours, it is his or her right. It is the responsibility of the staff, advocates, and family members to uphold that right to sexual self-expression for all individuals who do not abuse it.

CONCLUDING REMARKS

I know that the concepts expressed in this chapter will fit for some and be uncomfortable for others. That is fine. On very sensitive topics, everyone will not agree. The important point is for staff, parents, and families to be able to accept the PS development of the individual with mental retardation or developmental disabilities. If the individual makes the choice to masturbate, the staff, parents, and families should provide the education, counseling, and understanding to allow the individual to express his or her own sexuality through masturbation in a responsible way.

Chapter **6**

Same-Sex and Opposite-Sex Activity
Issues and Solutions

Since beginning my work in the area of sexuality education and counseling, I have chosen to speak of same-sex and opposite-sex activity rather than homosexuality and heterosexuality. The rationale behind this is my observation that the opportunities of individuals with mental retardation or developmental disabilities for sexual expression with a partner of choice are often so limited that these individuals simply learn to express themselves sexually with any available partners.

Is sex-role identity different in individuals with mental retardation or developmental disability? As reviewed by N. E. S. Gardner (1986), research indicates that this is not the case. However, the availability of education and counseling in sexuality, appropriate role models, and opportunities for socializing with the opposite sex have a great deal to do with an individual's gender identity and sexual self-concept.

In earlier chapters in this book I have stressed the rights of individuals with mental retardation or developmental disabilities to express themselves sexually. When I think of sexual relationships between individuals with mental retardation or developmental disabilities, I think of all of the parameters listed in Dailey's (1979) definition of sexuality (as quoted by N. E. S. Gardner, 1986, p. 48):

1. *Sensuality* An awareness of body and body image, sexual fantasy and memory, "satisfaction of skin hunger" (skin is the largest sex organ), physiology and anatomy, and the release of tension in orgasm
2. *Identity* The identity as male or female and the sex roles that are identified with each gender, as well as sex object preference (hetero- or homosexual); androgyny refers to the idea of combining the best of feminine and masculine role characteristics (like gentleness and nurturance combined with strength and assertiveness)

3. *Intimacy*   Spiritual feelings of closeness and caring that may go with sex
4. *Reproduction*   Creation of new life
5. *Sexualization*   The use of sex to control, influence, and manipulate others

Some of these components, such as reproduction, are difficult to actualize in a same-sex relationship, but all can and should be addressed for all individuals with mental retardation or developmental disabilities who are involved in sexual relationships, whether with same-sex or with opposite-sex partners.

Case Study 6-1

Suzanne and Wanda, two middle-aged women, were attending a community workshop for individuals with mental retardation. A sexuality counselor was asked to interview both women because the staff considered both Suzanne and Wanda promiscuous. During the interview, it became obvious that both women were sexually active, were enjoying sex, and had no intention of stopping their sexual activity. It was disturbing to hear from the caseworker that neither Suzanne nor Wanda was using any method of birth control. Both Wanda and Suzanne were willing to go to a doctor for birth control, but they were both from poor families and had not been seen by a physician in a long time. In the interview, the caseworker agreed to arrange for medical care to provide birth control.

In the past, Wanda and Suzanne's sexuality rights and needs would have been ignored. They would more easily have been victimized or gotten pregnant for lack of birth control or medical care to help deal with the issues. Both Wanda and Suzanne were sexually active, enjoyed sex, and planned to continue to have sex. Therefore, they were good candidates for sexuality education/counseling and were very responsive to it when it was provided.

Suzanne appeared to be in an enjoyable, nonabusive relationship. She was counseled about sexually transmitted diseases, shown how to use a condom for "safer sex," and advised to see a physician for birth control. Because the sexuality counselor suspected that Wanda was in an abusive relationship, she was advised about how to say, "No," to anyone who was abusing her. The use of a condom was also demonstrated to Wanda. She had a harder time grasping the information and required more follow-up work. The caseworker took steps to join together the efforts at home and in the community workshops to carry out the recommendations from the sexuality counselor. After this session, there was more cause for optimism regarding the future health and well-being of these two women.

Suzanne's and Wanda's families had not provided the sexuality education that was needed for them to avoid unwanted pregnancies or possible sexual abuse. Both women were capable of learning this information and were entitled to it. Some people might take the view that, by providing sexuality education and counseling for persons like Suzanne and Wanda, one is encouraging sexual activity and giving permission for it. I consider this a naive way to approach sexuality issues. It is accepted by professionals that all people are sexual from birth to death; why would it be any different for a person with mental retardation or developmental disability? Griffiths, Quinsey, and Hingsburger (1989) stated that "sexual behavior will occur regardless of accurate sexual knowledge. For this reason, the goal of sex and health education should be to provide individuals with information on how to appropriately express their sexuality in the most healthy way" (p. 73). The authors also noted that any agency that advocates sexual rights and freedoms for individuals with handicaps must also stress that these freedoms be expressed in ways that are safe for the individuals.

SAME-SEX ACTIVITY

In a large residential facility where 20–40 persons of the same sex live in the same building, rarely being given the opportunity to socialize with people of the opposite sex, it is understandable and predictable that one would observe more overt same-sex activity. Does "same-sex" mean "homosexual"? I do not believe it does. The term "same-sex" refers to sexual activity with a person of the same sex for purposes of sexual exploration or because that is who is available. To me "homosexual" implies that, if given a choice and the freedom to make the choice, a person would choose a sexual partner of the same sex rather than of the opposite sex. This indicates a chosen preference and a sexual orientation that is an integral part of the individual's sexual self-identity. If a sexualized person is never allowed or encouraged to socialize or be close to other persons of the opposite sex, it should not be surprising if he or she "chooses" to develop same-sex affectionate and physical bonds with persons he or she is living with.

In the past, there has been a great deal of focus on large residential environments. However, the reader should remember that a community residential facility for six or eight individuals of the same sex could become as restrictive as a large residential facility if it is miles away from locations where the opportunity for mixing with individuals of the opposite sex exists. Sometimes a "mini-institution" can be just as restrictive to the establishment of healthy opposite-sex relationships as a large residential facility.

Acceptability Issues

Dealing with Public Perceptions
When individuals with mental retardation or developmental disabilities engage in same-sex activity, the public often perceives this as homosexual behavior, and generally disapproves of it. I prefer to think of sexual

relationships between people of the same sex as same-sex activities until an individual is absolutely sure that his or her sexual preference is for someone of the same sex. When counseling individuals who have a sexual preference for same-sex activity and choose to enter the "homosexual life-style" in the community, the sexuality counselor needs to include these issues in the treatment plan so that work can be addressed toward those issues encountered in society by anyone choosing a homosexual life-style.

Morgenstern (1973) noted that more attention should be paid to the need of persons with mental retardation to have wider opportunities to form relationships, to date, to become engaged, to marry, and, if desired, to enjoy homosexual experiences. This was written in the 1970s but the same precepts hold true today. Morgenstern spoke of society's changing sexual mores and the demands of such young people for greater freedom to make their own decisions. He suggested that this may lead to other problems among these individuals. I believe that this is indeed what has happened. Advocates have pushed for more rights and now those rights exist. In this decade individuals with mental retardation or developmental disabilities must learn to accept all of the responsibilities that accompany these rights, especially in relationship to same-sex behavior and the accompanying high risk for contracting AIDS.

Restrictions of the Living Environment

I believe that all efforts should be made to help an individual live in the least restrictive environment. Individuals with mental retardation and developmental disabilities need to be aware that interdisciplinary teams that are trying to help them transfer to a less restrictive environment will need to know whether supervision is required for their psychosocial-sexual (PSS) behaviors. We need to help individuals understand that sexual behaviors do not exist within a vacuum. In order to move to less restrictive environments, individuals need to prove that they can manage their lives, including their psychosexual (PS) selves.

Case Study 6-2

Joshua, Lewis, and Rudy, adults with mental retardation, were pals who hung out together at their residential facility. Joshua, Lewis, and Rudy engaged in mutual masturbation and have participated in sexual activity that culminates by all three of them having anal intercourse with each other. However, all three claimed they were not experiencing positive feelings but were rather just having a better time than "jerking off."

The central issue here is what stand the professionals in their living environment should take regarding this behavior. Joshua, Lewis, and Rudy were capable of living in the community, so their life in the residential facility should be focused on developing skills and behaviors that would help them adjust to life in the community. In sexuality counseling, Joshua, Lewis, and Rudy were urged to examine the appropriateness of the behavior they had exhibited. They were encouraged to satisfy their sexual needs using masturbation as a private act, done alone, and not involving others.

In many communities, Joshua, Lewis, and Rudy's sexual expression would have been considered unacceptable if known to the public. Since all three men had the potential to live in the community, it was the responsibility of the residential staff to help them learn what behavior would be acceptable to society. In this case, private masturbation was the suggested solution to help these men fulfill their sexual needs and still function within the confines of their potential environment. In other cases, helping the individual to explore options for alternative sexual activity may be the best solution.

Case Study 6-3

Tyler was a young adult male with mental retardation and a severe speech handicap. Tyler also had a medical condition that resulted in a physical appearance quite different from his peers. He felt very self-conscious and had a very poor self-concept. Tyler did not understand why he looked different and why others made fun of him. As Tyler passed through puberty and began developing sexual feelings, he experimented extensively with masturbation. Tyler then wanted to participate in mutual masturbation. However, his past experiences at dances and other social events was that females would not pay attention to him, even if he worked up the courage to try to interact with them.

Tyler therefore began to look at the male population for a willing partner. Here Tyler also found difficulty unless he "bought" his way with gifts or food items. Tyler became quite successful at getting other males to cooperate with him in a passive role during anal intercourse, which he enjoyed. Tyler did not consider himself homosexual and was offended when someone called him "gay" or "queer," but he was making no effort to develop his sexuality in a heterosexual way.

Because Tyler wanted to live in the community, he entered sexuality counseling. The goals of his counseling sessions were to increase his self-esteem, ego, and body imagery, to learn the necessary sexual information, and to make sure that he was aware of the positives and negatives of being involved in the homosexual community at large. He was apprised of what special risks he might be taking because his disabilities render him more vulnerable to sexual exploitation and abuse. The sexuality counselor helped Tyler accept himself and look for an alternate solution to expressing his sexual feelings. In this case masturbation was encouraged, and the use of magazines with erotic pictures was suggested to help him develop the ability to fantasize. Privacy was also stressed, as was careful choosing of partners from those Tyler knew (without purchasing their favors).

Tyler was also encouraged to explore his ability to be more social and develop more skills in interacting with females on a nonsexual basis, so that eventually a friendship might lead to an affectionate opposite-sex relationship and possibly to a heterosexual experience. In the course of his sessions in a coeducational sexuality counseling group Tyler's self-image improved, and his behavior subsequently became more acceptable and appropriate to his current living environment.

Safety Considerations

Are same-sex relationships harmful? There are two important points to be made in considering this topic. The first is that there is always a possibility of physical harm if unsafe techniques are used or if one partner is unwilling. However, among the population of individuals with mental retardation or developmental disabilities there is a greater possibility of associated physical disabilities that can have unforeseen consequences in the realm of sexual activity.

Case Study 6-4

In a sexuality counseling group for males with mental retardation the topic of discussion was oral sex. These men were asked, "What would Jim do if Eric was giving oral sex to Jim and Eric had a grand mal seizure and bit down on Jim's penis?" The unanimous answer was, "Take him to the hospital and sew it back on." This answer holds no humor in reality because serious physical damage would be done to Jim, who was the passive partner. Oral sex was discussed as an expression of mutual masturbation in same-sex activity, and it was stressed that it usually is not harmful but that some precautions may be necessary.

A second point in regard to the potential for harm in same-sex activity has a more serious tone. In the 1990s, one important part of sexual relationships is conducting them in such a way as to avoid contracting AIDS, or hepatitis, in addition to herpes, and any of the other sexually transmitted diseases. As stated earlier, the practice of "safer sex" offers some protection, but is no guarantee. It is often difficult to determine whether individuals with mental retardation or developmental disabilities can process, integrate, and pragmatically use the information given to them about "safer sex." However, the risks incurred by the failure to do so are overwhelmingly high, so I believe that the right to sexual expression must absolutely be paired with the capability of being responsible for one's own sexual behavior and its consequences.

Such responsibility includes developing a life-long partner of one's choice and, until this is accomplished, not engaging in sexual practices of any kind in which there is an exchange of bodily fluids without using appropriate methods of protection. Individuals with mental retardation or developmental disabilities can and should learn to conduct their sexual lives in such a manner, whether they participate in same-sex or opposite-sex activities. There will be many individuals with mental retardation and developmental disability who will be able to heed and live by this advice. For them, the choice to participate in "same-sex" relationships that are consensual and nonexploitative should be honored. I believe that these individuals should be given this choice within the same parameters as anyone else in society. The important element is that the individual must be ready and able to accept the responsibilities that accompany this choice. It is important that the individual experiencing the behaviors should recognize and honor state laws.

OPPOSITE-SEX ACTIVITY

For purposes of differentiating between sexual behavior based on free choice and formed sexual orientation and sexual behavior based on exploration and availability of partners, I use the term "opposite-sex activity" rather than "heterosexuality." In general, however, the two terms describe a life-style that is much the same for individuals with or without mental retardation or developmental disabilities. Schepp (1986) referred to the heterosexual life-style as the process of expressing one's sexuality with members of the other sex, both in fantasy and in behavior, over the life span. She stated that this appears to be the experience of about half of the population of the United States, and that many of the other half are predominantly heterosexual in behavior, with an occasional experience or recurrent fantasy about people of their own sex. She noted that the dominant, approved cultural mode in much of the world is for men to select women as sexual partners and vice versa. Unfortunately, individuals with mental retardation often encounter difficulties in expressing themselves sexually even in a socially approved manner.

The Right to Sexual Self-Expression

For years, advocates, family members, professionals, and the individuals themselves have been fighting to be treated like everyone else and to be given the sexual rights that they are entitled to and yet have been denied over the years.

Case Study 6-5

Selma never let you forget that she was a mother, even though she had to give her child up for adoption. Selma, a woman with mental retardation who was in her mid-forties, was living in a residential center. Periodically, she went through cycles of being very sexually active, choosing any willing partner. When her sexual behavior became blatantly obvious, the staff referred Selma to a sexuality counselor. During one of the sexuality counseling sessions, Selma asked, in reference to sexual intercourse, "What is it supposed to feel like?"

Here was a woman who had given birth many years before, had lived in several different facilities, and had had a multitude of sexual partners. Yet, in total honesty and innocence, she wanted her question answered. It appeared that Selma had never had an orgasm; she was simply enjoying the male attention and closeness of the male body. However, on some level Selma knew that there should have been more.

Selma was encouraged to masturbate to see if she could achieve some positive feelings from clitoral stimulation. Selma was also encouraged to stop being promiscuous. Follow-up counseling sessions showed that Selma was beginning to have some positive sexual feelings. She was more aware of the orgasmic response, and she was being more discriminating about her overt sexual activity. In essence, Selma was developing more inner control over her sexual feelings and responses. During the sessions, Selma was never told that it was bad to act out sexually. Rather, she was told that she was choosing inappropriate behavior in an environment that had rules against sexual intercourse. Therefore, Selma was calling attention to herself and giving staff no option but to report her behavior when she exhibited it so publicly.

This situation is similar to the experience of many individuals with average intelligence who have not been helped to feel good about their sexuality and the feelings that they could have with sexual activity. With all individuals with mental retardation, it can easily be seen that they have the potential for developing good, positive feelings about their sexuality. It takes only information giving and permission giving, along with a supportive, nonjudgmental environment in which they can grow.

Personal Responsibility and Community Support

When individuals with mental retardation and developmental disability are being considered, I believe that the majority of the public is more comfortable with discussions of opposite-sex activity. Translating this receptiveness to the topic into support for sexuality education and counseling for such individuals has been a slow process, however. For this reason many have had relatively little success in establishing positive, healthy opposite-sex relationships, thus reinforcing in the minds of the public the myth that persons with mental retardation should be discouraged in these attempts. It is my belief that, with public approval and community support, appropriate sexuality education and counseling can break the cycle of failure and enable these individuals to achieve the level of sexual self-expression that is their right. The key factor in the success of the relationship is the ability of each of the individuals to take responsibility for his or her sexuality and for the consequences of expressing that sexuality.

Birth control is one of the responsibilities that accompanies the right to being sexual. If a couple chooses to be sexually active, they have the responsibility to go to the physician of their choice or to a family planning clinic or community health department and receive the information and support that they need to plan an appropriate birth control program that they will be able to carry out independently. If special sexuality education or counseling is needed to make this process easier, it should be provided by professionals specifically skilled in this area.

In my experiences with sexuality education and counseling, I have found it much easier to gain acceptance for the work that I do with opposite-sex couples than for my work with same-sex couples. More tolerance has been encountered and it is easier to build a support system for the couple and the relationship, once it has been ascertained that the two individuals can manage their adult lives. Many couples will choose to be together with or without marriage, and they deserve the necessary counseling and community support for this choice. If it is a committed relationship, it has become fairly easy to support a couple through the process of marriage and living together, either independently or in a residential facility where support personnel are available.

Historically, one of the strongest reasons for heterosexuality has been the establishment and maintenance of families; a female and a male parent are assumed to provide a balanced model of adult behavior and can share the tasks needed to give children a secure family life (Schepp, 1986). Many couples accept that they are capable of a loving, positive, committed relationship but fear that they will not be able to handle children. In such cases sterilization may be an appropriate choice for birth control. However, many couples will want to have children, and community resources must be developed to assure the proper nurture of the children and to provide support systems for child care, medical management, nutritional planning, and the like.

There are archaic laws on the books in many states that do not allow marriage for a person with mental retardation. Current advocacy systems are strong and able to fight these hurdles when they are encountered by a couple. However, it must be remembered that society expects any couple choosing to marry and have children to be able to take care of themselves and their children as much as possible. Advocates who act in the interest of children want them to be in environments capable of support and nurture rather than neglect or abuse. If there is a suspicion of neglect or abuse, the department of social services will step in to see that protective action is taken, often removing the child or children from the environment. For these reasons, those who advocate for the rights of individuals with mental retardation to marry and have children should also advocate for sexuality education and counseling, as well as community support, for these individuals in order to minimize the likelihood of such problems.

Avoiding Exploitation in Relationships

For individuals with mental retardation or developmental disabilities who have the ability to comprehend human sexuality and act on it, one of the most important concepts to teach is that of personal privacy. They must be told that "Your body is a private part of you. You are responsible for your own body and no one else can touch or hurt your body without force, unless you want them to or allow them to touch you. If someone wants to touch you or do something that you do not want, say 'No,' yell for help, get help, or fight." Learning not to be compliant is important for individuals with mental retardation or developmental disabilities, who must adjust to peer pressure from persons with average intelligence when living in the community or from other residents when living in a residential facility or group home.

Case Study 6-6

Lisa, an individual with mental retardation who lived in a residential facility, had a hard time communicating. She could talk, but only in simple words and phrases, and she had a severe articulation problem. Lisa was very sexually active with a variety of partners but, when counseled about her sexual activity, she admitted that she enjoyed sex with only one of these partners. However, because the other men would always buy her an extra soda, she would let them have sex with her. Lisa had to be taught to say "no" when she did not want to have sex, to separate her sexual feelings from her desire for sodas, and to be given a way to earn money so that she could buy the sodas without having to barter for sex to procure them.

The goal of the sexuality counseling was not to extinguish Lisa's sexual behavior, but to make it more meaningful and appropriate. This was accomplished as Lisa began to refuse the partners she did not like and found a way to earn money to buy treats. Lisa began to focus more of her attention on the man that she did like and thus began to develop a more meaningful relationship within which to explore her sexuality.

Individuals with mental retardation are often viewed as having a very poor self-image and sense of self-worth. Consequently, they sometimes sell themselves short or, literally, sell themselves cheaply with respect to sexuality. In a residential facility, it is not uncommon to find a barter system in effect: "I'll buy you a soda if you'll go behind the bushes and f--- with me." Since sexual intercourse is usually seen as a pleasurable activity, the individual will often cooperate and not "tell." The sexuality educator/counselor's task is to improve self-concept and self-worth, emphasize that friendship and sex should not be bought, and teach that saying "no" is a very acceptable and desired behavior.

PERSONAL HEALTH ISSUES

Birth Control

Sexuality education/counseling should include general information on birth control. In most cases it should also include pragmatic information that is specifically appropriate to the situation and the individuals involved. Overall, it is important to give useful and usable information to the individual with mental retardation or developmental disabilities. However, just providing the information is not enough. Making sure that the individual understands the information and can utilize it in real-world situations is crucial. It is important to realize that it may be difficult to adequately convey this information to some individuals. All efforts should be made to make this information easy to comprehend.

The sexuality educator/counselor should emphasize that not all birth control methods are equally effective for all persons, and each individual should decide which works best for him or her. The session should concentrate on communicating the basics of conception and contraception and devote less time to esoteric information that the individual may find difficult to effectively use. There is no point in giving birth control information that is beyond the ability of a specific individual to understand or use. Careful assessment of each individual should indicate the correct approach. Appropriate and necessary information should be given in a clear, concise manner and reviewed to ensure comprehension and retention.

Beyond the basics of conception/contraception, individuals with mental retardation or developmental disabilities need to learn where to obtain birth control and how to use it properly. Some contraceptives are readily available in the community—for example, condoms, foams, vaginal suppositories, and sponges—whereas others, such as birth control pills, Depo-Provera shots, intrauterine devices, and sterilization, can only be obtained from a physician. Also, different birth control methods must be utilized differently. For example, the pill must be taken regularly whether the person is sexually active or not, but foam or condoms should be used before each act of intercourse (and not after the act of intercourse). Since individuals with mental retardation often have trouble with multiple-step instructions, this information should be relayed in simple terms and repeated until comprehension is assured.

I believe very strongly that both men and women with mental retardation or developmental disabilities should be given the same information regarding birth control and the same opportunity to obtain and use it. In particular, women need to know why condoms provide some safety in sex, what kind to buy, and how to purchase them. If purchasing condoms is difficult for a woman, she should be able to go to a central, private place in her living, learning, and/or working environment to get condoms. Women should be encouraged to handle a condom, learning how to put it on her male partner and how to safely take it off and dispose of it. It is also important to teach both men and women that a new condom should be used for each act of sexual intercourse. In addition, use of

condoms should be encouraged even when participating in mutual masturbation because exchange of bodily fluids might be involved.

There are many community resources, such as family planning clinics, where contraceptives can be obtained, as well as information on birth
control for both males and females. Individuals should be made aware of
community resources that will be supportive and helpful and should
know how to access these services. It is helpful to review the process of
obtaining birth control, whether at a clinic or from a private physician.
Discuss the questions that may be asked. If there is going to be a physical
exam, go over what will happen in detail. Make sure the individual is
comfortable with the process.

Individuals with mental retardation or developmental disabilities
should also be given information on abortions. Abortion is a sensitive
topic, and there are probably as many feelings and opinions about it as
there are people. It is important to present information about abortion in
a nonjudgmental way. The individual needs to receive and understand all
necessary information about the issue: what an abortion is, how one can
be legally obtained, who has to pay for it, and general cost in terms of
both money and health. Educators and counselors must be aware of state
and federal laws on this issue. They should also ask about family views
and honor the family's position. When the family views abortion as an
acceptable alternative, they can be involved in the decision making process. When this is not the case, local protection and advocacy systems
may need to be used.

Case Study 6-7

Eloise, an individual with mental retardation, was 3 months pregnant
when she appeared at an abortion clinic. The abortion counselor found at
the intake interview that Eloise had no knowledge of what caused her
pregnancy—only that there was a baby inside her. She also showed no
knowledge of birth control or interest in using birth control after the desired abortion. The abortion counselor was leery of the situation because
she did not think that Eloise was able to understand the informed consent
form.

Eloise knew that she had trouble learning about sexual topics because
they embarrassed her. The abortion counselor handled the situation by
providing basic sexuality education using drawings and discussions of
anatomy, physiology, conception, contraception, pregnancy, and so forth.
Eloise was then sent home to think about the information and consider use
of birth control after the abortion. A few days later, Eloise returned to the
abortion clinic to see the counselor. She understood the information provided on the previous visit, and now freely admitted that she had had sexual intercourse with a man, which was how she became pregnant. Eloise
also verbalized a willingness to use birth control after the abortion. At this
point, the abortion counselor felt comfortable enough with Eloise's knowl-

edge to allow her to sign the informed consent form and proceed with the abortion arrangements.

This example shows appropriate caution and good counseling skills on the part of the abortion counselor, who accepted the task of helping Eloise become more responsible for herself sexually. If necessary, a certified sexuality educator/counselor involved with community agencies can apprise abortion counselors of the best methods of counseling people with mental retardation or developmental disabilities. The job of the sexuality educator/counselor is to give information and deal with feelings. The counselor should not advocate for or against abortion, but should help the individual receive and process the information at a level that is easily understood.

The sexuality educator/counselor should periodically check with public health officials to be sure that the most currently available information on birth control is provided. In order to assure the availability of community resources, health educators in local and state health departments need to become familiar with techniques of teaching that will be beneficial for the individual with mental retardation or developmental disabilities. The sexuality counselor should offer his or her support for this process by providing in-service training.

Sexually Transmitted Diseases

Until AIDS came onto the scene, sexuality education and counseling regarding sexually transmitted diseases centered around giving information about signs or symptoms that would enable individuals with mental retardation or developmental disabilities to know that they needed medical attention and teaching them how to obtain it. In addition, it was important to know how to recognize signs and symptoms, such as herpes blisters, in a partner and then to avoid sexual contact with that partner until he or she was well. With the advent of AIDS, a very different situation exists. AIDS is essentially an invisible killer, and there is no way to know if a partner or potential partner carries the AIDS virus unless reliable blood testing is done. Even blood tests involve a degree of uncertainty because the virus does not show up in the blood immediately after exposure.

I have found that the AIDS situation has presented special problems in working with individuals with mental retardation or developmental disabilities. It has been difficult to convince such individuals of the abstract concept that a person who looks very healthy could be very sick, carrying a deadly virus that can be exchanged through bodily fluids during sexual intercourse or sexual play. It is often difficult to develop a concrete appreciation of getting sick, hospital care that does not make a person well, dying, and of the more abstract concept that death is permanent. The sexuality educator/counselor then must relate the death back to the sexual contact with the person carrying the AIDS virus.

I have listened to individuals with mental retardation answer questions about the information I give them in a way that indicates understanding, but I doubt that internalization and integration of the material has taken place. I base this conclusion on the fact that most individuals I have counseled continue to have sexual intercourse with multiple partners while reporting that condoms, which would provide some protection, are used inconsistently, even though they know the dangers.

Availability of condoms and contraceptive sponges containing nonoxynol-9, the spermicide that is reported to kill the AIDS virus, is part of the answer to the problem. All residential facilities, sheltered workshops, and supervised apartments should provide an ample supply of the nonoxynol-9 condoms that individuals can access without embarrassment or questioning.

Case Study 6-8

Jeremy, a man with mental retardation who was entering his thirties, had never understood his sexual feelings of attraction to men. He was very sexualized and, while living in the community, had had many enjoyable sexual experiences with men. Jeremy never forced sex on anyone, but he had participated in anal intercourse and oral sex with many young teenagers that he saw as willing and eager partners. He never felt at risk, unusual, or different. Suddenly, Jeremy's family and members of the community started questioning him about why he was a homosexual and whether he knew that he could get AIDS. Jeremy was very confused. People were telling him that this pleasurable thing called sex could kill him.

Sexuality education and counseling were difficult with Jeremy because he could not see the abstract relationship between pleasurable sex and death. Role-play situations were set up to help demonstrate this relationship in a concrete manner but were not very successful. Jeremy understood that if he died, he would be buried and not be able to come back, but it still did not make sense to him. He also had trouble understanding why it was wrong for him to have sex with someone who was younger than he as long as that person wanted to have sex.

In desperation, the sexuality educator/counselor decided on two realistic goals. The first goal was to convince Jeremy not to have sex with anyone under the age of 18, which was a difficult concept since Jeremy had little understanding of the idea of age and could not even tell his own age. The counselor talked about choosing people who were as tall or as big as Jeremy and lived and worked in similar environments. Jeremy seemed to understand that he should not approach or be involved with people who went to public school because they were too young. The second goal was to convince Jeremy that he should wear a condom with nonoxynol-9 spermicide for each and every sexual encounter. Jeremy was taken to the drugstore, taught how to recognize the condom package he should buy, and instructed in how to put on the condom, take it off, and dispose of it properly. This process was made concrete enough so that the counselor was sure that Jeremy understood what to do.

Jeremy then became involved with a man who had active hepatitis. Many hours were spent in counseling with Jeremy, trying to teach him that the transmission of the hepatitis virus could be similar to that of the HIV virus. Again, this instruction was not very successful because it was just too abstract. Jeremy had not had a hepatitis vaccination, and he agreed to give informed consent to receive the vaccine, which offered him some protection against the hepatitis virus. However, Jeremy never understood why he could not have a shot to protect himself against AIDS.

The difficulty in providing sexuality education/counseling for Jeremy was that no matter how concrete the information was, Jeremy had such a strong sex drive and so little ability to generalize and internalize information that it was often a losing battle. The counselor's hope was that Jeremy would find a partner to bond with who was free of any sexually transmitted disease and with whom Jeremy could develop a meaningful and purposeful relationship. If not, the prognostic indicators all led to Jeremy continuing to interact with others in a promiscuous way, and thereby endangering his life and the lives of his future sexual partners.

Gordon (1987) noted that "Safer sex demands the use of a condom. It's no guarantee against pregnancy and sexually transmitted diseases such as AIDS. And of course you wouldn't want to have sex with anyone whom you suspect may be infected" (p. 15). Gordon suggested new rules for using condoms, which include using only a lubricated condom with the spermicide nonoxynol-9 and a reservoir tip.

> The couple should incorporate the condom into sexual foreplay and put it on at the point of erecting. After ejaculation (coming), the base of the condom should be held in place as the man withdraws his penis so that the condom will not come off inside the woman's vagina. Never use a condom more than once. It's also a good idea to wash thoroughly and urinate after sex. (p. 14)

This information also applies to individuals with mental retardation and developmental disabilities. It is the job of the sexuality educator/counselor to provide this information in such a way that it is comprehensible and usable for those individuals who need to receive such information in a very concrete manner. I have often encouraged males with mental retardation to use condoms when they are masturbating in private so that they will become comfortable with handling condoms—putting them on, taking them off, and disposing of them properly. This information on handling condoms should be given on a regular basis and should be communicated consistently by all adults in the environment. Family members should be informed of the instruction being given so that they can reinforce it and also have a supply of the condoms at home. Information on condom use and access to condoms should be made available to women as well. Ideally, men and women with mental retardation should be able to go to a store, find or ask for nonoxynol-9 condoms, and purchase them. If individuals are not capable of making the purchase themselves, they should be assured that they can get the condoms in their living, learning, or working environments.

I have changed many of my education and counseling techniques over the years in response to the AIDS epidemic. Until there is a vaccine and/or a cure for AIDS, community placement, the Individual Program Plan (IPP) planning, supported employment, and independent living must all be focused on the absolute necessity to have all acts of sexual expression be responsible. The connection between a pleasurable sexual act and death seems to be a very abstract concept that is difficult to teach to any individual, regardless of his or her age or level of ability or disability.

In reviewing recently published books that address sexuality, sexual abuse, and so forth, I was struck with the paucity of information on what to do about sexuality education and counseling with any population in the era of AIDS. Practicing "safer sex" is helpful and somewhat protecting, but abstinence is the only sure way not to be exposed to AIDS through sexual contact. Persistent problems with feelings of invincibility regarding AIDS make it hard to advocate for individuals with mental retardation and developmental disabilities who are living in the community and rightfully want to have all of the privileges that others have concerning sexuality issues. With privileges come responsibilities, and giving privileges before ensuring that the individual understands all of the responsibilities is poor professional practice. With individuals with mental retardation or developmental disabilities it is difficult to tell when the feeling of responsibility has been internalized and integrated into the ego structure. Just knowing the information and being able to explain it back to an instructor is not assurance that the information will be used or is pragmatic for that individual.

For administrators running residential facilities or independent living environments, the dilemma is more severe. Even with appropriate sexuality education and counseling, the risks are too high for multiple partner sexual behavior involving sexual intercourse or any sexual activity that involves the exchange of bodily fluids. I believe responsible professionals should be encouraging monogamous, lifelong relationships with emotional commitment. Individuals with developmental disabilities or mental retardation will need to heed the same restrictions as the rest of society if they are to be safe from this dread disease of the 1990s.

It is obvious that there will have to be a real effort to take the newly emerging findings on AIDS and translate them into understandable and purposeful information that might break through the feelings of invincibility that so many individuals seem to have regarding AIDS. No quick, easy answers are anticipated, but constant awareness of new information and a willingness to try to promote understanding in a proactive way to all persons is desired. Without this effort, the battle will not only be lost, it will be hard even to begin.

Individuals with mental retardation and developmental disabilities also need to know as much as they can comprehend about all sexually transmitted diseases. I would encourage the person providing the sexuality education and counseling to work closely with the health department to arrange visits for cooperative educational sessions and to make sure that parents and staff of sheltered employment or living environments receive the same information so that they can also reinforce what is being taught.

This is certainly a topic with no easy answers. Maybe the important point is to keep trying and modifying, and above all to recognize that individuals with mental retardation and developmental disabilities are going to behave sexually just as anyone else. Therefore, these individuals require and deserve the information necessary to help them make safe and responsible choices. The fact that this information is difficult to impart and very sensitive in nature does not excuse the professional from doing the very best job possible, modifying his or her technique as necessary for each individual. Creative solutions should also be devised with input from individuals with mental retardation and developmental disabilities and perhaps their parents and friends regarding special precautions to be taken under specific situations. The sexuality educator/ counselor should always keep the best interest of the individual in the forefront, recognizing the right of each individual to receive as much information as he or she can process.

CONCLUDING REMARKS

It is anticipated that professionals will advocate for societal recognition of individuals with mental retardation or developmental disabilities as being fully sexual. As this advocacy increases, many persons with mental retardation or developmental disabilities will choose their own sexual partners. However, there are still many persons with mental retardation or developmental disability who will never enter into a faithful and monogamous, lifelong relationship but will desire to be sexually active and will choose one or more partners of the same or opposite sex. I believe it would be a rare occurrence for an individual with mental retardation or developmental disabilities to come to me and ask for permission to have sexual intercourse. Of course, if this did occur, it would provide the perfect teachable moment to talk about sexually transmitted diseases, "safer sex," nonoxynol-9 condoms, and so forth. It would also be a time to talk about caring relationships, how to avoid abuse and what to do if it happens—in general, how to have a positive, loving relationship.

Sexuality education and counseling often focuses on communication, friendships, dating, enjoying another person without sexual intimacy, and avoiding having sexual intercourse if it was not desired. No one seems to be very bothered by this kind of information, but when a sexuality educator/counselor starts talking about having sexual intercourse, parents, staff, and community personnel begin to get nervous. In order to avoid the many problems inherent in human sexual expression, these topics must be discussed, and information and feelings need to be shared—not for the purpose of frightening the individual, but for the purpose of teaching and educating the person toward more responsible behavior.

Chapter 7

Marriage and Parenthood

THE ISSUE OF INTIMACY

Intimacy is usually conceived of as a relationship in which two people share intellectual, emotional, and physical closeness. Not everyone is capable of developing an intimate relationship even though they may want to or work at it very diligently. However, a certain level of intelligence is not a prerequisite. Individuals with mental retardation or developmental disabilities are capable of developing intimate relationships.

Individuals with less significant levels of mental retardation or developmental disabilities have capabilities similar to those persons without mental retardation or developmental disabilities. However, for individuals with more significant levels of mental retardation or developmental disabilities, true intimate relationships, as defined above, are not readily or easily achievable. Relational abilities must be examined on an individual basis; generalities should not be drawn.

Case Study 7-1

Dottie and Tom, a couple in mid-life, had both grown up in residential facilities. They were sweethearts and cared very much for each other. Dottie had mental retardation and cerebral palsy. She could not speak clearly at all but was able to use an augmentative communication system involving a typewriter and a printer that allowed her to communicate. Tom was diagnosed with mental retardation and could not ambulate on his own; he had lived his life in a wheelchair. Dottie and Tom approached an advocate and the administration at their facility about being married so that they would always be together.

They were living in a residential facility that by regulation had to allow them to marry and continue living on the premises, if that was what they decided. Dottie and Tom did marry, but because of their need for physical assistance they chose to stay in the facility. Their general activity program did not change and their adjustment seemed quite good. Having previously provided premarital counseling, the staff and the sexuality counselor continued to provide verbal assistance.

> Dottie and Tom were interested in the warmth and closeness that they thought marriage would bring them. They were not interested in expressing their affection physically; they asked for and received two single beds in the same room. The administration seemed supportive in providing them with whatever they needed to make the adjustment. One professional asked, "What if they want a divorce?" The team answered, "That would be their right also."

Such support for Dottie and Tom would not have been evident in many living environments in past years, but the situation has changed. What appears to be important today is whether two adult people can manage their lives and, if not, what support they need to be able to do so and how that support is going to be provided.

When intimacy encompasses an intellectual or emotional support system and closeness, society and families will rarely dispute the rights and needs of the individuals to participate in the relationship. However, when intimacy involves sexual intercourse, many of these same people shy away from helping individuals develop the skills necessary to deal with the feelings, emotions, and behaviors associated with intimate sexual activity. This stumbling block of public opinion and family acceptance needs to be overcome. At the same time, it should be the role of the sexuality educator/counselor to work with the individuals, alone and as a couple, to help them assume the responsibility for their intimate relationship, especially in the areas of birth control and feelings of closeness, love, sexuality, and sensuality. Through guidance and awareness of himself or herself and of the other person involved in the relationship, an individual with mental retardation or developmental disabilities can be helped to have a fulfilling intimate relationship.

Two important functions of the sexuality counselor when helping an individual develop an intimate relationship are: 1) determining what skills the individual has in developing and sustaining an intimate relationship, and 2) offering a support system for the individual who is working toward this goal. The emotional and psychosocial-sexual (PSS) abilities and developmental level of the individual must be assessed so that counseling will give the person a good chance of achieving some success.

Developing intimacy skills enables the individual to develop a more satisfying relationship, rather than just accepting a relationship with anyone who responds to him or her. The individual should understand that he or she has a choice about developing an intimate relationship and that there are responsibilities accompanying this choice.

The sexuality counselor must work within the constraints of the environment in which the individual resides. The counselor should also work with the expectations of the extended family, the staff of the residential facility, or the community. For example, the extended family may support a couple (e.g., by having a mobile home on the family property), or they may offer no support whatsoever or even attempt to prevent their relative from entering into an intimate relationship of which they do not approve. When such situations occur, it is appropriate for the counselor to involve the legal advocate for the individual to see that his or her legal rights are protected.

If the goal of the individual or couple is totally unrealistic, or it is determined that the couple is truly incapable of forming a meaningful and supportive intimate relationship, it is the counselor's responsibility to help the couple dissolve the relationship and move toward more appropriate and meaningful friendships, relationships, and social situations. Social opportunities in the community may enable individuals with mental retardation or developmental disabilities to meet appropriate friends or companions with whom they might enter into a nonintimate relationship. By providing information and aid, the individual can be assisted in finding other individuals who share similar interests.

MARRIAGE

In *The Right to Grow Up,* Haavik (1986) stated:

> Although [it is] illegal in many states, a considerable number of developmentally disabled persons do marry. Attitudes of parents and caregivers stem from the level of functioning of the individual. Parents of trainable level children for the most part disapprove of the prospect of marriage for their children, while parents of more mildly involved adolescents are more likely to view marriage for their offspring in a positive light. Similarly, administrators of institutions largely disapprove of marriage of institutional residents but are more approving of marriages of community-residing mentally retarded persons. The incidence of marriage among developmentally disabled persons is lower than the incidence among the nondisabled population. Studies investigating marital satisfaction or success have shown that many developmentally disabled couples function quite adequately and happily in marriage. . . (p. 86)

Haavik and Menninger (1981) provide an excellent overview of laws restricting marriage between individuals with mental retardation in their Chapter 2.

Many individuals are capable and desirous of entering into marriage. When faced with the decision to support or not support a couple or individual in their choice to enter into marriage, the professional must be able to evaluate and assess each individual's capability to cope with the necessary and appropriate skills that will make the goal of marriage an achievable one. If the determination is made that the adults involved can manage their lives in a way that is conducive to marriage, it is the responsibility of the sexuality educator/counselor to provide as much support and training as necessary to prepare the individuals for marriage. When it is determined that the individual or couple is not capable of functioning in the desired situation, guidance toward alternate decisions should be offered so that new and obtainable goals can be set and achieved.

Individuals with mental retardation or developmental disabilities who are contemplating marriage must be given support to make necessary adjustments to their living situation. Professionals need to be aware of options in regard to birth control counseling, sexuality education and counseling, education and training of life skills, alternative living arrangements, and availability of health care in the community. Parents or caregivers, staff, and support personnel working with the individuals need to be involved in the efforts to provide adequate training to help ensure success.

Developing Support Systems

Experienced educators should present information in all areas of daily living, emphasizing how to utilize various support systems without the supervision experienced in the past. This is an important issue for individuals who have moved from a more protective residential facility to the community. In the facility many decisions are already made for an individual, limiting his or her experience with situations requiring expression of preference or problem solving. In the community it is quite different. The "protective layer" provided by the residential facility is gone, and the phrase "responsibility for self" has more meaning.

Haavik and Menninger (1981) stated that:

> Workable alternative living arrangements are needed in order to maximize the possibility of harmonious and mutually beneficial marriages. It is also very important to develop premarital training programs that prepare the developmentally disabled person for the demands and obligations of marriage, as well as providing ongoing access to critically needed resources such as counseling, financial, legal, and vocational assistance. . . . After the clients have been judged capable, they can then move out into more independent community living settings . . . regulations specify that if a resident of an institution is married, he or she must be assured privacy during visits of the spouse. If a married couple are residents of the same institution, the regulations also specify that they be allowed to share a room. (p. 57)

All efforts should be made to keep together any married couple who desires it. With appropriate support systems, the probability for success in the marriage is greatly increased. Such support is a basic ingredient in enabling married individuals with mental retardation or developmental disabilities to achieve happiness.

Case Study 7-2

Emmy Lou Elisha and Elrod were individuals with mental retardation who married after knowing each other for a long time. Since marrying, they have lived in a mobile home on the extended family's property. The extended family approached a residential facility to see if the couple could move, as a married unit, to the facility because the family did not feel that it was offering enough supervision and support. The residential facility did not have accommodations for married couples but arranged to have the mobile home moved to the facility, where support systems were established to help Emmy Lou Elisha and Elrod function in their new environment.

Emmy Lou Elisha and Elrod were both given jobs and/or activities at the facility and were encouraged to participate in the recreation available there. Someone on the staff was assigned to provide support counseling and someone else made periodic checks on the mobile home for cleanliness and safety. Arrangements were made for the couple to receive their meals in the cafeteria. The staff at the facility worked with both Emmy Lou Elisha and Elrod as a couple, ascertaining their strengths and weaknesses. In this case, Emmy Lou Elisha was found to be the stronger of the pair. Elrod needed more support, which was given. However, the couple had tremendous difficulty separating from their extended family and eventually moved back to their original family location.

The important factor in this case study is that the residential facility, as an alternate living environment, was willing to accommodate Emmy Lou Elisha and Elrod without separating them or disturbing the already established marital relationship. This kind of willingness and support on the part of the residential facility certainly is needed. However, what happens to the couple who marries, attempts to live in the community, fails at this living arrangement, and has no extended family for support or shelter? What is the job of the residential facility at that point? Bringing the couple back to a residential facility where they must live separately in male and female dormitories is not a reasonable solution. It would be better for the community to develop resources such as supervised apartment complexes where married couples who are having trouble surviving alone could live together. Minimum supervision could be offered for the activities of daily living, whether they be budgeting, child rearing, or birth control. This seems to be the direction to look toward in the future.

Learning Skills for Daily Living

Issues such as these highlight the importance of comprehensive premarital counseling and education for individuals with mental retardation or developmental disabilities. All areas of physical and mental health must be addressed, from nutrition and food preparation to self-care, including birth control and its proper use. Both individuals must learn coping strategies for all aspects of life, including the very difficult strategy of decision making. Counseling and support should not stop once the couple is married but should continue until it is ascertained that the couple can function independently.

Haavik and Menninger (1981) stated that "there is an urgent need for training programs that provide [such] persons with reasonable expectations and needed skills for marriage" (p. 58). They suggested the following topics for a premarital preparation program (p. 58):

1. Sex education, including birth control, venereal disease, and training in appropriate sociosexual relationships
2. Money management, e.g., learning to prepare an anticipated monthly budget
3. Housing alternatives, including different types, costs, and maintenance needs
4. Domestic and home maintenance duties, such as food preparation, shopping, cleaning, clothes washing, and minor repairs
5. Transportation alternatives for work, leisure activities, and health and related appointments (different types, cost, and reliability of method should be explored)
6. Use of community resources such as health, social service, educational, and legal agencies
7. Relationships with relatives, including anticipated support or problems
8. Use of leisure time and social activities
9. Child-rearing choices, including responsibilities, duties, cost, and inevitable changes of marital relationships

Perhaps most important among these topics is the first. There are many men and women with mental retardation or developmental disabilities who might have the desire and skills to enter into and sustain a marriage, but they do not have the functional or cognitive skills necessary to parent. For these couples, counseling should emphasize that the prospect of developing a successful intimate relationship will be better if they do not have children. These couples can use continuous birth control if they so desire and are responsible enough to use it effectively.

The main objective of counseling is to inform the couple that sexual intercourse is a responsible act and that pregnancy can result if birth control is not used. The couple should be informed of available community resources and provided with the necessary education and counseling for developing a positive marital relationship and responsible decision making about birth control and possible parenthood. The couple can be referred to local family planning clinics or private physicians who have experience in working with persons with mental retardation or developmental disabilities. The counselor should ensure that the couple receive positive and consistent information from all people with whom they interact.

When birth control is not considered a reliable option and the couple does not desire children, they should be counseled about the possibilities of vasectomy and/or tubal ligation. Only if total, comprehensive informed consent is achieved should these sterilization procedures be used, because they are extremely difficult to successfully reverse. This option can also be used with someone who runs a high risk of producing children with mental retardation and, after having genetic counseling, chooses sterilization.

PARENTHOOD

Many professionals and parents are comfortable with marriage between persons with mental retardation or developmental disability; however, when the topic turns to parenthood there are outcries of fear and resistance.

> Many professionals and others are advocating marriage as long as contraception and appropriate community support are available. Parenthood among developmentally disabled people is oftentimes not viewed as positively, however. One of the principal dilemmas in the controversy of marriage and family rights is separating the rights and responsibilities of marriage from the rights, responsibilities, and duties involved in parenthood . . . usually the right to marry automatically implies the right to procreate. (Haavik & Menninger, 1981, p. 65)

Whitman and Accardo (1990) concluded that the prevalence of parents with mental disabilities is unknown and possibly unknowable. They found that poor judgment was most frequently mentioned as being the most difficult problem for these parents.

> The overwhelming majority of these parents report significant problems with their children, with their parenting role, and in their role as income providers. Almost none have been prepared in any way for any of these roles. Further, there are few, if any resources to support them in this effort. Many of these parents are remanded to protective services, which tends to be more punitive than supportive. (p. 28)

Haavik (1986) believes that if support is provided, it will be possible for some parents with mental retardation to do a successful and satisfying job raising their children.

Case Study 7-3

Jeannette, an individual with mental retardation who had spent most of her life in a residential facility, met Heyward, a man with mental retardation from the community. Jeannette and Heyward fell in love and desired to marry. The staff at the residential facility provided counseling for Jeannette and determined that she was capable of handling a marital relationship. The residential staff also arranged for a community-based counselor to work with Heyward. The couple were counseled about the responsibilities of marriage and developing the coping skills necessary to function in a marital relationship.

Because Jeannette has no extended family, it became the responsibility of the staff to provide the training and counseling to prepare her for marriage. After marriage, Jeannette and Heyward still required a support system for a time. This was provided by the community resources with backup from the residential staff. When Jeannette and Heyward decided to have a baby, they used community resources for prenatal care and other services. This marriage became meaningful for both people involved. However, without the support offered by the involved professional staff there would have been significant problems, because the couple did not have the skills to deal with many aspects of marriage and parenthood alone.

Potential for Retardation in Children

One of the main concerns voiced in the community is whether individuals with mental retardation or developmental disability will have children who are similarly affected. As noted by Haavik (1990), "measures of intelligence have suggested that many children of developmentally disabled parents function within the normal range of intelligence, although the percentages of children who are mentally retarded and need special schooling are substantially higher than percentages in the nonretarded population" (p. 87).

In *When a Parent Is Mentally Retarded*, D'Souza (1990) discussed common causes of mental retardation. A list adapted from Berini and Kahn (1987) indicates common causes of mental retardation (Table 7.1.). D'Souza concluded that,

> Mental retardation is of heterogenous etiology, including genetic as well as nongenetic causes. Genetic evaluation for etiology, management, and counseling is an integral component of modern medical care. An important factor is the recognition of different levels of mental retardation. The great majority of adults with mental retardation fall into the mild to moderate range of mental retardation and live in the community. Health care personnel need to realize that the offspring of these individuals do not necessarily have mental retardation and are more likely not to have mental disability. . . . It is important that all caregivers be aware of the needs of adults with mental retardation and their family members for genetic evaluation and counseling. Mentally retarded adults in the community should be provided with comprehensive genetic services. (p. 45)

Responsibilities of Parenthood

Responsibilities involved in marriage are fairly obvious, and some individuals will succeed in achieving them whereas others will not. Responsibilities involved in parenthood are harder to define, evaluate, and prepare for adequately. Each child is a unique individual with specific needs that differ from those of other children. However, all children need protection, nurturance, nourishment, love, and stimulation, in addition to proper medical and environmental care. Not all people are capable of providing these ingredients. If the parent is an individual with mental retardation, the community will probably scrutinize the situation and the first indicators of inadequate parenting will bring interference from various agencies.

The responsibilities of parenthood range from prenatal care to understanding pregnancy and recognizing problems that require medical assistance to preparation for childbirth. After birth, coping with the demands of parenthood includes knowing how to stimulate children at different levels of child development, knowing the signs of and caring for illness in children, and such routine tasks as food preparation, handling a baby, following doctor's orders and giving medications, ensuring safety in

Table 7.1.   Common causes of mental retardation

Genetic

Chromosomal disorders
Inborn errors of metabolism
Hereditary degenerative disorders
Hormonal deficiencies
Primary CNS defects
Malformation syndromes
Sporadic syndromes with unidentified etiology, possibly genetic
Low end of normal distribution

Acquired

Prenatal

Infection (e.g., syphilis, rubella, toxoplasmosis, cytomegalic inclusion disease)
Fetal irradiation
Toxins (e.g., fetal alcohol syndrome, lead poisoning, mercury poisoning, fetal
    hydantoin syndrome)
Maternal metabolic problems (e.g., maternal PKU)

Perinatal

Prematurity
Asphyxia (e.g., abruptio placentae, cord prolapse, meconium aspiration)
Infection [e.g., meningitis, encephalitis, TORCH (toxoplasmosis, rubella,
    cytomegalovirus, herpes) agents, syphilis, herpes simplex]
Trauma (e.g., breech delivery, intracerebral hemorrhage)
Hypoglycemia
Kernicterus

Postnatal

Brain injury (e.g., trauma, drowning, lightning)
Poisoning (e.g., lead, carbon monoxide)
Cerebrovascular accidents
Postimmunization encephalopathy (e.g., pertussis, rabies)
Infection (meningitis, encephalitis, abscess)
Early severe malnutrition
Hormonal deficiency
Psychosocial deprivation, abuse or neglect

From Whitman, B. Y. and Accardo, P. J. (1990). *When a parent is mentally retarded*, p. 34., as adapted from Berini and Kahn (1987). Reprinted by permission.

the home and crib, properly clothing infants and children, and overall nurturing. These are significant tasks to learn in caring for a baby or small child, and they are more difficult for an individual with mental retardation, who may not know how to accomplish all of these tasks in caring for himself or herself. For example, if a person's own hygiene is poor, how can he or she be expected to adequately and appropriately clean and dress a baby or young child? Educators and social service agencies will have to assume roles of advocacy and monitorship to protect the rights of parents and children.

Case Study 7-4

Ruby and Dan, individuals with borderline mental retardation, both came from very poor families with limited resources. Unable to provide stable home environments for them, their families had placed them in a residential facility as teenagers. They fell in love, ran away from the facility, and got married. The residential staff tried to remain in contact with them to provide a support system, but Ruby and Dan refused help and wandered from place to place, never with enough money or resources. They eventually had a baby, and were living on social welfare. On occasions when staff from the residential facility managed to contact Ruby and Dan, they reported that the couple looked unkempt. Ruby and Dan, however, claimed that everything was all right. The baby appeared well nourished and healthy, but was unstimulated and rather listless.

Ruby and Dan did not have enough training in coping with new situations or sufficient survival skills to live successfully in the community. They were clinging to each other but were not handling their lives in a responsible way. The baby was not receiving the stimulation that it needed. Ruby and Dan refused offers of counseling and support, which of course could not be forced on them. With proper counseling and preparation in job skills, homemaking, nutrition, and family planning, this couple would have a better chance at survival as a family unit. As it is, they are doing quite poorly.

The right to bear children leads to the responsibility of having the skills and knowledge to rear children. Many individuals with mental retardation or developmental disabilities can learn the necessary skills to perform parental duties and should be given the chance. Others will try and fail, at which time social service agencies will step in to act in the best interest of the child. Courts will be involved to protect the rights of all and, it is hoped, to act in the best interest of the child. Extreme measures of terminating parental rights will be initiated when necessary. Also, creative living environments will emerge that challenge existing systems. These may range from a cluster of supervised apartments with 24-hour supervision in parenting to communal group homes containing more than one family unit where supervision in all aspects of family planning and parenting skill training and relationship counseling is available.

In a good system, the support network will be in place so that all parts of the system will act to help the other parts, but this is more of a reactive than a proactive process. It would be better to develop proactive processes that enhance existing skills through needs assessments, building self-esteem in parents and children. The sexuality educator/counselor must be able to evaluate whether the individual with mental retardation or developmental disabilities possesses the necessary skills to become a parent. It is important to assess whether the individual will need assistance with any or all of the responsibilities of parenthood. [The reader is referred to *When A Parent Is Mentally Retarded* (Whitman & Accardo, 1990), in which many of these topics are explored in depth, with sensitivity and understanding.] In view of the extensive nature of the issues involved, sexuality educators turning their focus to family planning needs will undoubtedly reach out to existing community resources for help in this area.

Utilizing Community Resources

Parenting skills for adults with mental retardation and developmental disability become a community concern. Departments of social services are concerned with the "neglect" issue. Whitman, Graves, and Accardo (1990) stated that parental, especially maternal, mental retardation can be considered as a recognized risk factor for medical, emotional, and cognitive problems in children (see also Crain & Millor, 1978; Kaminer & Cohen, 1983; Sheridan, 1956). According to Whitman et al., the principal cause of these problems does not appear to be either child abuse or hereditary influence, but rather child neglect secondary to lack of parental education combined with the unavailability of supportive services (see also Schilling, Schinke, Blythe, & Barth, 1982; Seagull & Scheurer, 1986).

Whitman et al. (1990) noted that:

> One of the most difficult aspects of working with parents who have mental retardation is their strong tendency to become very dependent on the help of one or more of their professional workers. They seem to need to assure themselves that the professional cares and will respond. The usual ways of avoiding unhealthy dependency never seem to work as well with clients who have mental retardation. Part of the problem lies in their constant crisis orientation. . . . The problem for the helping professional is to know when the crisis is immediate and when a delay of a day or two will make little significant difference. (p. 59)

I have often been called in as a consultant to handle a "crisis situation" that could well have waited until a later time or been handled by a person in the normal support environment. When the professional responds to the situation as if it were a crisis, the individual with mental retardation or developmental disabilities learns that someone will come immediately to help resolve problems. To create an environment in which more individuation can occur and the individual can develop a sense of ego strength and self-esteem, it is important to first give the individual time to try to resolve his or her problem from a personal, independent perspective.

Whitman et al. (1990) also asserted:

> Parents with mental retardation are first and foremost adults with mental retardation. The specific problems encountered in attempting to teach parenting skills were direct reflections of the limitations in adaptive behavior and social skills observed in adults who have mental retardation. Typical problems included speech and language disorders; difficulties with organizing, sequencing, and adhering to time schedules; overgeneralization and undergeneralization; low self-esteem; previously undiagnosed

hearing loss; dental emergency (80%); homelessness (46% in one year); previous and current history of abuse; inability to read social and nonverbal cues; a tendency for recurrent crises to overtax and ultimately burn out existing social supports; and themselves becoming a focus of contention among multiple agencies. . . . Working with parents who have mental retardation is difficult in the extreme. The disorganization of every facet of their lives, as well as their inability to understand many everyday givens, can be frustrating beyond belief. Their unrelenting 24 hours-a-day needs, wants and demands make professional burnout an ever-present specter. (pp. 60–61)

Specialized education and counseling should be made available to parents who are mentally retarded. I believe that creative planning, supervision to make sure good child care and stimulation occur, and the use of supplemental community services can help ensure success in these areas.

I believe that there are probably many wonderful community resources available to assist individuals with mental retardation and developmental disabilities. The only problem is that these resources do not yet see the possibilities of what they can contribute in this area. It is our job as professionals and family members to seek out community resources and to convince them with education and support that they have something to offer individuals with mental retardation and developmental disabilities. For the newcomer to this process of exploration, I would suggest exploring local mental health clinics and family planning clinics, in addition to seeking out therapists and medical staff who have an interest in developing proficiency and expertise in these areas. Investigating day care centers may turn up an individual who is very willing to develop and could operate a specialized program to assist individuals with mental retardation and developmental disabilities as they learn how to cope with the job of parenting. We are beginning a new era of dedication to meeting these goals in the community. This will be an exciting decade for all professionals and agencies who are willing to take the risk to explore this new territory.

CONCLUDING REMARKS

I feel our job as professionals and parents is to help each individual begin and achieve the process of individuation in which he or she develops the necessary skills and coping mechanisms to make responsible and smart choices as he or she learns to understand and express his or her own sexuality. In this way, the educational and counseling process will work toward each person having an individual program plan that will deal with PSS and psychosexual (PS) development in a proactive way.

PART **III**

Counseling and
Community Issues

Chapter **8**

Sexual Exploitation and Abuse

◇◇◇◇◇◇◇◇◇◇◇◇◇◇◇◇◇◇◇◇◇◇◇◇◇◇◇◇◇◇

What makes individuals with mental retardation and developmental disabilities more susceptible to sexual victimization? The simplest answer seems to lie in the belief of the perpetrator either that no one will find out that the victimization has occurred, because the individual with mental retardation or developmental disabilities will not have the communication skills to inform others of the abuse or, if the victim does inform others, that no one will believe him or her. This is a real misconception. Physicians have become more skilled in recognizing physical signs of sexual abuse, and the medical community is more able and ready to testify in court when they find evidence of sexual abuse. Counselors and therapists have begun to specialize in interviewing children who are victims of sexual abuse and are beginning to show more interest in exploring these issues with children with mental retardation and/or developmental disabilities. Interdisciplinary and transdisciplinary work has opened up new avenues of support and cooperation so that everyone is working in the best interest of the child who has been victimized.

Longo and Gochenor (1981) estimated that, among both male and female children without disabilities, one out of five is sexually abused during childhood and adolescence. N. E. S. Gardner (1986) stated that there are no clear statistics on how many sexually exploited individuals have developmental disabilities and estimated that the rate might be even higher. She also discussed the vulnerability of adults with disabilities as victims of abuse and provided information on working with victims of abuse.

THE CONCEPT OF SEXUAL EXPLOITATION AND ABUSE

N. E. S. Gardner (1986) stated that

> Sexual exploitation exists when one person gratifies his or her sexual desires without the full and informed consent of his or her partner or victim. Such exploitation may be

without physical contact, as in cases of displaying pornographic materials to another
or exposing genitals inappropriately, or may refer to physical contact, as in rape, molestation, and incest. (p. 56)

Thus the scope of the problem can be seen to be wide. Sexual abuse victims may be children or adults, and the perpetrators may be strangers or
individuals known to the victims.

An excellent reference for the reader interested in pursuing an in-
depth study of sexual abuse is *Handbook of Clinical Intervention in Child
Sexual Abuse*, edited by Suzanne M. Sgroi, M.D. In this book, Sgroi, Blick,
and Porter (1982) defined child sexual abuse as:

A sexual act imposed on a child who lacks emotional, maturational, and cognitive
development. The ability to lure a child into a sexual relationship is based upon the
all-powerful and dominant position of the adult or older adolescent perpetrator,
which is in sharp contrast to the child's age, dependency, and subordinate position.
Authority and power enable the perpetrator, implicitly or directly, to coerce the child
into sexual compliance. (p. 9)

These authors defined incest from a psychosocial perspective, stating that:

Incestuous child sexual abuse encompasses any form of sexual activity between a
child and a parent or stepparent or extended family member (for example, grand-
parent, aunt, or uncle) or surrogate parent figure (for example, common-law spouse
or foster parent). . . . The crucial psychosocial dynamic is the familial relationship
between the incest participants. This is especially important when the incestuous sexual relationship involves a child. (p. 10)

N. E. S. Gardner (1986) pointed out that the problem of sexual abuse
is compounded because the abuse is often invisible:

It is important to realize that persons who have difficulties with abstract thinking do
not describe incidents in detail unless they have actually experienced such acts. It is a
strongly held belief of nearly all professionals in this field that vulnerable populations
(i.e., children and persons with developmental disabilities) do not lie about sexual
abuse (Assault Prevention Training Project, 1984). However, the victim does not report the incident for fear of reprisal or rejection. (p. 57)

Children do not easily lie about things that embarrass them or that are
painful. The public needs to understand that children are to be believed.

Increased Vulnerability of Persons with Retardation

N. E. S. Gardner (1986) stated that a common trait of victims of sexual
exploitation is vulnerability, and thus it is more crucial to examine what
makes persons with disabilities more vulnerable than other groups. An
individual with mental retardation or developmental disabilities might
have significant difficulties in communication, making him or her very
vulnerable to victimization because the perpetrator believes that he or
she will not be able to talk or tell the "secret." In addition, this individual
may not have the defensive skills to say "no" or to push away unwanted
sexual advances. Often, a person with a disability may have a physical
feature that sets him or her off as looking different from the average per-

son in society. It is possible that this marks the individual for easier prey from perpetrators seeking out victims.

Sanford (1980) concluded that:

> Probably the best protection for retarded children would be high visibility in the neighborhood; if the child is a familiar sight in the neighborhood, people will be able to tell something is wrong if the child's routine is off. . . . Anyone who lives in a community with a retarded child has a responsibility to do everything in his power to protect the child from tragedies such as child molestation. If only they would, it could, if only slightly, lighten the burden for the parents. (p. 345)

The problem of impaired communicative abilities is especially significant for individuals with physical conditions that require them to use nonverbal communication modes. However, there are ways to communicate with nonverbal individuals and some people are specially skilled in working with nonverbal individuals. In cases of suspected abuse, professionals need to determine the communication system of the individual and work with that system, regardless of the possible limitations and difficulty of the situation.

Case Study 8-1

Cindy, a public school teenager with severe cerebral palsy, used a language board to communicate. One day at school, Cindy used her language board to tell her teacher that her father had engaged in sexually inappropriate actions with her. The father never dreamed that Cindy would be capable of communicating what he did on the language board or that anyone would believe her. However, Cindy's teacher did believe her, and the department of social services was called in immediately. The teacher was present to show the social worker how to use the language board. The social worker also believed Cindy, and criminal charges were filed against Cindy's father. At the hearing, Cindy communicated the sexual abuse to the judge on the language board, and her father was convicted and jailed. Cindy was placed in foster care because her mother did not seem capable of protecting her. The department of social services made sure that Cindy received therapy from a therapist who was able to work with her nonverbal communication system.

This case sends a strong message that will begin to be heard by potential perpetrators who think they can do what they wish to an individual with a disability who is unable to speak. It is anticipated that more individuals, social service agencies, and courts will begin to listen to these individuals. Sexual abuse of persons with disabilities can be stopped if all professionals, parents, and agencies will take this attitude.

The Issue of Informed Consent

Griffiths, Quinsey, and Hingsburger (1989) stated that: "Given that many individuals with handicaps who display inappropriate sexual behavior may have, themselves, been abused, it is understandable that one of the critical elements of appropriate sexuality—consent—may be difficult for these individuals to grasp" (p. 20).

Haavik and Menninger (1981) noted the interesting concept that:

> The more normal living style and increased community access provided by group homes bring sexual expression and adjustment problems to the forefront. The question is no longer whether to allow sexual behavior, but how to provide for reasonably satisfying sexual relationships while developing procedures for dealing with problem situations. Often, an overriding area of concern for group home staff involves the issue of mutual consent of a retarded couple involved in sexual activity. With retarded individuals who are suggestible and lack knowledge and experience, it is sometimes difficult to define mutual consent in a pragmatic sense, with the implications of forethought and comprehension of the consequences of the activity. Situations having the appearance of mutual consent may sometimes come closer to exploitation. Determining situations and clients with whom mutual consent is feasible is an arduous task for staff and administrators. (p. 22)

The authors also stated that "It is difficult to balance the client's need and right to freedom of sexual expression with the equally important need to protect other clients from sexual exploitation" (p. 22).

The frequency of incest with individuals with mental retardation may be quite high. Those individuals with less significant levels of retardation may respond to the pleasure of the act and can easily be led or coerced into behavior that is abusive or inappropriate.

Case Study 8-2

Samantha, an adolescent with mental retardation living at home with her mother and stepfather, was attractive and sexually well developed for her age. She was very sexualized; she had been masturbating and enjoying it for years. Samantha's stepfather approached her, began fondling her breasts, and enticed her to have sexual intercourse but threatened to punish her if she told her mother. Samantha enjoyed sex with her stepfather but wondered if there was something wrong with this behavior because of the warning against telling her mother. The incidents continued frequently.

Samantha later moved to a residential facility and was sexually active there. When counseled about her sexual activity, Samantha related her experiences with her stepfather. This was not a typical case of rape since Samantha was an eager and willing partner, but the stepfather, legally and ethically, certainly was not an appropriate sexual partner for her. Samantha's mother was called and the stepfather was confronted. He did not deny the incidents but the mother refused to bring legal charges. The most the residential facility could do was take the matter to court and make the recommendation that Samantha not be allowed to visit her home as long as the stepfather was there. Samantha was then counseled about appropriate sex partners and incest.

For individuals with mental retardation and developmental disability, the problem of "informed consent" complicates cases of sexual abuse and incest. Court-determined ability to give "informed consent" is a complex issue that makes it more difficult to prosecute individuals accused of perpetrating acts of sexual abuse upon victims with mental retardation or developmental disabilities.

HELPING TO PREVENT VICTIMIZATION

Sexuality educators/counselors can help individuals with mental retardation and developmental disabilities avoid victimization. Therefore, efforts must be made to provide sexuality education to all individuals. This process should include working with the individuals so that they can recognize "dangerous and inappropriate" touching and know when to push away, call for help in whatever way they can, tell or show an adult that something has happened to them, and so forth. Parents and staff should receive the same information in in-service training programs. Extensive role-playing in many different environments should be encouraged to ensure generalization to all settings. Professionals should be familiar with and trained in the use of augmentative and alternative communication modes to help the individual with poorly developed communicatory skills. Repetition is important, and "booster" sessions should be given at periodic intervals to make sure that the information has been retained.

Victimization can also be prevented by taking steps to eliminate an environment in which abuse is easy. Many elements play a part in setting up a "victimizing environment." One significant factor is a lack of administrative policies concerning appropriate and inappropriate sexual behavior for persons with mental retardation and developmental disabilities in different living and working environments. Administrators are responsible for developing and enforcing policies that protect the rights of individuals with mental retardation or developmental disabilities. Once such policies are written, it is the responsibility of administrators to implement the policies in the most responsible and ethical way possible. Legal counsel should be obtained in the development of these policies.

Victimization can also occur in residential facilities and group homes when professional staff have an attitude of complacency. This can happen if professionals wrongly treat any sexual behavior as a part of an overall behavior pattern. Instead, staff should treat sexual aggression as rape to protect the rights of the victim. If the perpetrator is a person with mental retardation or developmental disabilities, he or she should be treated by a therapist or counselor trained in working with persons who commit sexual offenses (see Chapter 10).

Unfortunately, victimization can occur even when policies governing sexual behavior exist and caregivers and staff take measures to prevent sexual abuse among residents. Increased supervision may be the only solution in such instances.

Case Study 8-3

Mickey, an adult with profound mental retardation and multiple disabilities, was living in a private room in a residential facility. Mickey was bedridden unless he was put in a wheelchair. He could not talk, walk, feed himself, or meet any of his basic needs. Mickey could not communicate verbally, but sometimes he made pleasurable or distressed noises. On routine examination, the physician found Mickey to have a sexually transmitted disease (STD). Further lab work showed that Mickey had gonorrhea.

Mickey clearly is not capable of contracting a STD through his own actions. The assumption of the staff was that either a staff member or a visitor had performed fellatio or had sexual intercourse with Mickey and transmitted the disease. Mickey was treated for the STD and was moved from a private room to a ward of four people so that he would never be alone. Further action could not be taken against any individual because there was no way to find out who had participated in sex with Mickey.

Professionals might neglect to refer a person to an appropriate person or agency that could provide support and assistance. To reduce victimization of such persons in the community, counseling services from all agencies should be readily available to all individuals. Every effort should be made to protect the rights of persons with mental retardation and developmental disabilities in the same way the rights of any citizen would be protected.

RESPONDING TO REPORTED OR SUSPECTED ABUSE

A suspicion or claim of sexual abuse necessitates a report and the beginning of an investigation to validate the possibility or to find the information "unfounded." Most states require professionals to report to the department of social services any suspicion of child sexual abuse, and refusal to do so is illegal. Once the original report is made, the department of social services will initiate and carry out the investigation. Professionals in the field of mental retardation and developmental disabilities function as members of the investigating team and as advocates for the rights of the individual to receive all medical, counseling, protective and court-ordered services. The fact that an individual is mentally retarded or has developmental disabilities does not mean that he or she should not have the full attention necessary to stop any possible abuse.

Recognizing Signs of Abuse

Aguilar (1984) listed the following major physical and behavioral indicators of sexual abuse (p. 57):

1. Difficulty in walking or sitting
2. Torn, stained, or bloody underclothing
3. Pain or itching in the genital area
4. Bruises or bleeding in genital or anal areas

   5.   Venereal disease
   6.   Pregnancy
   7.   Difficulty sleeping, or sudden and frequent nightmares
   8.   Avoidance of a previously trusted and well-liked person, especially anyone in a position of authority, or a caregiver of the victim
   9.   Unexplained stomachaches or change in eating habits
  10.   Fear of being left alone, or the desire to be alone
  11.   Bedwetting
  12.   Change in leisure habits, or reluctance to join in previously enjoyed recreational activities
  13.   Delinquency or running away
  14.   Bizarre, sophisticated, or unusual sexual behavior or knowledge
  15.   Hypochondria
  16.   Sudden infantile behavior (sucking, biting, rocking)
  17.   Refusal to undress, to bathe, or to be bathed

Sgroi, Porter, and Blick (1982) listed the following behavioral indicators of child sexual abuse (pp. 40–41):

   1.   Overly compliant behavior
   2.   Acting-out, aggressive behavior
   3.   Pseudomature behavior
   4.   Hints about sexual activity
   5.   Persistent and inappropriate sexual play with peers or toys or with themselves, or sexually aggressive behavior with others
   6.   Detailed and age-inappropriate understanding of sexual behavior (especially by young children)
   7.   Arriving early at school and leaving late with few, if any, absences
   8.   Poor peer relationships or inability to make friends
   9.   Lack of trust, particularly with significant others
  10.   Nonparticipation in school and social activities
  11.   Inability to concentrate in school
  12.   Sudden drop in school performance
  13.   Extraordinary fears of males (in cases of male perpetrator and female victim)
  14.   Seductive behavior with males (in cases of male perpetrator and female victim)
  15.   Running away from home
  16.   Sleep disturbances
  17.   Regressive behavior
  18.   Withdrawal
  19.   Clinical depression
  20.   Suicidal feelings

Both of the above lists have a few items that do not fit well with a population of individuals with mental retardation or developmental disability. However, on the whole, the characteristics in both lists are indicators that should make family members, staff, and counselors suspicious that some form of sexual abuse may have occurred.

Response by the Counselor

The sexuality counselor provides treatment for individuals with mental retardation and developmental disability who have been sexually abused. Treatment issues focus on assuring the individual that the courts and appropriate community agencies will be contacted to give the individual protective services in any area necessary, including placement in another living environment if this is recommended by the investigating team. The actual counseling intervention with the individual involves teaching the child or adult that what happened was not his or her fault. Therapy is directed toward building self-esteem and developing the ability to say "no" and push away unwanted sexual advances. In addition, the individual must become capable of and have a system for reporting any further abuse as soon as it occurs so that it can be stopped. When appropriate, group therapy and family therapy are provided and specialized techniques using puppets, anatomically correct dolls, and art therapy are incorporated into the counseling regimen.

Response by the Residential Facility

If sexual victimization of an individual with mental retardation or developmental disabilities living in a residential facility occurs, professionals should be prepared to organize the services of a physician and sexuality counselor to help evaluate the needs of the individual. If there is a known perpetrator, criminal charges should be brought. All legal requirements in the city and state in which the individual resides should be observed. Most states have a mandatory reporting law that requires that instances of suspected abuse be reported to the appropriate social service agency, which will investigate in a thorough manner. Efforts should also be made to provide supportive family therapy to parents and extended family members who might be experiencing feelings of guilt over not having protected the child and prevented the abuse from taking place.

Staff of the residential facility should be involved in the sexuality education and counseling. Staff members also should participate in the family therapy sessions to learn more about how to help the individual during the therapy process. Staff can become effective in assisting in the healing and coping efforts.

Administrators and staff of residential facilities should be aware that community programs often do not have professionals trained in the field of developmental disabilities, and community mental health counselors are often uncomfortable dealing with such individuals. In these instances, assistance can be offered to support the process by involving a counselor familiar with individuals with mental retardation or developmental disabilities until the community mental health worker feels more skilled.

Resources in the Community

Once an individual with mental retardation or developmental disabilities moves out into the community, child and adult protective custody divisions of departments of social services are responsible for investigating instances of sexual abuse and taking necessary action in the courts and communities. These individuals and their families must be able to rely on these resources and must learn how to access them.

All states have laws that protect children. These laws are enforced by state departments of protective social services. Reporting laws exist that require professionals to notify authorities of suspected child abuse or neglect. All communities have facilities that can be accessed to help deal with these specific needs, such as medical examinations, necessary interviews, and work with the police and solicitor's office to see that advocacy is provided in the best interest of the child or adult. Since some communities' resources are more developed than others, research will have to be done to find out what resources are available in a specific community. Some areas have victim advocate groups that do an excellent job in coordinating services.

I would encourage persons involved with individuals with mental retardation and developmental disabilities to promote their community's efforts at growth in these areas. In addition, agencies and professionals must become better advocates for citizens with mental retardation and developmental disabilities in order to ensure that all appropriate services are readily available, accessible, and used.

EFFECTS OF MOVEMENT TO LEAST RESTRICTIVE ENVIRONMENT

Since the late 1970s, there has been an intense effort toward deinstitutionalization of all individuals with mental retardation and developmental disabilities. However, many individuals have lived in confined residential facilities where they have not had the opportunity to develop normal sexual outlets and awareness of heterosexual behavior. Therefore, once these individuals are deinstitutionalized, this lack of knowledge may lead to inappropriate sexual behavior in the community. Also, the ease with which an individual with mental retardation or developmental disabilities becomes victimized is heightened because of the individual's lack of understanding of normal societal rules regarding sexual behavior. All professionals need to take a stand of involvement so that we can promote the education and therapeutic intervention to the individual, arrange support services, and be there for the total process.

In the best of circumstances, individuals with mental retardation and developmental disabilities move from one living situation to another as they progress from more restrictive to less restrictive environments. When such a move occurs, new staff are made aware of the sexuality education and counseling that has been provided in the previous environment. This enables them to continue to reinforce appropriate responses and behavior that helps protect the individual from victimization. However, sexuality education/counseling should always be made available when needed, regardless of what may have been received in the previous living environment.

CONCLUDING REMARKS

As professionals become more skilled at interviewing individuals with mental retardation and developmental disabilities to determine if sexual abuse has occurred, it becomes easier to uncover and remedy the abusive incidents. Physicians are trained to examine babies, toddlers, and young children for possible physical evidence of sexual abuse. Counselors and therapists are more skilled in child interview techniques, using anatomically correct dolls, drawings, or items such as a doll house in play therapy to elicit responses and piece together stories the children are not able to verbally communicate.

Continued efforts ought to be made to reduce victimization of persons with mental retardation and developmental disabilities. Professionals should develop educational programs that teach mechanisms for avoiding and reporting abuse as well as emphasize the ability to form positive, appropriate personal relationships. There must be more opportunities for interagency referrals for individuals with mental retardation and developmental disabilities. All professionals and parents should assume an advocacy role to make sure that individuals do not become victimized. Mental health professionals and sexuality counselors in the community should accept individuals with mental retardation and developmental disabilities into their practices and, if necessary, employ a professional co-counselor who can assist with the aspects of counseling specific to the issue of victimization. Schools should continue progressing toward providing sexuality education to children in special education programs. Courts should vigilantly continue to prosecute and incarcerate those people who commit such crimes. Communities should band together to form support groups and services for victims of sexual abuse.

Chapter **9**

Undesirable Sexual Behavior

The public is often very suspicious of sexual behavior in individuals with mental retardation or developmental disabilities because it does not expect any expression of sexuality from these individuals. People without retardation are expected to be sexual, to experiment, and to occasionally do things that differ from the sexual activity norms. However, individuals with mental retardation are not supposed to behave in this manner. They are not expected to have the capability of imagining sexual activities beyond simple exploration of their physical sexual responses, masturbation, and perhaps sexual intercourse. When incidents of undesirable sexual behavior do occur, members of the community may become very upset and exaggerate the antisocial or anticommunity orientation of the behavior—the response may be much more intolerant than that shown toward such behavior by persons without mental retardation or developmental disabilities.

It must be recognized that individuals with mental retardation may explore and participate in all aspects of sexual behavior in much the same manner as persons without retardation. This experimentation may lead to incidents of undesirable sexual behavior that ought to be confronted when they occur. Failure to deal promptly and appropriately with such situations may lead to the individual's return to a more restricted environment—or to jail.

As individuals with mental retardation or developmental disabilities are deinstitutionalized, they become much more subject to being charged with or involved in sexual crimes. Because of the emotional aspect of this issue, citizens with mental retardation or developmental disabilities may more often be sentenced to jail, may serve longer terms in jail, and may not receive the necessary counseling and behavior modification to prevent recurrence.

The following are some areas in which an individual with mental retardation or developmental disabilities may have trouble in the community with respect to undesirable sexual activity. It may be noted that the environment in which the individual lives may determine the likelihood of involvement.

UNDESIRABLE BEHAVIORS

Indecent Exposure

Exposing of the genitals, or "flashing," is a major problem for individuals with mental retardation and leads to confrontations with the law. However, indecent exposure may arise from situations as simple as being in a public park and needing to urinate when no bathroom is available.

Case Study 9-1

Juan, a man with mental retardation, enjoyed going on outings in the community. He was very outgoing and often talked to strangers. Juan was taken on a field trip into the community and, while walking through an open park, he felt the need to urinate. Juan had learned to sight-read the bathroom words "Boys" and "Men" but this did him no good because there were no bathrooms in sight. Disregarding the fact that there were children and adults around him, Juan went to the nearest bush, unzipped his pants, took out his penis, and commenced urinating. A parent in the park observed Juan's actions, was highly disturbed, and found a policeman. Juan was arrested for indecent exposure and taken to jail, where it was ascertained that he was an individual with mental retardation and the charges were dropped.

Such a situation is a tremendous problem for the person who has significantly lowered adaptive skills. The individual may urinate openly and be arrested for indecent exposure when the act was not intended to shock or excite witnesses. Careful training in appropriate public behavior will help to prevent these kinds of problems for persons who do or will live in the community. In this case, Juan's parents and educators were remiss in sending him into the community without first teaching him the difference between appropriate and inappropriate responses to having to urinate when there is no bathroom available.

Of course, there are individuals with mental retardation or developmental disabilities who derive sexual excitement from exposing themselves to helpless victims. When this occurs, the person should not be allowed free access to the community until appropriate public behavior is learned.

Lewd and Lascivious Behavior

Lewd and lascivious behavior includes actions that are sexually unchaste, lack legal or moral restraints, or exhibit disregard for sexual restraints. Such behavior is also marked by disregard for strict rules or correctness, and in this sense becomes a "catchall" category covering any type of behavior on the part of an individual that society does not like. If this is the understanding of lewd and lascivious behavior, the actions of many individuals could fall into this category. In some cases the category may become so distorted as to allow the filing of charges against an individual with mental retardation if he or she merely expresses sexual interest in another individual.

Many laws regarding sexuality and individuals with mental retardation or developmental disabilities are archaic and unconstitutional. Before behavior is labeled as lewd and lascivious, all efforts should be made to ascertain whether the behavior is appropriate. The laws restricting the right to privacy of an individual with mental retardation may be what are undesirable and in need of change.

Sexual Abuse and Rape

Sexual abuse and rape are areas of concern for individuals with mental retardation because such individuals often innocently engage in sexual relations with persons under the age of consent. The individual with mental retardation must be taught that fondling or having sexual activity with someone under a certain age is considered child abuse or statutory rape depending on the sexual actions involved. These individuals must understand that court actions and jail sentences are the consequences of this type of behavior. The public seems to believe that statutory rape is a major area of concern for individuals with mental retardation. In actuality, many individuals simply need to be taught the concept of age of consent and what that age is in the state in which they reside.

I have had the experience of working with sex offenders who are mentally retarded or developmentally disabled who knowingly commit rape and/or sexual molestation. My impression is that this behavior is often similar to that of the average person in society who commits these acts because of a deviant sexual arousal pattern, in addition to poor impulse control and distorted thinking with erroneous internal justification for the behavior, resulting in cognitive distortions. I feel these individuals are entitled to treatment to see if they can develop moral behavior, improve their empathic responses, and begin to exhibit internalized control of their behavior. I am afraid that, just as with the average population, recidivism will be high. Therefore, we need to assume the responsibility to develop treatment programs and modalities that increase the probability of cognitive material being processed because of its presentation in a very concrete manner.

To extinguish inappropriate behavior and replace it with appropriate behavior, efforts need to be made by everyone involved in the interdisciplinary process, including the family. It is difficult to teach abstract material to many individuals. Since the pleasure principle is very tied in to sexual expression, repetition in teaching, including role-playing and concrete and therapeutic approaches, are imperative.

Fetishism

Fetishes (objects used for sexual gratification) are difficult to deal with in sexuality counseling because they are often so fixed. Often, the rights and needs of others are not foremost in the minds of the individual with the fetish.

Case Study 9-2

Carl, a person with mental retardation, had very high verbal, reading, and writing skills; he also had a motor disorder and problems with his speech that made him hard to understand. Carl had a fetish for women's shoes, and also engaged in cross-dressing.

At first, Carl would just approach a woman and ask to try on her shoes or touch them. As his family and the staff of his residential facility tried to get Carl to redirect or give up his fetish, he became more forceful with his approaches and actually attempted to assault a woman to get her shoes. Desensitization activities were tried. Efforts were also made to allow Carl to wear women's attire and makeup in private where he would not be ridiculed. None of these techniques was very successful. In addition to acting on his fetishes, Carl lied about his actions, angering his family. Carl thought nothing of wrongly accusing others if he believed it would help him be seen in a better light.

The situation contained an added dimension of danger: Carl was a pyromaniac and had set a very expensive fire in his home and had set smaller fires in the facility in which he lived. There also appeared to be a correlation between Carl's shoe fetish, his cross-dressing, and the fire setting. When the fetish behavior became assaultive, the staff and Carl's parents increased supervision and consequences for the behavior. However, more supervision was then needed to see that Carl did not get hold of matches or lighters because his pyromania behavior increased.

Carl functioned at a very high academic level for an individual with mental retardation and strongly desired to live in the community. The difficulty with Carl's fetish was that he used it as an excuse to violate the rights of others. It will be difficult for him to move into community living as long as he exhibits this behavior. Carl's parents did not think they could control him at home, and community residences were afraid to admit Carl because of the pyromania.

In this situation, it is not primarily the cross-dressing or the fetish for women's shoes that keeps Carl in a restrictive environment. Rather, it is the pyromania. If Carl can achieve and maintain appropriate behavior for any length of time, he may get his chance to live in the community and try to be gainfully employed. This outcome might be more likely if a "shadow" is employed so that essentially Carl is under one-to-one supervision at all times to ensure the safety of others.

Case Study 9-3

Jacob, who has spent most of his life in facilities for individuals with mental retardation, liked to collect shoes and other articles of clothing of young children and women, as well as pictures of other residents or their family members. In addition, he collected various other objects, frequently changing to a different item. For a long time Jacob had been able to convince the people in his environment that his behavior was harmless. However, a sexuality counselor who worked with child molesters interviewed Jacob and thought that his fetish was not as innocent as it may have appeared to others. Jacob acknowledged to the sexuality counselor that he was using the clothing articles to masturbate. It also appeared that he was using the pictures of the children in the same fashion.

Jacob had no concern for the feelings of the people he approached for personal articles or photos of family members (some of whom were living and some of whom had passed away). He did not seem willing or able to develop an empathic response and strongly denied that he was abusing anyone else's rights. Jacob also suffered from depression, for which he was being treated by a psychiatrist.

One day Jacob went up to a female resident and fondled her breast. This was seen by a staff person. The psychiatrist agreed that Jacob had now escalated to a different level of inappropriate behavior and he would have to accept some restrictions about his fetish or face legal consequences. Jacob was counseled firmly that he would not be allowed to ask people for their personal possessions but that what he chose to do in the privacy of his bedroom when he was alone would be his business. This was hard for Jacob to accept, but once he saw that the staff were serious and that he really had no choice, he became more compliant.

In both of these examples of the use of a fetish for sexual gratification, the situation is complicated by the fact that the men are individuals with mental retardation. If Carl and Jacob were men without retardation living independently in the community, it is possible that no one would ever have become aware of their behavior or tried to stop it. However, if they were living in the community at large, they might have to answer to the police, courts, and jail, with some protection from advocacy groups that work for individuals with mental retardation or developmental disabilities.

It is my experience that it is very hard to extinguish fetish behavior. I have not seen the adoption of more appropriate behaviors, but I have experienced individuals becoming more discreet about exhibiting their fetish behaviors.

Once a person like Carl or Jacob enters counseling for inappropriate sexual behavior that is backed up by supervision and reinforcement from caregivers, he or she might have a more difficult time achieving sexual gratification through the fetish because of increased supervision.

Sodomy

Many cultures, peoples, and even state laws consider sodomy an illegal act, whether it occurs between two consenting adults, a married couple, or two single people, regardless of gender. Therefore, it is considered by many to be undesirable sexual behavior. In reality, especially in the homosexual culture, sodomy is one of the acceptable ways of expressing sexuality.

When a man with mental retardation or developmental disabilities lives in a large dormitory or male-only residence, sexual exploration more frequently involves anal intercourse. It seems wise to consider this as same-sex activity rather than homosexual behavior, since it occurs more because of availability of partners than by choice or preference. The individuals involved need to be informed about the possible legal consequences of participating in this activity in any community where it is illegal. Counseling about contracting sexually transmitted diseases, especially AIDS, through anal intercourse is also important. If there is a person who tests HIV positive living in a residential facility where anal intercourse is common, administrators should provide one-on-one supervision to ensure that the individual is not sexually active. In this situation, counseling about the use of condoms for "safer sex" is not sufficient to protect the other individuals living in the environment.

There will probably always be arguments about whether or not sodomy is undesirable sexual behavior. Legality aside, however, the main issue is the need to present proper sexuality education to both men and women so that no one will be taken advantage of or forced to participate in an unwanted sexual activity. Individuals with mental retardation or developmental disabilities have to be taught that it is all right to say "no."

Bestiality

Individuals with mental retardation who live in rural areas and on farms are just as apt to experiment sexually with animals—such as sheep, dogs, and horses—as any other individual living in such environments. These animals openly exhibit sexual behavior toward each other and generate sexual curiosity in the individual, as well as providing instruction by example. It should not be surprising when the individual proceeds to experiment with the animals, since the animals are available and relatively cooperative.

In institutions for individuals with mental retardation where horses are kept for recreational activity, it is not unusual for a male resident to have intercourse with a horse. The horse is an available partner and the individual probably does not perceive that he will get into trouble for his behavior. When this happens, the staff must intervene with proper sexuality education counseling and training in more appropriate behavior. The individual can be taught that sexual experimentation with animals is unacceptable behavior in our society.

Sadomasochism

Deriving pleasure from inflicting pain on others (sadism) or inflicting pain on oneself (masochism), sexual practices that develop when the brain's pain and pleasure mechanisms become confused, are both dangerous. Bondage (tying up someone while having sex with them), whipping or flagellating oneself or another, scratching until bleeding occurs, slapping hard, hitting, or spanking all belong to this group of dangerous and nondesirable behaviors. As the sexuality counselor explores sexual behavior with a client, efforts should be made to ascertain if any inappropriate and harmful acts are included in his or her sexual activity. If so, efforts must be made to provide as much counseling and follow-up services as indicated to determine that the person will not continue these harmful acts. The individual should be helped to find pleasurable, nonharmful ways to self-stimulate or participate in sexual activity. Support from medical and/or psychological personnel in the community should be enlisted to ensure compliance. The individual needs to be informed that permanent damage or death can occur if sadomasochistic activities continue or intensify.

Professionals need to realize that they may encounter situations they find uncomfortable to deal with in counseling. Pain-oriented sexual pleasuring is one area with which many professionals feel uncomfortable. One of the important roles of the professional is knowing when to refer to someone for extra help—when to seek support and guidance in handling a problem. No problem is too hard to handle, but sometimes it is too hard to handle alone. Knowing when to call for help and where to go to find what is needed is the sign of a good professional. The ability to draw together a team to deal with a serious and dangerous problem like sadomasochism is vital to professional competency.

Autoerotic Asphyxiation

Any professional providing sexuality counseling for persons with mental retardation or developmental disabilities should be aware of the practice of autoerotic asphyxiation, sometimes called "scarfing," in which a man tightens something around his neck while masturbating. The reduced flow of oxygen gives a very intense erection. As Simon, a man with a more significant level of mental retardation, described this behavior: "When I tie the towel around my neck and play with myself, my penis goes up; and when I let go, my penis goes down." This behavior appears to be easily taught and imitated, so staff and parents should be made aware of it. Unfortunately, although the goal is sexual gratification, the result can be strangulation. Many times apparent suicides by hanging are later discovered to be accidental deaths resulting while the individuals were performing this dangerous masturbatory practice. Staff and parents should immediately obtain psychiatric evaluation and counseling for anyone suspected of engaging in autoerotic asphyxiation.

SEXUAL ACTIVITY AND THE LAW

There are many archaic laws governing the sexuality, sexual expression, and privacy of individuals with mental retardation. There are numerous states that forbid marriages between such individuals, and many state statutes remove their constitutional right to privacy. If any change is to occur in the laws, it will have to come from the individuals and their advocates, whether those be family members, friends, protection and advocacy systems, or legal aid groups.

This section is not intended to be a legal treatise. For those readers interested in this topic, a valuable source of information is *Sexuality, Law, and the Developmentally Disabled Person* (Haavik & Menninger, 1981). The information in this book is organized according to state, so the reader can simply turn to the section for the state where the individual with mental retardation resides. Also, professionals working in the field of sexuality education for individuals with mental retardation or developmental disabilities should thoroughly ascertain from legal counsel the laws governing the actions of the individuals in the particular state in which he or she resides. Legal counselors will know exactly where to find the appropriate statutes and interpret the information needed to handle a specific situation.

Legal Information the Counselor Should Possess

The sexuality counselor interested in working with individuals with mental retardation or developmental disabilities should be aware of the following information for effective counseling:

Current laws in the state where the professional resides and the implications of these laws with regard to federal regulations and constitutional rights (this information can be obtained through legal counsel, the attorney general's office, protection and advocacy systems, etc.)
Conflicts in laws and how they can deny innate human rights and constitutional rights to privacy

Laws restricting marriage in certain states

Use of local, state, and federal court systems to achieve changes in the laws, where appropriate

Use of protection and advocacy systems by parents, guardians, community, mental retardation advocates, and professionals

Legal issues in birth control for individuals with mental retardation or developmental disabilities

Legal issues in abortion for individuals with mental retardation

Legal issues in sterilization for individuals with mental retardation or developmental disabilities

Legal issues in confidentiality of HIV testing for the AIDS virus

Comprehension of due process and effective use of court systems so that procedures can be used by lay persons

Legal issues of informed consent for individuals with mental retardation or developmental disabilities

The sexuality counselor should know where to obtain appropriate and necessary advice and guidance. Thus, help will be available to lead the individual with mental retardation to a position in which he or she can enjoy full constitutional rights regardless of his or her state of residence or relative level of mental retardation.

The Legal Process for Persons with Mental Retardation or Developmental Disabilities

The legal process for persons with mental retardation or developmental disabilities tends to vary from state to state. Anyone interested in this topic should seek council with someone in their state who is knowledgeable of that state's statutes. The sexuality counselor can assist by assessing the legal system and creating an environment in which due process can be honored and achieved. This is a difficult process because most courts will refer these individuals to the local department of mental retardation. Unfortunately, it may be that the most the sexuality counselor can assist in will be to explore current local and state resources and help the individual utilize them so that he or she receives full benefit under the law.

CONCLUDING REMARKS

It is important to recognize and admit that all individuals will explore and exhibit all categories of sexuality—both those considered to be within the norm and those considered to be undesirable or antisocial. Since an individual with mental retardation or developmental disabilities is also a sexual being, it must be realized that the individual might exhibit appropriate and inappropriate sexual behavior, just as a person without

mental retardation or developmental disabilities might. Society must recognize the need to treat individuals with mental retardation or developmental disabilities the same as others and not jump to conclusions that
certain sexual behavior is undesirable because it is exhibited by an individual with mental retardation or developmental disabilities. Complex
legal issues need to be confronted and resolved, working toward responsible choices that are in the best interest of the individual with mental
retardation or developmental disabilities. I hope the time will come
when the legal system will help each individual go forward on the journey of meeting his or her human potential.

Chapter 10

Sexual Offenders

Criminal sexual conduct has many different definitions in different states. When charged with criminal sexual conduct, an individual with mental retardation or developmental disabilities is often prosecuted through the state's legal system. Protection and advocacy groups usually get involved and try to get the individual remanded to a facility for individuals with mental retardation instead of a penal facility. There are various philosophies regarding the usefulness of this approach.

The individual with mental retardation or developmental disabilities should be held accountable for his or her behavior. An individual with mental retardation or developmental disabilities must also assume responsibility for himself or herself and his or her behavior. With good sexuality education and counseling, the individual can learn to distinguish between appropriate and inappropriate sexual behavior. The individual can learn what is illegal and acknowledge the consequences for breaking the law.

Therapeutic programs to deal with sex offenders are not successful unless the perpetrator has acknowledged his or her guilt. Success is more probable if there is some leverage, preferably from a judge and court system, that forces the person to participate in therapy. This is often done by means of probation, where one of the conditions of probation is that the person regularly attends a group for individuals who commit sex offenses.

Unfortunately, most groups for sex offenders require a minimum intelligence quotient of 80. This judgment is based on the fact that so much of the group process is cognitive and abstract. However, I have found that the principles used in these groups can easily be adapted for use with persons with mental retardation or developmental disabilities. Success can be achieved with individuals whose intelligence quotients are as low as 40, as long as the therapist knows how to work with concrete language systems. Also, significant energy must be put into transdisciplinary planning for supervision in working and living environments and family support so that the individual can receive support from all surrounding systems.

THERAPY FOR SEX OFFENDERS WITH MENTAL RETARDATION

The first course of action when working with an individual with mental retardation who is accused or convicted of committing sex offenses is to have a sexuality counselor who is skilled in working with sex offenders with mental retardation conduct an individual interview. At that time it can be decided, along with the family and other professionals involved, whether the individual will be an appropriate candidate for group therapy. The group process is preferred in dealing with sexual offenses because peer pressure seems to break down denial systems more quickly. Progress cannot be made until the therapist works through the denial and the individual acknowledges that the sexual offense took place. Denial usually fades gradually, as more of the truth surfaces.

Case Study 10-1

Joseph was a middle-age man with mental retardation and a secondary stuttering problem. Joseph appeared sweet and needy and had a passive, "poor me" stance that had conned a psychiatrist, a psychologist, and others in the community into feeling sorry for him. Joseph had been accused of molesting several children, and the professionals believed that the children were accusing Joseph unfairly to make fun of him. Because of his speech defect, Joseph convinced professionals that he would have a hard time getting a fair trial in court. The public defender was trying to keep Joseph out of jail.

A sexuality counselor experienced in working with sex offenders with mental retardation was consulted. She interviewed Joseph with directness and the assumption that he was responsible for his behavior. She asked Joseph if he had molested the girls, and Joseph acknowledged his inappropriate and sexually abusive behavior. When asked why he had not admitted it before, he answered, "They did not ask me that question." (Unfortunately, this is often the case. In order to get an answer, the counselor or therapist must ask the appropriate question.)

In court, Joseph pled guilty and was given probation, with the condition that he attend the sexual offender group run by the sexuality counselor who interviewed him. Joseph entered the group, already past the first and most difficult hurdle of "denial." (This breakdown in the denial system is the beginning of the healing, therapeutic process.) Joseph was ready to begin the real therapeutic process. The counselor or therapist who learns to use direct and confrontational methods will be best able to help the perpetrator acknowledge his or her guilt and responsibility.

Structure and Composition of the Group

Groups that are developed to work with sex offenders with mental retardation do better if they are run by two therapists, one as the lead therapist and one as the support therapist. Groups can vary in size from 4 to 10 members. This particular kind of sexuality counseling is very confrontative and should be provided only by those individuals who have received specific training in working with persons who have committed sexual offenses (Caparulo, 1988; Loss & Ross, 1988a, 1988b; Ralston, 1991). Groups can be a good training opportunity for other professionals who want to learn to deal with the problems of sex offenders. Often these professionals will join in the process to learn the specific techniques needed to work with this population.

The presenting problems in a group of sex offenders are generally sexual assaults against young female and male children in the community. However, some individuals who enter the group will do so for other types of sexual offenses, including indecent exposure or flashing, "Peeping Tom" incidents, voyeurism, inappropriate behavior with fetishes, date rape, and violent rape. One of the main points to understand about sexual offenses is that the behavior does not usually happen in isolation. It is part of a continuum within which the offender is experimenting with many different inappropriate behaviors. The aberrant sexual behavior usually continues until the offender is caught and punished in some way that makes him or her accountable for his or her behavior. This often includes a requirement that the sex offender participate in the group therapy process.

When the person enters the group, he or she will speak and act as if he or she feels no responsibility to society. In some cases the offender is not concerned with the victim, does not understand why what he or she did is considered wrong, and has no desire to give up the deviant behavior. The offender is only sorry that he or she has been caught and has to attend a therapy group and receive more supervision. In other cases the perpetrator knows right from wrong and chooses to do wrong, with no empathy for the victim. These offenders will be able to communicate their past and present behavior with an understanding of society's rules regarding appropriate and inappropriate conduct.

When working with individuals with mental retardation who have committed sex offenses, the therapist is probably going to see adaptive behavior that is considered streetwise. The individuals in the group will often be noncompliant in other environmental situations but will make an effort to be compliant in the group. They will begin to see it as an empowered situation, with leverage being on the side of the courts, family members, residential facilities, and therapists.

Individuals with less significant levels of mental retardation can work effectively in a group. Experience shows that the actual ages of the individuals with mental retardation that form the group is not as relevant as their psychosocial-sexual (PSS) developmental stage. Another consideration is their ability to verbally communicate their thoughts and actions. The counseling group can be developed to meet the needs of adolescents or adults who have been accused or convicted of a variety of sexual crimes or can be focused on those who have been involved in one particular sexual offense, such as rape. Participants can be living in the community or in residential facilities.

Components of the Therapeutic Process

The group should meet weekly. Parents and family members should be involved in the counseling sessions through direct participation, and weekly clinical reports should be written. It is helpful to designate a secretarial person to be the recorder, taking down verbatim quotes from the participants that can be used to generate the final reports. This frees the therapists to interact with group members.

In the group therapy sessions, self-monitoring and self-rating on appropriate behavior are emphasized. The group members can be rated on their level of participation, telling the truth, carrying through with assignments, and general progress for a given week. Representatives of community services with which these individuals interact can be involved in the therapeutic process and should be sent weekly progress reports.

Issues emphasized in the group can include the following:

1. Learning responsibility for self
2. Recognizing deviant sexual arousal patterns
3. Trying to develop age-appropriate socialization skills through community activities
4. Emphasis on telling the truth, including very small details
5. Developing communication skills with family members
6. Attempting to develop an interest in age-appropriate individuals to date
7. Developing the skill of controlling impulses and thinking of alternate ways to behave when placed in a situation in which a sexual offense has previously occurred
8. Developing skills and behavior that enable community agencies to reestablish trust in the individual, which in turn allows the individual freedom in the community

Every 6 months, a transdisciplinary team should convene to determine progress and future goals for the participants. In my experience, the average length of stay in a group for sex offenders with mental retardation or developmental disabilities is 2–2½ years.

COMMON SEX OFFENSES

Deviant Sexual Arousal

The deviant sexual arousal pattern exists in individuals with mental retardation and developmental disabilities just as it does in others. The sex offenders who molest children do so because they are sexually excited by them. Anyone, male or female, can exhibit a deviant sexual arousal pattern when sexually excited by looking at or touching or having sex with children. In medical schools and clinics, this response can be measured by the use of a plethysmograph; exercises in masturbatory satiation can be used to control the response. However, it seems unlikely that protection and advocacy groups would be comfortable with these techniques being used with persons with mental retardation or developmental disabilities. With this in mind, I have developed a Relapse Prevention Chart that enables the individual to cope with the problem in an acceptable, nonthreatening way (see Appendix C).

Case Study 10-2

Imagine being in your 70s and finding out that your 50-year-old son has been accused of sexually molesting little girls while giving them rides on his moped around the church. Neal was caught because a frightened child told her mother; other mothers started asking the other little girls in the neighborhood if anything had happened. Everyone was surprised because they thought that Neal was harmless. Neal could not read or write, but he seemed quiet and lived with his aging parents, riding his moped to a job he performed adequately with no problems. The job supervisor did not find it odd that Neal looked for discarded adult magazines in the trash. Neal had never had an adult girlfriend. He had very poor social skills and did not express his feelings well to males or females.

When Neal was arrested for criminal sexual conduct, it was hard for anyone who knew him to believe the charges. A clinical psychologist appointed by the court asked a sexuality counselor who worked with sex offenders with mental retardation to see Neal. No one expected Neal to open up and talk. However, the sexuality counselor used confrontation techniques and very direct questioning, and in the first session Neal acknowledged his inappropriate behavior. He would ask the young girls to ride on his moped. When they agreed, he would fondle their genitals under their panties and then go to a private place where he would masturbate to orgasm. Neal was exhibiting a deviant sexual arousal pattern. Neal had been masturbating using pictures of adult naked women for a long time, but his only true physical sexual contact was with the children. Neal's aging parents had no idea of his deviant sexual behavior and were horrified by it. They thought that Neal was just shy and afraid of adults and therefore played with children.

In court Neal pled "guilty" on all counts and was remanded to a sex offender group. Neal's parents participated with him, giving him their loving and firm support to change and accept responsibility for his behavior. Neal began to feel tremendous guilt for his actions. He was able to identify with the pain of his victims. Neal accepted the anger of the children's parents and society. He began to see that there were adult and appropriate ways to meet his sexual needs. Counseling was given in the area of masturbation fantasy, helping Neal realize he could masturbate to orgasm using pictures and fantasies of adult women. Neal began going to community dances for individuals with mental retardation, where he gradually reached out and met some people his own age. Although he was shy, as Neal's social and communication skills increased, so did his ability to relate in socially acceptable ways.

Instead of being such a loner in his home, Neal began to interact more with his parents and other family members, decreasing his isolation. Neal's behavior continued to improve in all environments and gradually the probation officer gave him more freedom. Eventually Neal was allowed to ride his moped to work or on short errands. Neal understood that he had lost the trust of the community and that interacting with children was off limits and would have violated his probation. He was compliant with this, and all adults in the environment supported his efforts in this area by offering supervision when necessary.

Neal's parents felt that, because of their age, other living arrangements needed to be provided for Neal. Now that he was accepting responsibility for his behavior, a recommendation was made for semi-independent living that would allow Neal to move out of his parents' home. Neal realized there still would always be some supervision and accepted this fact as part of the appropriate consequence for his inappropriate sexual behavior. Since he no longer appeared to be a risk to the community, Neal was allowed to terminate participation in the group with the understanding that, if there was any recidivism, he would have to return to the group immediately. The sexuality counselor made periodic checks with Neal's parents on his status and found that he was continuing to progress and was doing quite well in adjusting to his working and living environments. Occasionally, he took an evening adult education course to help him with reading survival skills and basic money management.

Neal made great strides in the development of self-esteem and moral development. In relapse prevention training, where he learned to change his deviant sexual arousal pattern to one of arousal in response to age-appropriate persons, Neal showed that age did not have to be a negative factor. The involvement of Neal's parents showed the importance of involving family members in the therapeutic process, regardless of their ages.

Incest

Individuals with mental retardation and developmental disabilities are often the victims of incest, as noted in Case Study 8-1. However, incest can also occur in family units made up of individuals with mental retardation who are married and have children. When these problems exist, all community resources need to be engaged in the therapeutic process.

Case Study 10-3

Franklin could not read or write and had a severe learning disability and borderline mental retardation. He was a very depressed young man. He was married and had two children. Franklin had recently been in jail and was now on probation, for molesting his daughter. A condition of Franklin's probation was that he attend counseling. A community mental health clinic had placed him in a sex offender group, but he was soon expelled from the group because he could not do the written exercises and he rambled and perseverated verbally in his own personal language, creating frustration for the other group members. Franklin was referred for individual therapy with a therapist skilled in working with sex offenders with mental retardation and developmental disabilities.

Franklin had never acknowledged exactly what had happened concerning his conviction for molesting his daughter. Using a confrontational model to break down the denial, the therapist discovered that Franklin had a book that belonged to his prepubescent daughter. This book discussed the changes in a young female body and included pictures of what a changing body would look like. Franklin liked to look at the childlike pictures in this book and masturbate. Sometimes he coerced his daughter into letting him feel her breasts and vagina, and then he put his erect penis between her legs and ejaculated. Franklin had been beaten and punished severely for masturbating with pictures of nude women when he was a teenager.

At the time this occurred, Franklin was not getting along well with his wife, who was a person with average intelligence but with limited capabilities. No one had ever talked to Franklin about relationships and what to do about problems with his marriage. When he entered therapy, Franklin was upset that he had been caught. He did not like having to spend time in jail, and he resented being on probation. He expressed anger that the court would not allow him to see his children. (This fact seemed irrelevant since his wife had filed for divorce, taken the children to another state, and refused to let him see the children anyway.) It was difficult for Franklin to deal with his behavior in a realistic way, accept responsibility for what he had done, and also accept the reality of the consequences. Furthermore, Franklin had no empathy for his daughter or her pain. He felt that he had not truly harmed her since he had not put his penis all the way inside her. He thought that she would still want to have a loving relationship with him as she grew up.

Franklin had great difficulty accepting the therapist's demand that he not be around any young children, male or female. (There was a suspicion that he had also molested his young son.) Franklin tried to reach out to other women to date and was adamant that he was going to date women his age who would want to have children. He wanted to have more children. He also saw no danger in his being around the young children of the women that he wanted to date.

The therapist worked with the probation officer and the supervisor at the plant where Franklin worked to help monitor his dating behavior. The therapist worked with Franklin in a concrete, didactic manner, having his relatives with whom he lived and his coworkers attend the therapy sessions. Since there was no professional group therapy available for Franklin, a group of family and friends was substituted. This group created an atmosphere of peer pressure consisting of individuals in Franklin's environment whom he valued.

Franklin became depressed when his wife and children moved out of state. He was referred to a psychiatrist and was given a prescription for antidepressant medication. Franklin refused to cooperate in taking his medication, even when it was prepared in dosage dispensers that were easy for him to understand. The physician assistant at the plant where Franklin worked even offered support.

Eventually, Franklin disintegrated at work. The physician assistant and local company doctor had to make the decision to admit him to a private residential psychiatric hospital under company insurance. When the insurance ran out, Franklin was transferred to the state hospital for persons with mental illness. It was not known if the company would be able to hold his job for him until he was released.

The psychiatrist thought that Franklin would probably establish some feeling of security in the state hospital and resist further treatment or assistance since it would force him to face the reality of what he had done. The reason Franklin did not make progress had very little to do with his cognitive levels. He was working with professionals who were patient and concrete with him. All therapeutic intervention had failed because of Franklin's intense denial and lack of motivation to change. The main problem that held Franklin back was that he refused to even try to develop an empathic response with his victim. In this situation, it is unlikely that Franklin will get better.

ADDITIONAL FACTORS IN SUCCESSFUL THERAPY

Working with issues of sexuality is complex. The best possible approach is a transdisciplinary one in which the individual with mental retardation or developmental disabilities receives input from all possible resources. Because so much of the therapeutic approach relies on creative energy, there is a need to share ideas and explore various possibilities for solutions. There is a need in the community for all agencies and private practitioners to work together to develop a cohesive transdisciplinary treatment. In this way, further victimization of children will be reduced, and adequate and appropriate treatment will be offered to individuals with mental retardation or developmental disabilities who have committed sex offenses.

As sex offenders learn to behave appropriately, they should be returned to the community as soon as possible, using a "shadow" technique to assist them in integrating back into society. Paying a person to act as a shadow is much cheaper than paying for residential care. A shadow is a person who is employed to follow the individual at all high-risk times in the community, with the responsibility of redirecting any inappropriate behavior. In this situation, the community is protected while the individual receives more freedom to move in the community. As the individual proves he or she has changed and can make good choices about behaving in the community, the shadow can gradually be faded. The use of a shadow and the reduction of "shadowed" time should always be a transdisciplinary team decision.

Other new and innovative ways of case management should be explored and developed to ensure that the proper support system is in place for optimum adjustment of the rehabilitated sex offender in the community.

A WORD ABOUT INCARCERATION

When an individual with mental retardation ends up in the penal system, there should be a special unit or prison that is protective in nature, enabling an individual with mental retardation to pay a societal debt for a sexual offense without being placed with hardened criminals. If this is not done, the incarcerated individual will be vulnerable to victimization and education in more violent crimes. For example, some states have special units in state correctional institutions that provide for sexual offenders to be in a therapeutic environment. Often, these units will accept individuals with mental retardation or developmental disabilities. State departments of mental retardation can be instrumental in supporting the development and continuation of these special units. The sexuality counselor should make referrals to these specialized units when the individual with mental retardation or developmental disabilities poses too high a risk for community living and outpatient treatment. The sexuality counselor has the responsibility to work with the defense lawyer and the solicitor to find the solution and proper programming environment that will be in the best interest of the individual with mental retardation or developmental disabilities.

Chapter 11

Issues for the Future

ISSUES IN SEXUALITY EDUCATION/COUNSELING

Need for and Right to Extensive Sexuality Counseling Information

The right of an individual with mental retardation or developmental disabilities to sexuality education and counseling has been well established in this book. But what of passion, clitoral and penile stimulation, different positions, lubricants, methods of masturbation, and alternative stimulation such as vibrators or oral sex? Can these topics ever be discussed, along with homosexuality, incest, bestiality, and other "problem areas"? We should not wait until the individual develops tremendous feelings of guilt, neglect, and rejection before it is considered justifiable to correct the situation. Individuals with mental retardation or developmental disabilities deserve to be taught how to achieve sexual satisfaction by means of the more esoteric as well as the basic methods. Will society and public opinion allow anyone or any group to do this? How might the legal domain interfere? Who overcomes the parents' fears?

It is easy enough to ask all of these questions, but to answer them we must take a stand, confront society, and make the public realize that such education is really needed. However, few among us can disregard community opinion, and there is little motivation to do so since it is unclear whether such confrontation would accomplish our goals. When will the individual with mental retardation or developmental disabilities be allowed and encouraged to develop sexual relationships that he or she can enjoy? Who will teach the individual how to enrich his or her life without hurting himself or herself or others? The average person is too leery to do anything about it. Can caregivers and professionals be part of this? It is hoped that a more enlightened approach is not too far in the future.

Living Environment versus Sexual Expression

There are many easy and clear examples of sexual limitations placed on persons living in certain situations. An individual living at home will usually be neither encouraged nor allowed to engage in sexual activity with a sibling or family member. Individuals living in a state residential facility may have to abide by archaic and rigid laws that are biased and that remove their constitutional rights to privacy. Still, these people have the daily opportunity to meet, greet, socialize, and relate to other peers. Even if sexual relating is against the rules, there will still be many opportunities for peer interaction.

The definition of "restrictive" in relation to sexual expression must be considered on an individual basis. The statement cannot simply be made that a particular living environment is restrictive. For example, persons with mental retardation or developmental disabilities are often encouraged to live independently in the community—the "least restrictive" environment. However, if these individuals have not developed the skills necessary to cope with community life they may break the laws because they lack the internal control systems necessary to modify their behavior. They may be incarcerated and thus placed in a "most restrictive" environment. In this case, a residential facility may have been the least restrictive environment for these persons.

The specific abilities and limitations of the individual should be considered when determining what makes an environment restrictive. Once external restrictions, such as making sure that there are ramps for wheelchairs, are conquered, the internal restrictions of coping skills and adaptive levels of the person should be studied by the professionals making the decision. The feelings of the person should always be considered within the scope of reality. The fact that a person wants to live independently does not necessarily mean that person should be encouraged to do so, if the necessary coping skills have not yet been developed.

It is important to counsel the person to develop his or her ability to move from one living environment to another. If certain levels of skill are necessary for the process, those should be made clear to the individual. Simple, easy processes should be established that will enable the person with mental retardation or developmental disabilities to progress from a more restrictive to a less restrictive environment.

Sterilization

It appears that part of the fear surrounding an intimate relationship between two individuals with mental retardation or developmental disabilities is that the couple will reproduce. Even if their baby does not have mental retardation or developmental disabilities, there is a continued fear that the couple might not possess the nurturing skills to raise the child properly. If this is the case, extensive and intensive birth control education is warranted—and perhaps even the consideration of the never-mentioned option of sterilization.

Sterilization may be appropriate for two people who can make the choice to live together, enjoy a rich sexual life, and become supportive and loving companions, but know that they do not have the skills to parent. Many people without mental retardation make this choice. Why cannot the individual with mental retardation or developmental disabilities receive professional and societal support for this option?

ISSUES IN THERAPY

Choice of Techniques

Even for the average individual, society is presently too conservative to feel comfortable with more than using a wooden or plastic penis and vagina to demonstrate normal anatomy and function and methods for interacting with one's own body parts. This is considered acceptable for people without mental retardation, so why is it considered wrong to help individuals with mental retardation by using these prostheses to enable them to understand human sexuality and relate it to their own bodies?

When will we develop techniques for teaching masturbation to individuals with mental retardation and developmental disabilities? They should have the same opportunities as any individual to successfully masturbate to climax and feel good about what they are doing. If a person cannot read but can imitate, is it wrong for an older sibling, parent, or caregiver to demonstrate masturbation and encourage the person to try it? Why is this kind of teaching severely criticized for individuals with mental retardation and developmental disabilities? Public opinion and the law may have a great deal to do with the problem. Some would label such teaching as child abuse or incest.

What about the use of surrogate partners? Very reputable sexuality therapists frequently use sexual surrogates in therapy with persons without mental retardation or developmental disabilities. Why cannot this be a good vehicle of learning for the individual? There is an understandable fear of lawsuits because the courts are indefinite about informed consent when an individual is judged incompetent. What can be done legally to make surrogates a more feasible option? A program could be established to give special training to sexual surrogates so that they are well informed about the needs and communication abilities of the individual. A sexuality therapist or counselor trained in working with individuals with mental retardation or developmental disabilities could then work with the couple. Of course, this concept is more difficult to employ for anyone in the 1990s because of the epidemic of AIDS. The real question is, if it were safe, would it be acceptable for individuals with mental retardation or developmental disability? Are we going to advocate that all people receive the same rights to make the same choices?

The solutions to these problems are not easy. No matter how uncomfortable, solutions must be found if individuals with mental retardation and developmental disabilities are to progress sexually. Often, such individuals develop undesirable and frustrating behavior as a substitute for appropriate and satisfying sexual behavior because they just do not know how to do what with whom.

For individuals without mental retardation who are having trouble developing sexual self-expression, there are books, courses, and clinics. These individuals are taught about available tools and techniques to enhance sexuality. Many of these things are applicable to individuals with mental retardation, and many of these aids can be useful and enjoyable to the person who is also physically disabled. However, society's rules, judgments, and constraints restrict use of these tools. Even open talk of the subject is barely tolerated, much less encouraged.

Consumer Protection in Choice of Counselor

Sexuality education/counseling programs have to be sure that they have qualified counselors who are rendering appropriate instruction and counseling. The counselor must develop ways to help the individual explore and feel positive about his or her sexuality. If parents, administrators, or society feel a little or very uncomfortable, well, that might be the price that has to be paid. A high price, perhaps, but at some time it needs to become an affordable one. If not, the "sneak around, find out on your own" variety of sex education, which is often unfulfilling or meaningless to the individual, will continue.

Sexuality issues are very personal and delicate. The privacy and personal rights of the individual should always be respected first. Individuals only communicate about sensitive issues with people with whom they are comfortable about the topic. This usually implies that the listener must be a person who is comfortable with his or her own sexuality, has had training in how to provide sexuality education and counseling, and has been supervised in this process so that the consumer is protected.

The American Association of Sex Educators, Counselors and Therapists (AASECT) is a national organization that certifies professionals in the areas of sex education, sex counseling, and sex therapy. Consumers can contact AASECT (see Appendix F) to find out who is certified in their geographic area. (Such certification is also often included in telephone directory listings.) These individuals should be able to join forces with experts in the fields of mental retardation and developmental disabilities to develop the resources for the individuals seeking assistance in this area. These trained professionals are very scarce and therefore often work on a consultative basis in which they come into a program, do in-service training workshops for parents and professionals, and do individual or couple consultation for brief counseling as needed.

Consumers need to be aware of credentials and qualifications. If there is not an AASECT-certified professional available, the consumers can turn to the licensure laws of the state in which they live, or have their personal physician or a community clinic help them locate a professional licensed in psychology, social work, or professional counseling who has experience in working with sexuality issues. It is most helpful if this person also has exposure to and knowledge of mental retardation and developmental disabilities. If there is no one individual available with these skills, it is good to look for a team of two or more professionals who can work together to help accomplish this task. Of course, if the client is already in a residential facility program, the Individual Program Plan (IPP) team can help identify individual professionals who can provide the service.

Street Language: Can It Be Accepted?

Adults often have a difficult time accepting street language. They need to realize that individuals with mental retardation and developmental disabilities know the words and their meanings and use them. If this book contained passages using explicit obscenities, readers might have immediately closed it and condemned the contents. This would have meant that many readers would not have obtained the information presented in this book, and that no future communication with them would have been possible. A corollary statement could be made about the results of counseling if the counselor overreacts to the use of street language by an individual.

For the reserved and conservative members of society, street language is often uncomfortable and ugly. Children are taught that such words are bad and naughty and that people who say these words are bad people. This is a concept that children without mental retardation can think about abstractly. They realize that using some of the language does not necessarily mean that they are bad people. This is not automatically true among individuals with mental retardation, who tend to have more concrete thought and language processes. These individuals often become consumed with guilt and negative feelings about themselves when they use street language and are chastised or ostracized for doing so. If caregivers and counselors learn to accept street language and understand particular words used, then it becomes easier to teach proper terminology to individuals with mental retardation or developmental disabilities.

Parents, caregivers, and professionals must learn not to react emotionally to street language. Adult inhibitions about this language, when presented to individuals with mental retardation or developmental disabilities, are useless and nonpurposeful. It is time for adults to accept that the individual will acquire street language, in the same way any other child might. Unlike most people, however, individuals with mental retardation may not have the discrimination to know when and where to use the words. This is where sexuality education/counseling help should be given.

Parenthood

Once two individuals with mental retardation or developmental disabilities decide that they want to live together, with or without marriage, there is much they can learn. Just as society willingly supplies birth control pills and instructions, it can also be responsible for supplying the counseling that would help make these individuals better parents if they choose to have a child. It is true that this is more likely to happen under the guise of matrimony, but even then professionals hesitate to provide anything but the barest information on what parenthood really entails.

What kind of program will be considered a success? Which communities will support parenthood among persons with mental retardation or developmental disabilities? Can a system help a couple succeed without family and community support? If more individuals with mental retardation marry, will more become divorced? Will the community be there to help individuals with the process of divorce and single parenting? What about child support, when the other parent's only income is social security funding? Is society ready to face these issues? It seems irresponsible in the 1990s to provide family planning and lessons on child rearing, without also being prepared to address divorce and all the legal, moral, and ethical issues that accompany this topic.

What happens when two individuals with mental retardation or developmental disabilities have a baby with mental retardation or developmental disability? What rights does the baby have to quality treatment and daily care from a person skilled in such techniques? If the parent with mental retardation cannot do this task, will he or she be at risk for losing the child, or will society take on the responsibility to pay for a caregiver to the child to provide the help that the parents are unable to give? These are tough questions with no simple answers. When rights are upheld for a person, responsibilities will be demanded of the individual to keep those rights. And what of the children who are born to parents with mental retardation or developmental disabilities? What are their rights?

The most important issue is rights of the children. For many individuals with mental retardation, marriage with supportive systems may be a viable option. However, parenthood may be a risk because the individuals may be unable or unprepared to fulfill the responsibilities involved. This might result in the child being removed and placed in foster care. Courts may take over, terminating parental rights, and placing the child or children up for adoption. Who deals with the emotional response of the parents when this happens?

Are there enough community resources to provide the support systems these considerations imply? Even with unlimited money, a 30-year-old individual with mental retardation may not have enough self-esteem and skills to parent a child through sickness and health, the various stages of development, and the ever-present need to develop a self-identity. What happens when the child's academic skills exceed those of the parent? Does role-reversal happen? Is it healthy for parents and children? What happens when a child needs help from a parent with homework and the parent cannot give it? Will there be homework telephone help-lines in rural areas and small towns? Who picks up the pieces of the parent's shattered self-esteem when he or she does not have the skills to help the child he or she loves?

These questions may sound hypothetical but they are all too real for the person who deals daily with young adults with mental retardation who go to friends, parents, and counselors saying they want to have lives like their siblings . . . they want to get married, live alone, have babies, and "be like everybody else." It takes a skilled counselor to help any individual deal with the reality that there may be many things that he or she may not be able to do. Accepting one's limitations while still feeling that one is meeting self-directed life challenges is what is important for each person. The skilled educator/counselor uses therapeutic techniques to help each individual focus on and develop his or her own unique potential to experience life to the fullest. For some, this process will include marriage. For some it will include parenthood and for others it will not. Searching for the possibilities includes finding and identifying the strengths and weaknesses of each individual, and then working to maximize the positives and minimize the negatives, in the best interests of the individuals involved.

ISSUES IN THE COMMUNITY

Change in Society's Attitudes

It is time to take a realistic, if slightly painful, look at what it means to be an individual with mental retardation or developmental disabilities who has sexual needs, desires, and frustrations. Everyone expects individuals with mental retardation or developmental disabilities not to notice sex or, worse yet, to act nonsexual or asexual. These individuals often are not considered as competitive in the job market or as capable of living independently. Must individuals with mental retardation and developmental disabilities be second-class citizens sexually, too? It is time to change this status. The first step in this process is to help society recognize the sexual fulfillment needs of all people.

Individuals with mental retardation and developmental disabilities are finally being recognized as sexual beings, but society has yet to accord them a need to develop their sexuality to a point that it is a positive and enjoyable part of their lives. Why is it so threatening for society to think that individuals with mental retardation or developmental disabilities can realize the meaning and fulfillment of orgasm, even if they cannot read or understand words such as "coitus" or "clitoral stimulation"?

Teenagers and young adults without mental retardation often enter into sexual relationships and decide to cohabit without great distress or notice from family or community. Why are two individuals with mental retardation who also have this desire forced to suffer society's disapproval? Should they not be given the support system to make it possible to have this same experience? With the proper knowledge and support, they might be successful and have fun, too, while learning to be responsible in a relationship.

Should society be so frightened of such relationships developing and being consumated, or at least explored? These fears just encourage ignorance. If this is the goal, society is achieving it well. If the goal is to develop responsible and enjoyable sexuality, then society is failing grossly, and it is time for a drastic change.

Legal Advocacy and Reform

The fact that laws exist does not mean they are good, fair, equal, or reasonable. How are bad, discriminatory laws changed and what does society do in the meantime? None of the discrimination in the American past would have ever been remedied if everyone sat around waiting for it to happen. It took activists and leaders to change things. Who are the activists who will lead the fight for the sexual rights and privileges of individuals with mental retardation and developmental disabilities?

Individuals need an advocate to say, "Why do people have to be sexually uninformed and frustrated all the time? Individuals have the right to express their sexuality openly and freely whether in heterosexual or homosexual experiences." The adults, caregivers, and professionals need to be helping in this process.

In the decade of the 1990s, I hope that more advocates will push society to recognize the rights to develop good PSS attitudes and behaviors in all persons with mental retardation and developmental disabilities, commensurate with their ability to accept responsibility for their PSS activities and behaviors. In this way, these individuals will be afforded the opportunity to grow and explore life as they develop their individual human potentials.

Development of Community Resources

For individuals with mental retardation and developmental disabilities to successfully live, learn, and work in the community, there has to be community participation in the process. J. F. Gardner and Chapman (1990) asserted that community participation is part of the normalization principle and is a measure of the extent to which people are socially integrated into the community. They stated that:

> Community participation includes both personal and impersonal interactions. Impersonal interactions take place, for example, while ordering a meal in a restaurant and during work or work training. Personal interactions include the opportunity to have meaningful relationships with friends and family. For children this includes parents, siblings, relatives, and school and neighborhood friends. For adults this interaction extends to friends, relatives, and perhaps, spouse and children. (p. 43)

How is the community responsible in accepting and dealing effectively with the sexuality issues surrounding individuals with mental retardation and developmental disabilities? Are community mental health clinics and departments of public health ready to deal with the medical, physical, and emotional aspects of these problems? I believe that the professionals working in the fields of mental retardation and developmental disability have a professional responsibility to reach out to community resources, modeling and teaching the idea that services offered to the public could be easily modified to meet the needs of individuals with mental retardation and developmental disability and that these individuals are entitled to the services of any citizen in society. Inexperience or lack of knowledge in how to provide these services on the part of a person or agency is not an excuse. The community agencies and the professionals in other fields have the responsibility to seek out in-service training by qualified mental retardation specialists who can help in the adaptation of the agency's service to the individual with different or special needs. Not knowing the answers does not give a group permission to withhold the service. Ignorance creates the need for skill development on the part of the provider. I provide workshop in-service training throughout the country, and have found many willing and capable professionals from the community attending my workshops in order to learn and implement new skills.

The individual with mental retardation or developmental disabilities has the right to make choices. This includes his or her right to choose where and how to get professional help in handling questions and issues surrounding sexuality education and counseling. Until community agencies are ready to stand on their own in their ability to provide sexuality education and counseling to such individuals, the agencies might consider contracting with a consultant who would participate in staffing and in-service training for other professionals who have skills in sexuality education and counseling but who have never worked with individuals who have mental retardation or developmental disability. This cooperative effort will ensure that the rights of the individuals are being upheld while community agencies develop the expertise that enables them to fulfill their responsibilities for providing services.

The community can contribute to the normalization process by recognizing individuals with mental retardation and developmental disability as citizens worthy of community service and programs. Growth that emanates from the community agencies will influence the vested interests of the community itself to accept and work with individuals with mental retardation and developmental disabilities. In this manner, community leaders and agencies can model attitudes toward such individuals that can generalize to the community as a whole.

I believe that the attitude of the total community toward individuals with mental retardation as being sexual beings needs to be changed. This change could be effected through church or synagogue groups, parent-teacher organizations, community service clubs, business and professional women's clubs, and other groups. Night courses might be offered in local colleges giving an orientation to sexuality among persons with mental retardation and developmental disabilities within the scope of understanding the whole person. Videos might be developed for use in the particular clubs or groups. Speakers trained in this area could make themselves available to reach out, inform, and disseminate information. Verbally skilled individuals with mental retardation or developmental disability could also speak to help break down stereotypes and barriers that presently exist.

Newspapers could advocate for the rights of individuals with mental retardation and developmental disability to live fulfilling lives through community integration and participation in all aspects of community living. Feature stories of success could appear on a regular basis. County libraries could have books and videos available to educate the community about the lives of individuals with mental retardation and developmental disability. As these individuals are presented as total people, their sexuality should also be addressed, with the aim of desensitizing the public to the myth of "infantilization of the mentally retarded." This is one approach I use in my workshops.

It would be beneficial to have individuals with mental retardation and developmental disabilities and their advocates meet with municipal or county councils to state their needs and make suggestions for ways the community can help implement models of successful interventions that benefit all citizens. Volunteerism by individuals with mental retardation and developmental disabilities could also help in eliminating community bias and promoting the notion of normalization. Community programs facilitating contact between those individuals or their advocates who offer to assist, and such places as senior citizens' housing, schools, shelters for the homeless, and nonprofit agencies should be instituted and developed. County agencies could try to utilize the skills of individuals with mental retardation and developmental disability, thereby demonstrating their capabilities to reach out supportively to other populations.

Businesses that employ individuals with mental retardation and developmental disability need to be aware of the PSS development of the individual so that any problems in this area that occur on the job will be treated with understanding, compassion, and knowledge of available resources that can be helpful.

I believe that the community has much to offer and contribute to the lives of individuals with mental retardation and developmental disabilities. Persons with mental retardation and developmental disabilities must be seen as whole people who deserve to go through the normal life cycle of sexualization. The gathering together and joining of existing and developing resources is the challenge of the 1990s.

FACING THE FUTURE

As the year 2000 approaches, let us use this last decade of the century to explore untested and rich ground. We must consider loosening the reins of protectiveness tied to individuals with mental retardation and developmental disabilities, chancing all of the possibilities of success and failure that might occur if the reins are untied. Putting judgments aside, let us look to see where society can be led toward the freedom of individuals to initiate, express, and grow in sexuality. This is a time for the development of community resources, which should follow the assessment of needs and delineation of what support services are necessary for implementation of new, innovative, and creative programs.

During this time, different uses for our residential treatment facilities will probably develop. They will be more therapeutic in nature, allowing for specific programs that give individuals with special problems such as sexual offenses a place to go for specialized individual and group treatment aimed toward reintegration into the community. Residential treatment of individuals who commit acts against society will be preferred until there are different community monitoring systems available, including electronic beeper location systems, supervised community living, and developing of "shadow" programs (see Chapter 10). I believe that such systems will be the wave of the future, being much less expensive options than residential care.

Gathering resources to help an individual live within his or her biological family unit is also emerging as being in the best interest of the individual and his or her family. Once legislators see that it is cost-efficient to help an individual stay with his or her natural family unit, money will be released for this purpose and family support funds will become the preferred means of support for these individuals.

New ideas require time for adjustment. In 1987, Dr. Virginia Satir taught me that the process of change requires the introduction of a foreign element, resultant chaos, and the need to practice, practice, practice before arriving at the new status quo. The 1990s have arrived in a state of chaos. Commitment to practice is needed so that by the year 2000 the new status quo will be evident. This will include having all members of society act in a way that is in the best interest of the individual with mental retardation or developmental disabilities so that each person receives the entitlement to reach his or her own human potential. Let each commit to the journey, enjoying the process!

Understanding and Expressing Sexuality:
Responsible Choices for Individuals with Developmental Disabilities
by Rosalyn Kramer Monat-Haller, M.Ed., LISW, LPC, CCC-SLP
AASECT Certified Sex Educator/Sex Counselor
copyright © 1992 by Paul H. Brookes Publishing Co., Inc.
Baltimore • London • Toronto • Sydney

APPENDIX **A**

The Pragmatics of Colored Chalk

◇◇◇◇◇◇◇◇◇◇◇◇◇◇◇◇◇◇◇◇◇◇◇◇◇◇◇◇◇◇◇◇◇◇

Often educators and counselors think that anything meaningful or beneficial must include expensive audiovisual materials. For presentations on sexuality, we feel that we need models, dolls that have genitalia or that will deliver babies, or other fancy equipment. The reality is that if simple, meaningful, concrete language is used with colored chalk and a chalkboard, all the information that is necessary can be provided.

Figures A.1 through A.13 at the end of this appendix illustrate a simple technique of providing sexuality education using only a chalkboard and colored chalk or paper and colored markers. It is important for the reader to understand that these drawings are meant to be primitive, expressionless, and similar to body stick figures that any parent, educator, or caregiver can draw easily. In fact, it is appealing to individuals with mental retardation to have unsophisticated drawings, very simplistic in nature, that can be drawn by anyone in any sexuality education session.

The important point is to use the drawings to show the differences between males and females. By using colored chalk on a chalkboard or colored markers on white paper, the adult can systematically and consistently show how anatomy, conception, and contraception occur. The choice of colors for body parts is insignificant except for the fact that *it is important to use the same color for the specified body part or function throughout all of the drawings.* The use of the same color for the same body part or function will help eliminate confusion in the learning process. Each body part or function should be shown with a different color.

EXAMPLE OF THE METHOD

Depending on the individual or group, decide whether to present the male or female anatomy first. On the chalkboard, with white chalk, draw two asexual bodies similar to those in Figure A.1. For each point to be made, add the appropriate anatomical or physiological information to the drawings using different colors as necessary (represented in step-by-step fashion in the remaining figures). For the female, say something like:

> We are going to pretend that this is Suzie. Let's give her long hair. She is growing into a woman now, so some changes have happened to her body. She has developed breasts [Figure A.2]. There is an opening between her legs called a vagina [Figure A.3]. Suzie is maturing and has grown some hair under her arms and around her vagina [Figure A.4]. Inside Suzie's body is a special place where a baby grows. It is called a womb or uterus [Figure A.5] and is connected to the outside of her body through the vagina [demonstrate]. There are two Fallopian tubes [Figure A.6], which lead to the ovaries [Figure A.7] where the eggs are.

At this point, go to the drawing of Johnny and say the following:

> Now let's see how Johnny looks different from Suzie. He has nipples but has not developed breasts [Figure A.8], and I guess that we give Johnny short hair. As Johnny has grown, his body has developed and his penis is now large [Figure A.9]. Sometimes it hangs down and sometimes, when he is excited and has an erection, it sticks out like this [demonstrate with a dotted line; Figure A.10]. Johnny also has grown some hair on different parts of his body. He has hair on his face now and he shaves. He has hair under his arms and around his penis [Figure A.11].
> Both Johnny and Suzie have glands that are developing. The glands will give off a body odor if Johnny and Suzie are not clean and have not used deodorant. This is something that we want to talk more about later.
> Now, let's continue looking at our drawings. If Johnny gets excited, a white sticky fluid comes out of the penis. The fluid is called semen and has sperm in it [draw this in white chalk; Figure A.12]. If the sperm gets inside Suzie's vagina, either by them having sexual intercourse or by it getting on Johnny's hand and then getting into the vagina, the sperm will swim up into the womb.
> Remember, the eggs are in Suzie's ovaries. Once a month, one of them comes down this tube and will be waiting in the womb to make a baby. If the sperm gets to the womb at the time that the egg is there, what will happen? [Wait for or prompt the response "A baby."]
> You are right. The egg and sperm will join together, making a baby [Figure A.12]. To review, let's go to another part of the chalkboard and draw a womb. [Use the same colors as in previous drawings, such as Figure A.5. Show by drawings how the baby begins to form and grow (Figure A.13).] If we don't want to make a baby but we do want to have sexual intercourse, what do we have to do? [Wait for or prompt the response "Use birth control."]
> Yes! On these drawings I can show you some of the different ways that you can stop the sperm from getting to the egg and causing conception.

At this point, illustrations using the same color system would show how various birth control methods would work.

USE OF THE METHOD IN ASSESSMENT

The Pragmatics of Colored Chalk can be used to assist the professional in understanding the level of knowledge of body parts being assessed on the Sexuality Assessment for Persons with Mental Retardation and Developmental Disabilities.

Using Figure A.12, the sexuality educator/counselor can review the body parts with the individual including the process of ejaculation and conception, circling the body parts and processes that the individual comprehends. Using the colored chalk provides a simple and inexpensive way to aid the professional or sexuality educator/counselor in obtaining and recording this information.

CONCLUDING REMARKS

By using good pragmatic and functional communication, and a box of colored chalk and a chalkboard, you can keep the techniques simple and inexpensive. At the same time, you can keep the individual or group interested and impart all of the necessary information in a simple way. I believe that this technique would work well with any individual, with or without mental retardation or developmental disability. The level of language is the important factor; the language used must be individualized.

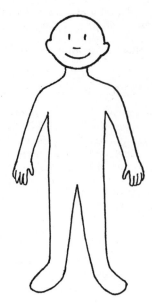
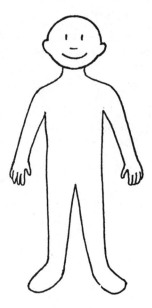

Figure A.1.

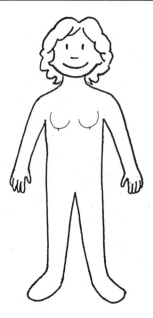
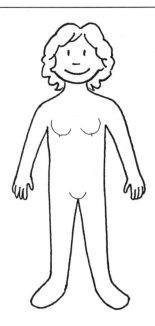

Figure A.3.

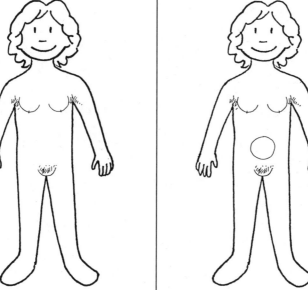

Figure A.4.   Figure A.5.

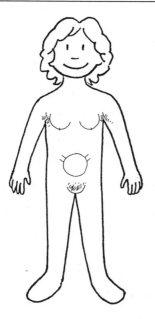

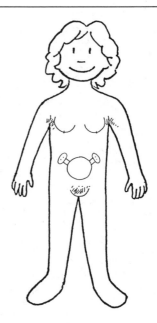

Figure A.6.   Figure A.7.

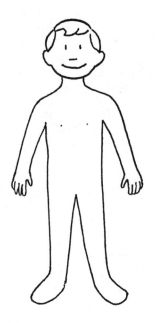

Figure A.8.

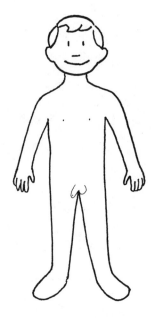

Figure A.9.

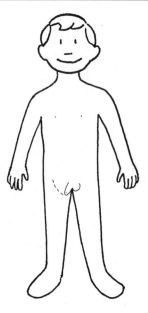

Figure A.10.

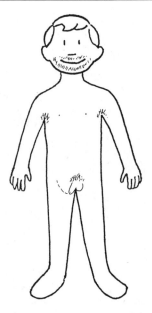

Figure A.11.

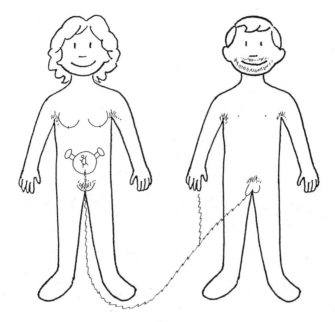

Figure A.12.

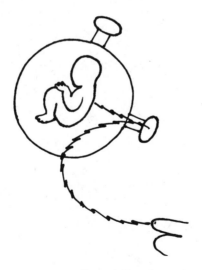

Figure A.13.

Understanding and Expressing Sexuality:
Responsible Choices for Individuals with Developmental Disabilities
by Rosalyn Kramer Monat-Haller, M.Ed., LISW, LPC, CCC-SLP
AASECT Certified Sex Educator/Sex Counselor
copyright © 1992 by Paul H. Brookes Publishing Co., Inc.
Baltimore • London • Toronto • Sydney

APPENDIX **B**

Sexuality Assessment

◇◇◇◇◇◇◇◇◇◇◇◇◇◇◇◇◇◇◇◇◇◇◇◇◇◇◇◇◇◇◇◇

All persons with mental retardation are entitled to receive the amount and level of sexuality education and sexuality counseling they need. A simple sexuality assessment written by this author can easily be used by caregivers, educators, nurses, counselors, and other professionals to help determine where to begin and identify who will start the process. It also helps identify goals that all persons in the individual's environment can emphasize. The content of this book provides the background necessary to use the assessment. Appendix A (Pragmatics of Colored Chalk) provides information on how to fill out the top part of the assessment.

After completion of the assessment, the results can be shared with the family and necessary professionals. The individual's program team can develop plans for education and counseling and determine who will carry out the program. Basic sexuality education can be provided by any responsible adult in the environment. Sexuality counseling should be provided by individuals trained and skilled in mental health counseling and sexuality issues. The American Association of Sexuality Educators, Counselors, and Therapists (AASECT) is the national certifying organization in sexology. A professional certified by AASECT would possess the necessary skills to provide sexuality education and counseling to persons with mental retardation.

Federal survey teams periodically review the records of each individual with mental retardation or developmental disabilities to see that the person's needs have been addressed and federal standards maintained. The assessment provided here should meet those standards, and its presence in the individual's record will show that the individual's needs and rights in the area of sexuality have been addressed. The assessment allows for the delineation of specific objectives and designates who will be responsible for implementing them.

Sexuality Assessment for Persons with Mental Retardation and Developmental Disabilities

Client: _____   Birthdate: _____

Client's residence: _____   Age: _____

Address: _____   Date of assessment: _____
_____

Person administering assessment: _____

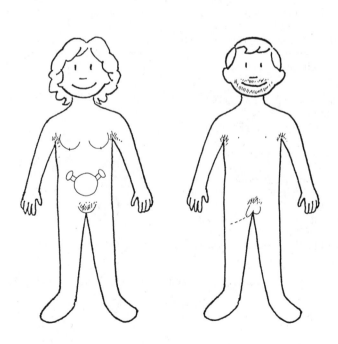

UNDERSTANDING OF BODY PARTS

Directions: Circle the body parts the client can identify. If slang terms are used for any body parts, write them here.

_____ _____ _____ _____ _____

Does client understand puberty and body changes? (   ) YES   (   ) NO

Whom do you recommend provide this new knowledge? _____

PSYCHOSOCIAL-SEXUAL DEVELOPMENT

Does client do the following?

		Yes	No	Same sex	Opposite sex
1.	Kiss	( )	( )	( )	( )
2.	Hold hands	( )	( )	( )	( )
3.	Hug	( )	( )	( )	( )
4.	Participate in vaginal intercourse	( )	( )	( )	( )
5.	Participate in oral intercourse	( )	( )	( )	( )
6.	Participate in anal intercourse	( )	( )	( )	( )
7.	Say "no" to unwanted sexual advances	( )	( )	( )	( )
8.	Push away unwanted sexual advances	( )	( )	( )	( )
9.	Call for help when someone is bothering him or her	( )	( )	( )	( )
10.	Masturbate appropriately	( )	( )	( )	( )
11.	Masturbate inappropriately or with harmful objects	( )	( )	( )	( )
12.	Approach others for sex	( )	( )	( )	( )

Additional factors:

		Yes	No	Same sex	Opposite sex
13.	Is client appropriate for a dating program?	( )	( )	( )	( )
14.	Has client been the victim of sexual assault?	( )	( )	( )	( )
15.	Has client ever perpetrated sexual assault?	( )	( )	( )	( )
16.	Does client have knowledge of sexually transmitted diseases, including AIDS?	( )	( )	( )	( )
17.	Does client have knowledge of birth control?	( )	( )	( )	( )
18.	Does client have knowledge of use of condoms for "safer sex"?	( )	( )	( )	( )

Of the above items, _____, _____, _____, need to be worked on in sexuality education/ counseling.

INDIVIDUAL PROGRAM PLAN

Sexuality education will be provided for the client in the following way:

_____

Understanding and Expressing Sexuality:
Responsible Choices for Individuals with Developmental Disabilities
by Rosalyn Kramer Monat-Haller, M.Ed., LISW, LPC, CCC-SLP
AASECT Certified Sex Educator/Sex Counselor
copyright © 1992 by Paul H. Brookes Publishing Co., Inc.
Baltimore • London • Toronto • Sydney

APPENDIX **C**

Relapse
Prevention Chart

◇◇◇◇◇◇◇◇◇◇◇◇◇◇◇◇◇◇◇◇◇◇◇◇◇◇◇◇◇◇◇

Sex offenders with mental retardation usually have a deviant sexual arousal pattern in which the person is sexually stimulated and excited by children or non–age-appropriate persons. In sexuality counseling with these individuals, it is helpful to use a Relapse Prevention Chart like the one proposed here. The chart is used in conjunction with an exercise in developing coping strategies for deviant sexual arousal, as described below. This relapse prevention training exercise should be performed as a part of individual or group counseling, with the sexuality counselor and the individual's peers in the group providing support. This chart is used repeatedly, helping the perpetrator develop many new and different coping strategies.

A chalkboard, white board, or large sheet of white paper is used so that colored chalk or colored markers can be used for nonreaders. The chart is divided into two sides, with the number of columns on each side being the same as the number of participants in the group (Fig. C.1). A different color is used for each person and the name of the person is written in the assigned color at the top of the chart on the right and left sides.

On the right-hand side of the chart the rows are numbered beginning with 10 at the top and descending to 0. This side represents a ladder that the person can "walk" down. An arrow can be drawn along the right of the chart indicating that the steps will be down on this side. A green star can be put by the 0, indicating that the 0 is the desired place to be. A red star can be put by the 10. The right-hand side of the chart is labeled "children."

	Name	Name	Name	Name	Name	Name	Name	Name	Name	Name	Name	Name	
*+10													10–**
9													9
8													8
7													7
6													6
5													5
4													4
3													3
2													2
1													1
**–0													0+*
		WOMEN			Adults or same age					CHILDREN			

Figure C.1. Sample relapse prevention chart (Green star = single asterisk, red star = double asterisk.)

The left-hand side of the chart is similar to the right except that the 10 is the desired outcome and has the green star by it. A red star can be by the 0, and there should be an arrow going up, indicating that on this side of the chart the objective is to climb up the ladder. The left-hand side of the chart is labeled "adults or same age."

During relapse prevention training, each perpetrator takes a turn filling in the columns under his or her name, using the appropriate color of chalk or marker. The perpetrator begins at the negative 10 on the right-hand side of the chart, saying "When I had sex with the child, I was feeling. . . . That was a poor choice. I could have chosen to do. . . . " Each time the perpetrator can think of an alternate appropriate action he or she could have taken in order to be in control of his or her behavior, he or she can mark a downward arrow with the colored chalk and move down one step on the ladder. When he or she eventually reaches 0, he or she is praised for the smart choices that allowed him or her to choose activities other than sexual abuse.

Next the perpetrator fills in the appropriate column on the left-hand side of the chart, where he or she is rewarded for making "smart choices." The individual moves up the ladder to the desired 10 by marking an upward arrow for each thing that he or she can think of to help become sexually aroused by and interested in persons of his or her own age. Verbal encouragement and rewards are given for each upward step that is made until he or she reaches 10.

I have found the Relapse Prevention Chart to be effective in working with sex offenders with mental retardation or developmental disabilities. It gives a concrete system for actualizing some of the fantasy work that has often been thought of as difficult for persons with mental retardation or developmental disabilities. In therapeutic groups the chart is used for group process and also on an individual basis with an individual when he or she is ready to assume responsibility for his or her behavior and is at the point of being ready to cognitively make choices and consider options to help deal with his or her deviant sexual arousal pattern. This is a good technique to use once the individual has broken through denial. It will help enable the individual to avoid further problems as he or she deals with lack of impulse control of his or her deviant sexual arousal pattern.

Understanding and Expressing Sexuality:
Responsible Choices for Individuals with Developmental Disabilities
by Rosalyn Kramer Monat-Haller, M.Ed., LISW, LPC, CCC-SLP
AASECT Certified Sex Educator/Sex Counselor
copyright © 1992 by Paul H. Brookes Publishing Co., Inc.
Baltimore • London • Toronto • Sydney

APPENDIX **D**

Anger Ladder
and Happy Steps

USE OF AN ANGER LADDER

The main focus of sexuality counseling is to deal with feelings. Often these feelings are of extreme anger. Usually, underneath the emotion of anger is a strong feeling of "helplessness" and "being out of control." It is the job of the counselor to help the person in counseling begin to feel more control over his or her life. This is often achieved by using concrete tools such as the Anger Ladder.

Figure D.1 is an example of an Anger Ladder for Rodney, a 21-year-old man with mild mental retardation. The 10 represents when Rodney is feeling angry and the 0 represents when he is feeling calm. The star at the 10 is colored red, symbolic of a stoplight indicating "stop." The star at the 0 is colored green, symbolic of a stoplight indicating "go." The rungs on the ladder are numbered and colored purple. (Colors are used to make the Anger Ladder more interesting and to help Rodney in retention.) Broken arrows go down the ladder step by step, indicating Rodney's choices of actions he can follow to lower his anger and increase his feeling of control (every person's Anger Ladder will be unique in the choice of actions at each step). When Rodney reaches 5, there is a yellow line indicating a caution light to signal that he is out of danger. At each step below the 5, soothing green wavy lines indicate that Rodney is entering a state in which he feels peaceful and in control.

Children, adolescents, and adults can use this symbolic technique. Anger Ladders can be made to fit in a wallet and can be laminated so that they can be carried at all times. When the person begins to feel out of control, he or she can pull out the Anger Ladder and remind himself or herself of the smart choices that he or she can make. If the person is a nonreader, symbols can be used instead of words. Multiple Anger Ladders can be made for different environments and are always specific to the individual and his or her needs.

USE OF HAPPY STEPS

Another helpful chart is a reverse of the Anger Ladder known as Happy Steps. This chart is constructed in the same way as the Anger Ladder, using colors and arrows to indicate the steps of progress, but everything is reversed since in this case the bottom step is "sad" and the top step is "happy." The person makes smart choices of action by climbing his or her Happy Steps to end up at the positive 10, which is marked by a green "go" star. Figure D.2 is an example of Happy Steps that were made by Sylvia, a young woman with mental retardation. As with the Anger Ladder, cards can be made showing Happy Steps so that they can be carried at all times.

CONCLUDING REMARKS

The use of concrete visual symbolic charts is beneficial in working with all individuals who have trouble seeing between the stages of growth that are needed to get to where one wants to be. Educators, counselors, and professionals are only limited by forgetting to use their own creative imagination to help open the door to others to learn. Being creative and approaching each person as a unique individual capable of learning, living, and loving, regardless of kind and degree of disability, leads all involved a long way down the road to becoming more fully human. This in turn allows others to participate in another individual's journey, a privilege and honor to be received humbly and with joy!

Anger Ladder

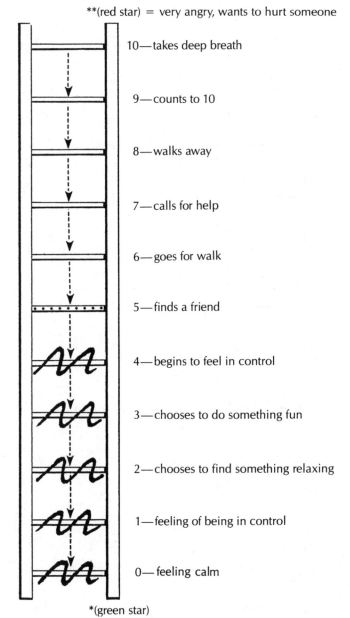

**(red star) = very angry, wants to hurt someone

10—takes deep breath

9—counts to 10

8—walks away

7—calls for help

6—goes for walk

5—finds a friend

4—begins to feel in control

3—chooses to do something fun

2—chooses to find something relaxing

1—feeling of being in control

0—feeling calm

*(green star)

Figure D.1. Rodney's anger ladder. (*Note:* Steps are different for each individual.) (Green star = single asterisk, red star = double asterisks, • • • = yellow line, ⋀⋀ = green wavy lines.)

Happy Steps

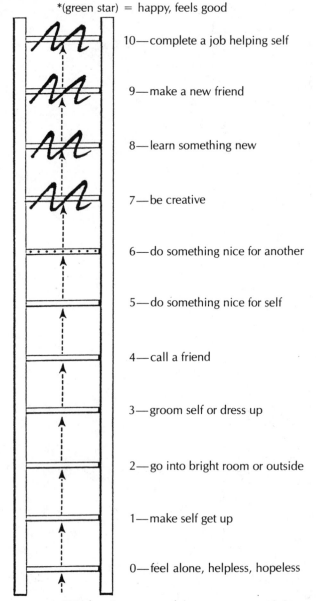

*(green star) = happy, feels good

10—complete a job helping self

9—make a new friend

8—learn something new

7—be creative

6—do something nice for another

5—do something nice for self

4—call a friend

3—groom self or dress up

2—go into bright room or outside

1—make self get up

0—feel alone, helpless, hopeless

**(red star) = very unhappy, wants to withdraw or hurt self

Figure D.2. Sylvia's happy steps. (*Note:* Steps are different for each individual.) (Green star = single asterisk, red star = double asterisks, • • •= yellow line, 〰 = green wavy lines.)

Understanding and Expressing Sexuality:
Responsible Choices for Individuals with Developmental Disabilities
by Rosalyn Kramer Monat-Haller, M.Ed., LISW, LPC, CCC-SLP
AASECT Certified Sex Educator/Sex Counselor
copyright © 1992 by Paul H. Brookes Publishing Co., Inc.
Baltimore • London • Toronto • Sydney

APPENDIX **E**

In-Service Training Workshop Curriculum

◇◇◇◇◇◇◇◇◇◇◇◇◇◇◇◇◇◇◇◇◇◇◇◇◇◇◇◇◇◇

With regard to sexuality education, each individual with mental retardation or developmental disabilities is unique, with his or her own set of needs. Learning styles are different, and the most important factor for the person providing the sexuality education is to communicate concretely with the individuals who are being educated. Public school teachers, employees of state departments of education, parents, interdisciplinary team members, caregivers, administrators, and community mental retardation board members all have one request in common. They all ask for a "curriculum" to tell them in simple terms how to "do" sexuality education for individuals with mental retardation.

To meet this purpose, I propose that all-day workshops be held to train the adults and professionals who will be providing the sexuality education. These workshops should be experiential in nature, allowing time for role-playing and discussion of relevant case studies, with creative problem solving by audience participation. The participants should achieve a level of comfort with issues of sexuality that will enable them to cover the material suggested in the curriculum handout proposed here. This handout follows the material presented in this book and takes the learner from the point of knowing how to use colored chalk for basic sexuality education (see Appendix A) to understanding how to use community resources for referrals and the development of policies necessary to implement the curriculum.

It is my opinion that all of the expensive materials in the world will not make a successful sexuality education curriculum program for individuals with mental retardation or developmental disabilities if staff and parent training is not presented first. Individual instructors tend to prefer to use their own techniques and/ or some of the other well-developed programs on the market. I suggest that by using the simple two-page sexuality assessment presented in Appendix B, the colored chalk education method presented in Appendix A, and the suggested topics in the curriculum handout below, a successful program can be implemented at a minimum cost.

A public school, residential facility, department of mental health, or the like can use the following curriculum at an all-day workshop for teachers, administrators, care providers, professionals, parents, and support personnel. Additional time can be set aside for reviewing the appropriate portions of their programs in order to integrate the information presented in the workshop. All of the information in this handout is discussed in detail in other parts of this book. The workshop presenter can find complete explanations of topics in the outline by studying this book.

Understanding and Expressing Sexuality:
Responsible Choices for Individuals with Developmental Disabilities
by Rosalyn Kramer Monat-Haller, M.Ed., LISW, LPC, CCC-SLP
Certified Sex Educator/Sex Counselor
copyright © 1992 by Paul H. Brookes Publishing Co., Inc.
Baltimore • London • Toronto • Sydney

Curriculum Handout for In-Service Workshops in Sexuality Education and Counseling for Individuals with Mental Retardation and Developmental Disabilities

I. SEXUALITY: Expression of sexual attitudes and activities in relationship to individuals with mental retardation and developmental disabilities

II. SEXUALITY EDUCATION FOR INDIVIDUALS WITH MENTAL RETARDATION AND DEVELOPMENTAL DISABILITIES
   A. Orientation for teachers, staff, caregivers
   B. Who provides instruction
   C. Videotape utilization and topics on tape staff can develop
      1. Overview of sexuality and the relationship to individuals with mental retardation or developmental disabilities; anatomy and physiology (use of colored chalk teaching method)
      2. Birth control for individuals with mental retardation or developmental disabilities
      3. Homosexuality, wet dreams, masturbation, fantasies, use of condoms, "safer sex," sexually transmitted diseases (including AIDS), sex offenses, and development of dating procedures for individuals with mental retardation or developmental disabilities
      4. Issues concerning parenthood and marriage for persons with mental retardation or developmental disabilities
   D. Goals of training staff
   E. Myths
   F. Desensitization to street language
   G. Developing administrative support
   H. Materials and techniques
      1. Be concrete
      2. Use low-level language or augmentative systems
      3. Use simple pictures
      4. Ask questions of the group to see what the participants understand
      5. Discuss appropriate and inappropriate social and sexual behavior

I. Factors imperative to a successful sexuality education program
   1. Policies need to be developed and supported by the administration and communicated to the parents as well as to all school personnel, caregivers, and professionals working with the group of individuals with mental retardation or developmental disabilities; individualization for each person must be emphasized
   2. Everyone involved with the individual with mental retardation or developmental disabilities needs to assume responsibility for at least feeling comfortable enough with their own sexuality so that they can deal with the sexuality of the individual with mental retardation
   3. Any dating rules or standards expected for appropriate social behavior in a given living, learning, or working environment should be clearly communicated to all and enforced by everyone involved
   4. Using videotapes specifically developed for the environment is an excellent tool that keeps material consistent; this technique allows for personal interchange and role-playing of feelings in response to the material on the tapes
   5. It is imperative that the sexuality program is administered by someone experienced both in sexuality education/counseling and in the field of mental retardation; this ensures that good teaching/counseling is provided for the participants that encompasses both fields
   6. Without good administrative support, well-informed staff, faculty, and parents, and a qualified programmer, there will be no adequate sexuality program for individuals with mental retardation or developmental disabilities; all of the above must exist to make the significant impact that is needed
J. Subject areas to be covered in sexuality education
   1. Anatomy and physiology
   2. Maturation and body changes
   3. Birth control
   4. Sexually transmitted diseases, AIDS, condoms, and "safer sex"
   5. Masturbation
   6. Responsibility of being sexual
   7. Same-sex and opposite-sex activity
   8. Psychosocial-sexual behavior (PSS) and psychosexual (PS) development
   9. Building friendships and relationships
   10. Marriage and parenthood
III. PURPOSE AND ROLE OF SEXUALITY COUNSELOR WITH INDIVIDUALS WITH MENTAL RETARDATION AND DEVELOPMENTAL DISABILITIES
   A. Primary purpose to discuss feelings and facilitate communication
   B. Societal input to make sure resources are used in the community
   C. Role of sexuality counselor
   D. Difference between sexuality education (dealing with facts) and sexuality counseling (dealing with feelings)
   E. Helping all individuals achieve living in the least restrictive environment
   F. Development of worksheets for developing a positive adult socialization program for different environments

1. Activities individuals with mental retardation or developmental disabilities can initiate and carry out on their own
    a. The person can be encouraged to own and place individual leisure-time equipment in his or her room for private use (e.g., radio, stereo, television, books, age-appropriate games)
    b. Individuals can learn to explore community recreational activities, either visually or verbally, by being aware of public media such as newspapers and television (these activities would include movies, concerts, bowling alleys, and special events); the person can learn to request that teachers, work staff, or staff in the living environment make arrangements for him or her to attend such events so that the school, work, or living environment can become the liaison between the person and the community
    c. In a group home environment, the person can initiate invitations to friends from the community or other residences into the group home for socialization activities such as watching television, making popcorn, and listening to records; staff would be responsible for providing appropriate supervision and other support services for the activity, guiding the individuals into more social interaction
2. Activities the family of the individual with mental retardation and developmental disabilities can initiate and carry out in a supportive way
    a. Family members can consider having one special day a month where they invite group home members into their family homes for socialization activities, such as cookouts or pizza parties (with all the families doing this on a rotational basis, each family would be responsible approximately one time per year); for this activity, the family could tell the group home leader what support staff and materials they would need for the event (e.g., transportation to and from the family home, any specified amount of money contributed from the participants to participate in the event, and request for a specific number of group home staff to assist)
    b. If the group home is not coeducational, family members may want to consider sharing some of these activities with a family from another group home so that the activity will be coeducational
    c. Another option for families to consider is providing tickets or entry passes to community ball games or skating rinks as their contribution to a socialization activity; in this way, families may be able to help in a supportive financial way if they are not able to offer the use of their homes
3. Activities the group home staff can initiate and carry out
    a. At least two times a month or every other week, group home staff should try to plan a special event that would involve participation in a community recreational activity or involve members of the opposite sex (e.g., members from another community residence) to provide an appropriate socialization experience

        b.   Group home staff can discuss and outline local recreational activities and locations that are appropriate and readily accessible for an individual to participate in the community; such activities might include signing oneself out to walk to a nearby grocery store to purchase a treat or walking to the bus station to attend an activity (the group home staff will have to teach skills such as bus riding before this is appropriate)

        c.   As a general rule, individuals should be encouraged to develop friends and enjoy socialization activities without pairing off into couples

        d.   After any socialization activity, the staff should take the opportunity to discuss socialization benefits and encourage continuation of all positive, appropriate socialization behavior

        e.   Individuals should be involved as much as possible in caring for their own rooms and shared living area by developing chore activity charts that would encourage helping each other as friends

        f.   Staff should make an effort to discourage unrealistic talk of love, marriage, boyfriends and girlfriends, and babies, while encouraging talk about having fun, going places, seeing new things, and choosing appropriate friends for these activities

        g.   Individuals should always be encouraged to exhibit appropriate social behavior, and they should be expected to abide by the socialization and dating rules of the group home as understood by the person, the family, and the administrative staff; positive reinforcement should be given for observing socialization behavior that is appropriate for the living environment

    4.   Activities that can be carried out through other community-regional resources

        a.   Staff should explore current available support systems and services available through community-vended programs (e.g., beginning square dance groups, appropriately rated and suitable movies)

        b.   Persons should be taught to use these resources

IV. LIVING ENVIRONMENTS

    A.   All efforts should be made to move the individual with mental retardation or developmental disabilities from the more restrictive to the least restrictive environment

    B.   Recognize all of the inherent sexual limitations and restrictions of each environment, helping the person adjust to the changes he or she finds in each environment

    C.   Explore valid questions that are relevant concerning living environments

    D.   Make sure the person with mental retardation or developmental disabilities understands the psychosocial-sexual rules of the environment in which he or she lives

V. DEVELOPING HEALTHY PSYCHOSOCIAL-SEXUAL ATTITUDES IN INDIVIDUALS WITH MENTAL RETARDATION AND DEVELOPMENTAL DISABILITIES

A. Working with other disciplines and the benefits of creating inter-disciplinary and transdisciplinary teams
    1. The nursing profession in schools, community resource agencies, and residential facilities is a wonderful resource to tap
    2. Speech pathologists are a good group to approach because these professionals know how to work with concrete language systems and augmentative communication; the speech pathologist can be of great assistance to the sexuality educator/counselor and the family
    3. Psychologists, counselors, and social workers can all become involved in evaluating, assessing, and meeting the sexuality education/counseling needs of persons with mental retardation
    4. Educators and adult training program providers are important to include because they see the individual with mental retardation for several hours each day
B. Special roles the other disciplines can assume
    1. Professionals can act as facilitators who are openly able to communicate about sexuality
    2. The professional can coordinate the interdisciplinary or transdisciplinary team and help all team members deal with sensitive topics of sexuality as they relate to persons with mental retardation
C. Other disciplines can function as facilitators for family interactions, especially in the area of sexuality
    1. A referral to a family therapist is one opportunity for family interaction
    2. Co-therapy with the family therapist or other significant professionals can provide open verbal forums where sexuality issues can be discussed
    3. Working with family members, clergy, physicians, or other professionals can bridge the gaps between disciplines
    4. In this process, the role of the other disciplines is to initiate and carry out effective communication systems for and with the person with mental retardation
D. Role of the other disciplines as sexuality educators with young children, developing adolescents, or young adults with mental retardation and developmental disabilities
    1. Reasons why other disciplines should function in the role of sexuality educators
        a. Any sexuality educator should have the ability to use appropriate anatomical and physiological language comfortably
        b. Sexuality educators should be aware that the individual is taught accountability for himself or herself and his or her own body in all respects; individuals with mental retardation or developmental disabilities must know how to protect themselves from sexual abuse
    2. The involvement of other disciplines guarantees that efforts at generalization into all learning, living, and working environments will be enhanced
E. Better and longer lasting results and retention of sexuality information with significant family members as co-sexuality educators and co-sexuality counselors

F. Topics of concern
    1. Individuals must know how to communicate "no," "stop," "don't bother me," and "help" when approached inappropriately
    2. Individuals must be taught "responsibility for self"
    3. Individuals must recognize that behavior is affected by handicaps, places of living, learning, and working, and the rules and attitudes of the society in which the person resides
    4. All people must recognize that "being a person with a handicap" is different from being a "handicapped person," especially in relationship to sexuality
G. Suggestions for how other disciplines can offer support services to local, state, and regional departmental needs in the area of sexuality education/counseling

VI. PUBLIC RELATIONS
A. Sexuality education programs can succeed if parents, community, and staff are given a chance for exposure to the material
B. In-service training for the public increases acceptance of the tenets of the program

VII. PROVIDING SEXUALITY EDUCATION FOR INDIVIDUALS WITH MENTAL RETARDATION AND DEVELOPMENTAL DISABILITIES IN PUBLIC SCHOOL SYSTEMS
A. Local, regional, and state authorities endorse the program
B. Sexuality education for individuals with mental retardation and developmental disabilities helps protect them from sexual abuse
C. Support and involvement of the parents and the Parent-Teacher Association in the schools
D. Sign a release for participants
E. Explore topics parents desire
F. Examples of previous incidences of protection from sexual abuse
G. Assure parents that goal is to help protect the child from unwanted sexual advances

VIII. GENITALLY DIRECTED SELF-STIMULATION
A. Masturbation
B. Relationship of masturbation to relative level of mental retardation or developmental disabilities
C. Value judgment
D. Look at program
E. Private versus public
F. Permission giving
G. Masturbation that becomes harmful
H. Mutual masturbation versus self-stimulation
I. Same-sex masturbatory behavior

IX. SOCIAL CONCERNS AND THE LAW
A. Individuals with mental retardation and developmental disabilities need to understand the meaning of "criminal sexual conduct" and the consequences for this behavior
B. Individuals with mental retardation and developmental disabilities need to understand right from wrong in relationship to morals, ethics, and the law
C. Individuals with mental retardation and developmental disabilities

need to understand that they will be held accountable for their behavior

D. Encouragement should be given to making smart choices that obey the law rather than poor choices that break the law

X. INTIMACY, MARRIAGE, AND PARENTHOOD

A. Explore the meaning of intimacy as a closeness between two people in physical, emotional, and intellectual ways

B. Discuss the responsibilities of marriage, including commitment, finances, housing, and medical care

C. Explore all of the skills necessary to adequately care for and provide for a baby, such as feeding, sickness, safety, schooling, and other components of nurture that parents must be able to provide.

XI. SEXUAL ABUSE ISSUES RELATING TO INDIVIDUALS WITH MENTAL RETARDATION OR DEVELOPMENTAL DISABILITIES

A. What behaviors make it easier to victimize an individual with mental retardation or developmental disabilities

B. If an individual with mental retardation or developmental disabilities is sexually abused, he or she is entitled to the best evaluation by a sexuality counselor that is available in the locale

C. If a child with mental retardation or developmental disabilities has been sexually abused or if there is any suspicion of abuse, by law it must be reported to the department of social services

D. Individuals with mental retardation suspected of being sexually abused should be examined by a physician skilled in looking for physical evidence that will hold up in court

E. Criminal prosecution should proceed if there is a suspected or known perpetrator

XII. WORKING WITH SEX OFFENDERS WITH MENTAL RETARDATION OR DEVELOPMENTAL DISABILITIES

A. The individual with mental retardation or developmental disabilities who commits a sexual offense should be responsible for his or her behavior

B. There should be an evaluation by a sexuality counselor skilled in working with sexual perpetrators with mental retardation and developmental disabilities

C. If appropriate, there should be adjudication in court

D. If court leverage is not available, family members or program areas such as leisure time and freedom to go out without supervision should provide the leverage in treatment

E. After initial interviews, the most appropriate treatment is group therapy using a direct, confrontational model

1. The sexual perpetrator must assume responsibility for his or her behavior

2. The therapist must be able to break down the perpetrator's denial system

3. The sexual perpetrator must develop an empathic response for the victim

4. The sexual perpetrator must move beyond the "law and order" stage of moral development and understand that the behavior is bad and hurts the victim

5. Deviant sexual arousal patterns usually exist, and relapse prevention training will probably be necessary

XIII. APPLICATIONS OF THESE PRINCIPLES TO ALL INDIVIDUALS WITH DEVELOPMENTAL DISABILITIES OR PHYSICAL HANDICAPS
- A. The process of sexuality education/counseling can be used and individualized for individuals with developmental disabilities
- B. Individuals with physical disabilities also have the need and right to sexuality information, which should be individualized to meet specific needs

XIV. USE OF THERAPY DOG IN SEXUALITY COUNSELING
- A. A therapy dog can be used in sexuality counseling sessions to build interactive response and increase trust and communication
- B. The therapy dog can enhance the development of the empathic response

XV. USE OF FAMILY THERAPY TECHNIQUES
- A. Bringing family members into counseling sessions empowers the system
- B. Having the individual with mental retardation or developmental disabilities participate in family therapy keeps him or her from becoming the "identified patient"
- C. When the individual's actual family is not available, the therapist can create a family therapy environment by involving other adults and peers from the person's current living environment

APPENDIX **F**

Resources

TRAINING IN SEXUALITY EDUCATION AND COUNSELING

In-service training workshops led by the author currently are available. These workshops emphasize the content of this book. They also explore the development of individualized multimedia, such as videotapes, that are appropriate for specific training settings. For information regarding costs and details, contact the author directly at P.O. Box 2103, Summerville, SC 29484-2103 (803-873-6935)

ADDITIONAL SOURCES OF INFORMATION

The following organizations may be contacted by readers interested in receiving further information or help with a particular need or problem.

American Association for Counseling and Development
5999 Stevenson Avenue
Alexandria, VA 22304
(703) 823-9800

American Association on Mental Retardation
1719 Kalorama Rd. N.W.
Washington, D.C. 20009
(202) 387-1968

Association for Retarded Citizens
P.O. Box 6109
Arlington, TX 76005
(817) 640-0204

American Association of Sex Educators, Counselors and Therapists
Suite 1717
435 N. Michigan Avenue
Chicago, IL 60611
(312) 644-0828

American Speech-Language-Hearing Association
10801 Rockville Pike
Rockville, MD 20852
(301) 897-5700

Autism Society of America
1234 Massachusetts Avenue N.W., Suite C-1017
Washington, D.C. 20005
(202) 783-0125

March of Dimes (Birth Defects) Foundation
1275 Mamaroneck Avenue
White Plains, NY 10605
(914) 428-7100

National Association of Protection and Advocacy Systems
900 Second St. N.E., Suite 211
Washington, D.C. 20002
(202) 408-9514

National Council on Alcoholism and Drug Dependence
12 West 21 Street, Suite 700
New York, NY 10010
(800) NCA-CALL

National Easter Seal Society
70 E. Lake Street
Chicago, IL 60601
(312) 726-6200

United Cerebral Palsy Associations
7 Penn Plaza, Suite 804
New York, NY 10001
(212) 268-6655

Williams Syndrome Association
P.O. Box 178373
San Diego, CA 92117-0910

Glossary

Augmentative/alternative communication mode: A method of supplementing or replacing verbal communication (speech) by using another method such as gestures, sign language, communication boards, or electronic devices.

Blissymbols: Part of the system of Blissymbolics, a copyrighted pictorial symbol language containing 100 basic symbols that serves as a bridge between pictures and written words.

Certified sex counselor: An individual meeting the criteria for sex counselor and being certified by the American Association of Sex Educators, Counselors and Therapists. Criteria include 90 hours of human sexuality education covering specialized core areas, 135 hours of sexuality counseling training, and 500 hours of supervised counseling.

Certified sex educator: An individual meeting the criteria for sex educator and being certified by the American Association of Sex Educators, Counselors and Therapists. Criteria include 90 hours of human sexuality education covering specialized core areas, and 2 years experience involving sex education (800 hours).

Certified sex therapist: An individual meeting the criteria for sex therapist and being certified by the American Association of Sex Educators, Counselors and Therapists. Criteria include 90 hours of human sexuality education covering specialized core areas, 90 hours of sex therapist training, and 500 hours of supervised clinical treatment.

Clarification process: A series of separate interviews that involves the perpetrator and the nonoffending parent together, and individual interviews with the victim where the therapist works toward preparation for the clarification process. The perpetrator, in the presence of the nonoffending parent, clarifies his or her behavior and accepts the responsibility of the crime against the child, assuming total responsibility, apologizing, and assuring the nonoffending parent that he or she will never do it again. Safeguards are put in place to prevent any further victimization. When the clarification is completed between the perpetrator and nonoffending parent, and the therapist has prepared the child for the session, a therapeutic intervention session is held with the therapist, the perpetrator, the victim, and the nonoffending parent or significant other who acts as a comfort to the victim. The session is always done in a way working toward the best interest of the child. The perpetrator tells the child the same things he told the nonoffending parent as he or she clarifies the responsibility for the offense to the child in the presence of the therapist.

Deinstitutionalization: The transfer of persons with developmental disabilities and mental retardation to community-based care systems, while making an effort to reduce the number of persons admitted to the institution.

Deviant sexual arousal: Sexual arousal to inappropriate visual or actual situations, objects, and people such as children. Often the arousal is to persons who are not age appropriate. This is an area to explore with pedophiliacs.

Fetishism: "Recurrent, intense, sexual urges and sexually arousing fantasies involving the use of nonliving objects (fetish). The persons with fetishism frequently masturbate by holding, rubbing, or smelling the fetish object, or may ask his sexual partner to wear the object during their sexual encounters" (American Psychiatric Association, 1987, p. 282).

Individual with mental retardation: Significant subaverage general intellectual functioning concomitant with deficits in adaptive behavior in occurrence during the developmental period, generally meaning IQs below 70.

Individual with developmental disability: Disability occurring during the developmental period, requiring special services. Disabilities in this category include mental retardation, cerebral palsy, seizure disorders, autism, significant language impairments, and any at-risk children including individuals with genetic disorders normally associated with developmental delays.

Individual program plan (IPP): The active treatment plan for the individual that originates from comprehensive functional assessments and describes all services the individual will be provided to meet all of his or her needs. Sometimes referred to as the Individualized Habilitation Plan (IHP).

Interdisciplinary team: A group of professionals from different training backgrounds who bring their individual expertise to the process of program planning and implementation.

Licensed independent social worker: An individual meeting requirements of the licensure law of the state in which he or she practices that allows the individual to provide services within the regulation of the law in that state. Social work involves a broad spectrum of services designed to help individuals and groups enhance social functioning. Social case work is centered on the individuals' needs, both personally and environmentally. The professional skills of the worker focus on enabling the individual to adjust psychologically and environmentally to the situation. This involves work with families, agencies, communities, and total environmental milieu. Social workers attempt to release resources for the betterment of the human condition. A social worker gives precedent to professional responsibility over financial gain and observes ethical areas of practice.

Licensed professional counselor: An individual meeting requirements of the licensure law of the state in which he or she practices that allows the individual to provide services within the regulation of the law in that state. A counselor can have various therapeutic backgrounds. The counselor works with the individual and family toward personal and family adjustment. The counselor works within the scope of training and skills.

Licensed psychologist: An individual meeting requirements of the state licensure law of the state in which he or she practices that allows the individual to provide services within the regulation of the law in that state. The function of the licensed psychologist includes psychometric testing, IPP planning, interdisciplinary interaction, development of life skills, and behavior programs and psychotherapy. Services are dependent on the specialty area of the license.

Masturbation: A form of self-stimulation that is focused on the genitals.

Moral development: "The process of developing through the Level I Premoral stages (Stage 1-obedience and punishment orientation, Stage 2-naively egoistic orientation), to Level II Conventional Role Conformity stages (Stage 3-good-boy orientation, Stage 4-authority and social–order-maintaining orientation [usually the intellectually disabled are arrested at this stage, sometimes referred to as the 'Law and Order' Stage]), to Level III Self-Accepted Moral Principles stages (Stage 5-contractual legalistic orientation, Stage 6-conscience or principle orientation)." (Caparulo, 1988, p. 7).

Normalization: N. E. S. Gardner defines as "providing the same services, risks, and opportunities to persons with developmental special needs as are provided to everyone else" (1986, p. 47).

Opposite-sex activity: Sexual activity between a male and female that involves touching, kissing, and the possibility of, or actual occurrence of, sexual intercourse. This behavior often is referred to as heterosexual.

Psychosexual (PS): The development within the self of attitudes relative to sexuality, including how one feels about one's sexual self and sexuality, and concepts of what sexuality means to the individual.

Psychosocial-sexual (PSS): The awareness of oneself sexually in relationship to the awareness of others sexually; the interplay of sexual feelings and responses in either heterosexual or homosexual development.

Same-sex activity: Sexual activity between either two males or two females that does not necessarily imply homosexual preference or homosexual lifestyle. This activity involves touching, kissing, and the possibility of, or actual occurrence of, sexual intercourse.

Sexuality education: The process of giving information about sexuality issues.

Sexuality counseling: The process of dealing with feelings about sexuality issues.

Shadow: The word used to describe the process where a staff member unobtrusively supervises the total movements of someone in any environment, allowing for accessibility to community participation with supervision. The shadow has the responsibility of redirecting any inappropriate behavior.

Street language: Words describing parts of the genitals or sexual activity that are commonly used on the street (usually slang).

Therapy dog: A dog used in a therapeutic environment to help create bonding and the empathic response. Therapy dogs are also used in working with individuals who are depressed or hospitalized. Other animals can become therapy animals, such as cats, horses, guinea pigs, rabbits, parrots, or any other cuddly or affectionate animal that can be handled in an interactive way.

Bibliography and Related Materials

ANATOMICAL DOLL MANUFACTURERS

Analeka Industries, Inc., P.O. Box 141, West Linn, OR 97068 (503)655-3596
Hylands Anatomical Dolls, Inc., 4455 Torrance Blvd., Suite 310, Torrance, CA
   90503 (213)316-0527
Migima Designs, Inc., P.O. Box 70064, Eugene, OR 97410 (503)726-5442
Teach-A-Bodies, 2544 Boyd St., Fort Worth, TX 76109 (817)923-2380

FILMS

About sex. (1972). New York: Texture Films, Inc.
Conception-contraception. (1973). Highland Park, IL: Perennial Education, Inc.
Feeling good about yourself: Breaking through the social and personal barriers of disappointment and fear. (1985). Kailua-Kona, HI: Feeling Good Associates.
Kempton, W. (1972). *Human sexuality and the mentally retarded.* Philadelphia: Planned Parenthood of Southeastern Pennsylvania.
Kempton, W., Bass, M., & Hanson, G. (1972). *ABC's of sex education for trainable persons (THE).* Owings Mills, MD: Hallmark Films.
Kempton, W., Bass, M., & Hanson, G. (1976a). *Fertility regulations for mentally handicapped persons.* Owings Mills, MD: Hallmark Films.
Kempton, W., Bass, M., & Hanson G. (1976b). *How and what of sex education for educable persons.* Owings Mills, MD: Hallmark Films.
Kempton, W., Bass, M., & Hanson, G. (1978). *Sexuality and the mentally handicapped.* Santa Monica, CA: Stanfield Film Associates.
Like other people. (1971). Highland Park, IL: Perennial Education, Inc.
Monat, R. K. (1982). *Sexuality and the mentally retarded* [Videotape]. (To accompany the book, *Sexuality and the mentally retarded, A clinical and therapeutic guidebook.*) Summerville, SC: Author.
St. Louis Association for Retarded Citizens (Producer). (1976). *On being sexual.* Santa Monica, CA: Stanfield Film Associates.
Silverman, M., & Lenz, R. (1979). *Active partners.* Akron, OH: Thomas Gertz and Associates, Inc.

WRITTEN MATERIAL

Aguilar, S. (1984). Prosecuting cases of physical and sexual assault of the mentally retarded. In *Sacramento County Prosecutor's Notebook*, Vol. III.

American Psychiatric Association. (1987). *Diagnostic and statistical manual of mental disorders—Revised* (3rd ed.). Washington, DC: Author.

Assault Prevention Training Project. (1984). *Women against rape.* Columbus, OH: Author.

Bachrach L. L. (1985). Deinstitutionalization: The meaning of the least restrictive environment. In R. H. Bruininks & K. C. Lakin (Eds.), *Living and learning in the least restrictive environment* (pp. 23–36). Baltimore: Paul H. Brookes Publishing Co.

Baldwin, M., & Satir, V. (Eds.). (1987). *The use of self in therapy.* New York: The Haworth Press.

Berini, R., & Kahn, E. (1987). *Clinical genetics handbook.* Oradell, NJ: Medical Economics Books.

Berkman, A. (1984–1986). Professional responsibility: Confronting sexual abuse of people with disabilities. *Sexuality and Disability, 7*(3/4), 89–95.

Bernstein, N. R. (1985). Psychotherapy of the retarded adolescent. *Adolescent Psychiatry, 12,* 406–413.

Blatt, B. (1980). The pariah industry. A diary from purgatory and other places. In G. Gerbner, C. J. Ross, & E. Zigler (Eds.), *Child abuse: An agenda for action* (pp. 185–203). New York: Oxford University Press.

Boat, B. W., & Everson, M. D. (1988). Use of anatomical dolls among professionals in sexual abuse evaluations. *Child Abuse and Neglect, 12*(2), 171–179.

Brandwein, H. (1973). The battered child: A definite and significant factor in mental retardation. *Mental Retardation, 11*(5), 50–51.

Brantlinger, E. A. (1985). Mildly mentally retarded secondary students' information about and attitudes toward sexuality and sexuality education. *Education and Training of the Mentally Retarded, 20*(2), 99–108.

Brantlinger, E. A. (1988). Teachers' perceptions of the parenting abilities of their secondary students with mild mental retardation. *Remedial and Special Education, 9*(4), 31–43.

Brashear, D. B. (1981). Contemporary patterns: Emerging issues of the sexual rights of adolescents in institutions. In D. A. Shore & H. L. Gochros (Eds.), *Sexual problems of adolescents in institutions* (pp. 17–26). Springfield, IL: Charles C Thomas.

Brookhauser, P. E. (1987). Medical issues. In J. Garbarino, P. E. Brookhauser, & K. J. Authler (Eds.), *Special children—special risks: The maltreatment of children with disabilities* (pp. 161–178). New York: Aldine de Gruyter.

Brown, H., & Craft, A. (1989). *Thinking the unthinkable: Papers on sexual abuse and people with learning difficulties.* London: FPA Education Unit.

Browning, D. H., & Boatman, B. (1977). Incest: Children at risk. *American Journal of Psychiatry, 134*(1), 69–72.

Calkins, C. F., & Walker, H. M. (Eds.). (1990). *Social competence for workers with developmental disabilities: A guide to enhancing employment outcomes in integrated settings.* Baltimore: Paul H. Brookes Publishing Co.

Caparulo, F. (1987). *A comprehensive evaluation of a victim/offender of sexual abuse who is intellectually disabled.* Orange, CT: The Centre of Sexual Health and Education, Inc.

Caparulo, F. (1988). *The victim/offender—case study of an intellectually disabled adolescent sex offender*. Paper presented at the University of Michigan Medical School, Ann Arbor, MI.

Caplan, P. (1986). Is there a relationship between child abuse and learning disability? *Canadian Journal of Behavioural Science, 18*(4), 367–380.

Carnes, P. (1983). *The sexual addiction: Out of the shadows*. Minneapolis, MN: Compcare Publications.

Champagne, M. P., & Walker-Hirsch, L. W. (1982). Circles: A self-organization system for teaching appropriate social/sexual behavior to mentally retarded/developmentally disabled persons. *Sexuality and Disability, 5*(3), 172–174.

Child abuse and cerebral palsy [Editorial]. (1983, May 21). *The Lancet*, p. 1143.

Child abuse and developmental disabilities: Essays. (1980). Washington, DC: National Center on Child Abuse and Neglect (DHEW).

Chipouras, S., Cornelius, D., Daniels, S., & Makas, E. (1979). *Who cares? A handbook on sex education and counseling services for disabled people*. Baltimore: University Park Press.

Clark, K. (1986). *Sexual abuse prevention education: An annotated bibliography* (rev. ed.). Santa Cruz, CA: Network Publications.

Cole, S. S. (1984–1986). Facing the challenges of sexual abuse in persons with disabilities. *Sexuality and Disability, 7*(3/4), 71–88.

Cole, S. S. (1988). Women, sexuality, and disabilities. *Women and Therapy, 7*(2/3), 277–294.

Cole, T. M., & Cole, S. S. (1977). Sexuality and disability: The physician's role. *Rehabilitation Medicine*, July, 525–529.

Coleman, E. M., & Murphy, W. D. (1980). A survey of sexual attitudes and sex education programs among facilities for the mentally retarded. *Applied Research in Mental Retardation, 1*, 269–276.

Comfort, A. (Ed.). (1972). *The joy of sex*. New York: Simon and Schuster.

Comfort, A. (1978). *Sexual consequences of disability*. New York: George F. Stickley Co. (distributed by Van Nostrand Reinhold).

Comfort, M. B. (1978). Sexuality in the institutionalized patient. In A. Comfort (Ed.), *Sexual consequences of disability* (pp. 249–253). New York: George F. Stickley Co.

Cooney, M. H. (1986). *Meeting the social and sexual needs of disabled students: A counseling challenge*. (ERIC Document Reproduction Service No. ED 290 248).

Corrigan, J. P., Terpstra, J., Rurrow, A. A., & Thomas, G. (1981). Protecting the rights of institutionalized individuals. In *Proceedings of the Fifth National Conference on Child Abuse and Neglect* (pp. 181–194). Milwaukee: University of Wisconsin, Region V Child Abuse and Neglect Resource Center.

Cozzolino, J. P. (1977). Criminal justice and the mentally retarded. *Dissertation Abstracts International, 38*(6A), 3751–3752.

Craft, A., (1982). *Sex educational counseling of the mentally handicapped*. Baltimore: University Park Press.

Craft, A., & Craft, M. (1978). *Sex and the mentally handicapped*. London: Routledge & Kegan Paul.

Craft, A., & Craft, M. (1983). *Sex education and counseling for mentally handicapped*. England: Costello.

Crain, L. S., & Millor, G. K. (1978). Forgotten children: Maltreated children of mentally retarded parents. *Pediatrics, 61*, 130–132.

Crossmaker, M. (1986). *Empowerment: A systems approach to preventing assaults against people with mental retardation and/or developmental disabilities*. Columbus, OH: The National Assault Prevention Center.

Cruz, V. K., Price-Williams, D., & Andron, L. (1988). Developmentally disabled women who were molested as children. *Social Casework: The Journal of Contemporary Social Work, 69*(7), 411–419.

Daniel, A. E., & Menninger, K. (1983). Mentally retarded defendants: Competency and criminal responsibility. *American Journal of Forensic Psychology, 1*(4), 11–22.

Daniels, S. M., Cornelius, D., Makas, E., & Chipouras, S. (1981). Sexuality and disability: The need for services. *Annual Review of Rehabilitation, 1,* 83–112.

Davies, M. (1986). Sex education for young disabled people. *Adoption and Fostering, 10*(1), 38–40.

Davies, R., & Johnston, P. R. (1986). Relationship education for people who live with mental handicaps [Special issue]. *Sieccan Journal, 1*(2), 43–46.

de la Cruz, F. F., & LaVeck, G. D. (Eds.). (1973). *Human sexuality and the mentally retarded.* New York: Brunner/Mazel, Publishers.

Demetral, G. D., Driessen, J., & Goff, G. A. (1983). A proactive training approach designed to assist developmentally disabled adolescents deal effectively with their menarche. *Sexuality and Disability, 6*(1), 38–46.

Denkowski, G. C., & Denkowski, K. M. (1985). The mentally retarded offender in the state prison system: Identification, prevalence, adjustment, and rehabilitation. *Criminal Justice and Behavior, 12*(1), 55–70.

Denkowski, G. C., Denkowski, K. M., & Mabil, J. (1983). A 50-state survey of the current status of residential treatment programs for mentally retarded offenders. *Mental Retardation, 21*(5), 197–203.

Deutsch, H., & Bustow, S. (1982). *Developmental disabilities: A training guide.* Boston: CBI Publishing.

Developmental Disabilities Project, Seattle Rape Relief. (1983). *Teacher training manual on sexual abuse of persons with disabilities: Techniques for planning and implementing a self protection program.* Seattle: Seattle Rape Relief.

Diamond, L. J., & Jaudes, P. K. (1983). Child abuse in a cerebral-palsied population. *Developmental Medicine and Child Neurology, 25,* 169–174.

Dixon, H. (1988). *Sexuality and mental handicap: An educator's resource book.* Cambridge, England: Learning Development Aids.

D'Souza, N. (1990). Genetics and mental retardation. In B. Y. Whitman, & P. J. Accardo (Eds.), *When a parent is mentally retarded* (pp. 31–48). Baltimore: Paul H. Brookes Publishing Co.

Edmondson, B., McCombs, K., & Wish, J. (1979). What retarded adults believe about sex. *American Journal of Mental Deficiency, 84*(1), 11–18.

Edwards, J. P., & Elkins, T. E. (1988). *Just between us: A social sexual guide for parents and professionals with concerns for persons with developmental disabilities.* Portland, OR: Ednick Communications.

Evans, A. L., & McKinlay, I. A. (1989). Sex education and the severely mentally retarded child. *Developmental Medicine & Child Neurology, 31*(1), 98–103.

Family planning services for disabled people: A manual for service providers. (1980). Rockville, MD: National Clearinghouse for Family Planning Information.

Feeling good about yourself. (1980). Highland Park, IL: Perennial Education, Inc.

Fidone, G. S. (1987). Homosexuality in institutionalized retardates [Letter]. *Infection Control, 8*(6), 231.

Finkelhor, D. (1984). *Child sexual abuse.* New York: The Free Press.

Fischer, H. L., & Krajicek, M. J. (1974). Sexual development of the moderately retarded child: Level of information and parental attitudes. *Mental Retardation, 12*(3), 28–30.

Fischer, H. L., Krajicek, M. J., & Borthick, W. A. (1983). *Sex education for the devel-*

opmentally disabled: A guide for parents, teachers, and professionals. Baltimore: University Park Press.

Fitz-Gerald, M., & Fitz-Gerald, D. (1983). How to develop and implement a comprehensive sex education program for the deaf. *Perspectives for Teachers of the Hearing Impaired, 1*(3), 8–12.

Fletcher, D., & Ogle, P. (1981). A realistic approach to sex education for the developmentally disabled: The human growth and development curriculum. *Journal for Special Educators, 17*(4), 316–325.

Frankl, V. E. (1984). *Man's search for meaning: An introduction to logotherapy* (3rd ed.). New York: Touchstone Books/Simon & Schuster, Inc.

Garbarino, J., & Authier, K. (1987). The role of the educators. In J. Garbarino, P. E. Brookhauser, & K. J. Authier (Eds.), *Special children—special risks: The maltreatment of children with disabilities* (pp. 69–81). New York: Aldine de Gruyter.

Gardner, J. F., & Chapman, M. S. (1990). *Program issues in developmental disabilities: A guide to effective habilitation and active treatment* (2nd ed.). Baltimore: Paul H. Brookes Publishing Co.

Gardner, J. F., & Chapman, M. S. (1985). *Staff development in mental retardation services.* Baltimore: Paul H. Brookes Publishing Co.

Gardner, N. E. S. (1986). Sexuality. In J. A. Summers (Ed.), *The right to grow up* (pp. 45–66). Baltimore: Paul H. Brookes Publishing Co.

Gendel, E. S. (1968). *Sex education of the mentally retarded child in the home.* Arlington, TX: National Association for Retarded Children.

Gillan, P. (1980). Psychological methods in sex therapy for the disabled. *Sexuality and Disability, 3*(3), 199–202.

Gimarc, J. D. (1979). *Social/sexual living skills.* Columbia, SC: University of South Carolina Press.

Gochros, H. L., Gochros, J. S., & Fischer, J. (1986). *Helping the sexually oppressed.* Englewoods Cliffs, NJ: Prentice-Hall.

Goodman, L. (1973). The sexual rights of the retarded—A dilemma for parents. *The Family Coordinator, 22,* 472–474.

Gordon, S. (1973). *The sexual adolescent, communicating with teenagers about sex.* North Scituate, MA: Duxbury Press.

Gordon, S. (1979a). *Facts about sex for today's youth.* New York: Ed-U Press.

Gordon, S. (1979b). *Girls are girls and boys are boys so what's the difference?* (rev. ed.). New York: Ed-U Press.

Gordon, S. (1987). *Seduction lines heard 'round the world and answers you can give: A world book of lines.* Buffalo, NY: Prometheus Books.

Gordon, S., & Biklen, D. (1979). *Sexual rights for the people who happen to be handicapped.* New York: Ed-U Press.

Gordon, S., & Gordon, J. (1987). *A better safe than sorry book* (rev. ed.). New York: Ed-U Press.

Green, D. T. (1983). A human sexuality program for developmentally disabled women in a sheltered workshop setting. *Sexuality and Disability, 6*(1), 20–24.

Greengross, W. (1976). *Entitled to love: The sexual and emotional needs of the handicapped.* London: National Marriage Guidance Council.

Griffiths, D., Hingsburger, D., & Christian, R. (1985). Treating developmentally handicapped sexual offenders: The York Behaviour Management Services Treatment Program. *Psychiatric Aspects of Mental Retardation Reviews, 4*(12), 49–52.

Griffiths, D. M., Quinsey, V. L., & Hingsburger, D. (1989). *Changing inappropriate sexual behavior: A community-based approach for persons with developmental disabilities.* Baltimore: Paul H. Brookes Publishing Co.

Haaven, J., Little, R., & Petre-Miller, D. (1990). *Treating intellectually disabled sex offenders: A model residential program.* VT: The Safer Society Press.

Haavik, S. (1986). Marriage and parenthood. In J. A. Summers (Ed.), *The right to grow up* (pp. 67–90). Baltimore: Paul H. Brookes Publishing Co.

Haavik, S. F., & Menninger, K. A., II. (1981). *Sexuality, law, and the developmentally disabled person.* Baltimore: Paul H. Brookes Publishing Co.

Hall, J. E. (1975). Sexuality and the mentally retarded. In J. R. Green (Ed.), *Human sexuality: A health practitioner's text* (pp. 165–174). Baltimore: Williams and Wilkins.

Hamre-Nietupski, S., & Ford, A. (1981). Sex education and related skills: A series of programs implemented with severely handicapped students. *Sexuality and Disability, 4*(3), 179–193.

Hanke, G. C. (1987). Sexuality of clients with mental retardation/developmental disability. *Asha, 29*(12), 31–33.

Hatcher, R., Steward, G., Stewart, F., Guest, F., Schwartz, D., & Jones, S. (1980). *Contraceptive technology* (10th ed., rev.). New York: Irvington Publishers.

Hill, G. (1987). Sexual abuse and the mentally handicapped. *Child Sexual Abuse Newsletter, 6,* 4–5.

Hingsburger, D. (1987). Sex counseling with the developmentally handicapped: The assessment and management of seven critical problems. *Psychiatric Aspects of Mental Retardation Reviews, 6*(9), 41–46.

Hingsburger, D. (1988). Clients and curriculum: Preparing for sex education. *Psychiatric Aspects of Mental Retardation Reviews, 7*(3), 13–17.

Hurley, A. D., & Sovner, R. (1983). Treatment of sexual deviation in mentally retarded persons. *Psychiatric Aspects of Mental Retardation Newsletter, 2*(4), 13–16.

The international and domestic training and technical assistance project in disability and mental health/reproduction health care. (1979). New York: Planned Parenthood of New York City, Inc.

Jaudes, P. K., & Diamond, L. J. (1985). The handicapped child and child abuse. *Child Abuse and Neglect, 9*(3), 341–347.

Johnson, R., & Kempton, W. (1981). *Sex education and counseling of special groups: The mentally and physically handicapped, ill, and elderly* (2nd ed.). Springfield, IL: Charles C Thomas.

Kaminer, R. K., & Cohen, H. J. (1983). Intellectually limited mothers. In *Developmental handicaps: Prevention and treatment* (pp. 24–44). Washington, D.C.: American Association of University Affiliated Programs for Persons with Developmental Disabilities.

Kempton, W. (1977a). The mentally retarded person. In H. L. Gochros & J. S. Gochros (Eds.), *The sexually oppressed* (pp. 239–256). New York: Association Press.

Kempton, W. (1977b). The sexual adolescent who is mentally retarded. *Journal of Pediatric Psychology, 2*(3), 104–107.

Kempton, W. (1979). *Sex education for persons with disabilities that hinder learning—A teacher's guide.* Philadelphia: Planned Parenthood of Southeastern Pennsylvania.

Kempton, W., Bass, M. S., & Gordon, S. (1980). *Love, sex, and birth control for the mentally retarded—A guide for parents* (3rd ed., rev.). Philadelphia: Planned Parenthood Association of Southeastern Pennsylvania.

Koller, H., Richardson, S. A., & Katz, M. (1988). Marriage in a young adult mentally retarded population. *Journal of Mental Deficiency Research, 32*(2), 93–102.

Krenk, C. J. (1984). Training residence staff for child abuse treatment. *Child Welfare, 63*(2), 167–173.

Leight, L. (1990). *Raising sexually healthy children.* New York: Ed-U Press.

Liskey, N., & Stephens, P. (1978). *Cerebral palsy and sexuality.* Fresno, CA: Disabled Students on Campus Organization (c/o Handicapped Student Services), California State University at Fresno.

Longo, R. E., & Gochenour, C. (1981). Sexual assault of handicapped individuals. *Journal of Rehabilitation, 47*(3), 24–27.

Loss, P., & Ross, J. E. (1988a). *Psychoeducation curriculum for the adolescent sex offender in treatment.* Mt. Pleasant, SC: Jonathan E. Ross, M.A., Inc.

Loss, P., & Ross, J. E. (1988b). *Risk assessment/interviewing protocol for adolescent sex offenders.* Mt. Pleasant, SC: Jonathan E. Ross, M.A., Inc.

Luterman, D. (1984). *Counseling the communicatively disordered and their families.* Boston: Little, Brown.

MacEachron, A. E. (1979). Mentally retarded offenders: Prevalence and characteristics. *American Journal of Mental Deficiency, 84*(2), 165–176.

Macleod, S. (1985). *For one and all: Sexuality and your disabled child.* Halifax, NS: Planned Parenthood Nova Scotia.

Madaras, L. (1988). *What's happening to my body?—A growing up guide for mothers and daughters.* New York: New Market Press.

Madaras, L., & Saavedra, D. (1988). *What's happening to my body? book for boys—A growing guide for parents and sons.* New York: Ed-U Press.

Masters, W. H., & Johnson, V. E. (1966). *Human sexual response.* Boston: Little, Brown.

Mayla, P. (1973). *Where did I come from?* Secaucus, NJ: Lyle Stuart, Inc.

McNab, W. L. (1978). The sexual needs of the handicapped. *Journal of School Health, 48*(5), 301–306.

Meler, J. H., & Nelson, W. P. (no date). *Relationship between child abuse and neglect and developmental disabilities.* Beaumont, CA: Children's Village, USA.

Merson, R. M. (1987). Sexuality in communication disorders. *Asha, 29*(12), 27–28.

Meyers, R. (1978). *Like normal people.* New York: McGraw-Hill.

Monat, R. K. (1982). *Sexuality and the mentally retarded. A clinical and therapeutic guidebook.* San Diego, CA: College-Hill Press.

Monat-Haller, R. K. (1987). Speech-language pathologists as counselors and sexuality educators. *Asha, 29*(12), 35–36.

Morgenstern, M. (1973). The psychosexual development of the retarded. In F. F. de la Cruz & G. D. LaVeck (Eds.), *Human sexuality and the mentally retarded* (pp. 15–28). New York: Brunner/Mazel.

Murphy, L., & Delia, S. (1987). Abuse and the special child. *Special Parent/Special Child, 3*(1). (ERIC Document Reproduction Service No. ED 288 323).

Murphy, W. D., Coleman, E. M., & Abel, G. G. (1983). Human sexuality in the mentally retarded. In J. L. Matson & F. Andrasik (Eds.), *Treatment issues and innovations in mental retardation* (pp. 581–643). New York: Plenum.

Murphy, W. D., Coleman, M. A., & Haynes, M. R. (1983). Treatment and evaluation issues with the mentally retarded sex offender. In J. G. Greer & I. R. Stuart (Eds.), *The sexual aggressor* (pp. 22–41). New York: Van Nostrand Reinhold Company, Inc.

National apostolate with mentally retarded persons quarterly publication. (1989). Volume 20/Number 2. Dayton, OH: National Apostolate with Mentally Retarded Persons.

Nelson, M., & Clark, K. (1986). *The educator's guide to preventing child sexual abuse.* Santa Cruz, CA: Network Publications.

Pattullo, A. (1969). *Puberty in the girl who is retarded.* Arlington, TX: National Association for Retarded Children.

Perske, R. (1973). *New directions for parents of persons who are retarded.* Nashville, TN: Abingdon Press.

Pincus, S. (1988). Sexuality in the mentally retarded patient. *American Family Physician, 37*(2), 319–323.

Pitceathly, A. S., & Chapman, J. W. (1985). Sexuality, marriage and parenthood of mentally retarded people. *International Journal for the Advancement of Counseling, 8*(3), 173–181.

Psycho-sexual development and sex education for the mentally retarded. (1974). Chapel Hill, NC: University of North Carolina Press.

Pueschel, S. M., & Scola, P. S. (1988). Parents' perception of social and sexual functions in adolescents with Down's syndrome. *Journal of Mental Deficiency Research, 32*(3), 215–220.

Ralston, M. E. (1990). *Incest: A community response to a family system problem* (rev. ed.). Sullivan's Island, SC: Author.

Reich, M. D., & Harshman, H. W. (1971). Sex education for the handicapped: Reality or repression. *The Journal of Special Education, 5,* 373–377.

A resource guide in sex education for the mentally retarded. (1971). New York: Behavioral Publications.

Rolett, K. (1976). *Organizing community resources in sexuality counseling and family planning for the retarded.* Chapel Hill, NC: State Services Office.

Rose, E., & Hardman, M. L. (1981). The abused mentally retarded child. *Education and Training of the Mentally Retarded Child, 16*(2), 114–118.

Rousso, M. (1982). Special considerations in counseling clients with cerebral palsy. *Sexuality and Disability 5*(2), 78–88.

Rowitz, L. (1988). The forgotten ones: Adolescence and mental retardation. *Mental Retardation, 26*(3), 115–117.

Rowitz, L. (Ed.). (1989). Developmental disabilities and HIV infection: A symposium on issues and public policy [Special issue]. *Mental Retardation, 27,* 197–262.

Ryerson, E. (1981). Sexual abuse of disabled persons and prevention alternatives. In D. G. Bullard & S. E. Knight (Eds.), *Sexuality and physical disability: Personal perspectives* (pp. 235–242). St. Louis: C. V. Mosby.

Ryerson, E. (1984). Sexual abuse and self-protection education for developmentally disabled youth: A priority need. *SIECUS Report, 13*(1), 1–3.

Sanders, G. L. (1984a). Relationships of the handicapped: Issues of sex and marriage. In E. I. Coppersmith (Ed.), *Families with handicapped members* (pp. 63–64). Rockville, MD: Aspen Systems Corporation.

Sanders, G. L. (1984b). Relationships of the handicapped: Issues of sexuality and marriage. *Family Therapy Collections, 11,* 63–74.

Sanford, L. R. (1980). *The silent children: A parent's guide to the prevention of child sexual abuse.* New York: McGraw-Hill Book Co.

Santamour, M., & West, B. (1977). *The mentally retarded offender and corrections.* Washington: National Institute of Law Enforcement and Criminal Justice, Law Enforcement Assistance Administration, U.S. Department of Justice.

Satir, V. (1972). *Peoplemaking.* Palo Alto, CA: Science and Behavior Books, Inc.

Satir, V. (1983). *Conjoint family therapy* (3d ed.). Palo Alto, CA: Science and Behavior Books, Inc.

Satir, V., & Baldwin, M. (1983). *Satir step by step; A guide to creating change in families.* Palo Alto, CA: Science and Behavior Books, Inc.

Schepp, K. F. (1986). *Sexuality counseling: A training program.* Muncie, IN: Accelerated Development Inc.

Schilit, J. (1979). The retarded offender and criminal justice personnel. *Exceptional Children, 46,* 16–22.

Schilling, R. F., Schinke, S. P., Blythe, B. J., & Barth, R. P. (1982). Child maltreatment and mentally retarded parents: Is there a relationship? *Mental Retardation, 20,* 201–209.

Schor, D. P. (1987). Sex and sexual abuse of developmentally disabled adolescents. *Seminars in Adolescent Medicine, 3*(1), 1–7.

Seagull, E. A. W., & Scheurer, S. L. (1986). Neglected and abused children of mentally retarded parents. *Child Abuse & Neglect, 10,* 493–500.

Seattle Rape Relief Developmental Disabilities Project. (1982a). *Special education curriculum on sexual exploitation. Level I Kit (Ages 6–11).* Seattle, WA: Comprehensive Health Education Foundation.

Seattle Rape Relief Developmental Disabilities Project. (1982b). *Special education curriculum on sexual exploitation. Level II Kit (Ages 12–19).* Seattle, WA: Comprehensive Health Education Foundation.

Self-protection for the handicapped: A curriculum designed to teach handicapped persons to avoid exploitation. (1985). Washington: Kent Public Schools. (ERIC Document Reproduction Service No. 263 705).

Sengstock, W. L., & Vergason, G. A. (1970). Issues in sex education for the retarded. *Education and Training of the Mentally Retarded, 5*(3), 99–103.

Sex education for the mentally retarded. (1969). San Leandro, CA: Alameda County Mental Retardation Service.

Sexual exploitation and abuse of people with disabilities. (1984). *Response to Violence in the Family, 7*(2), 7–8.

Sgroi, S. M. (Ed.). (1982). *Handbook of clinical intervention in child sexual abuse.* Lexington, MA: Lexington Books.

Sgroi, S. M., Blick, L. C., & Porter, F. S. (1982). A conceptual framework for child sexual abuse. In S. M. Sgroi (Ed.), *Handbook of clinical intervention in child sexual abuse* (pp. 9–37). Lexington, MA: Lexington Books.

Sgroi, S. M., Porter, F. S., & Blick, L. C. (1982). Validation of child sexual abuse. In S. M. Sgroi (Ed.), *Handbook of clinical intervention in child sexual abuse* (pp. 39–80). Lexington, MA: Lexington Books.

Sha'ked, A. (1978). *Human sexuality in physical and mental disabilities: An annotated bibliography.* Bloomington: Indiana University Press.

Shane, J. F. (1988). *Abuse against children with developmental handicaps: An annotated bibliography.* Toronto: Ontario Association for Community Living.

Sheridan, M. D. (1956). The intelligence of 100 neglected mothers. *British Journal of Medicine, 1,* 91–92.

Shuger, N. B. (1980). Procreation, marriage, and raising children. In R. L. Burgdorf, Jr. (Ed.), *The legal rights of handicapped persons: Cases, materials, and text* (pp. 857–992). Baltimore: Paul H. Brookes Publishing Co.

Smith, S. (1983). The link between sexual maturation and "adolescent grieving" in parents of the dependent disabled. *Sexuality and Disability, 6*(3/4), 150–154.

Sobsey, D. (1988a). Sexual offenses and disabled victims: Research and implications [in French & English]. *Vis-à-Vis: A National Newsletter on Family Violence, 6*(4), 2–3.

Sobsey, D. (1988b). Sexual victimization of people with disabilities: Professional & social responsibilities. *Alberta Psychology, 17*(6), 8–9.

Sobsey, D. (in press). Factors in the sexual abuse and exploitation of people with mental retardation. In J. M. Levy, P. L. Levy, & B. Nivin (Eds.), *Employment, integration, and community competence: The keys to quality of life and community coalescence.* New York: Young Adult Institute.

Sobsey, D., Gray, S., Varnhagen, C., Pyper, D., Reimer-Heck, B., & Wells, D. (1990). *Annotated bibliography: Disability, sexuality and abuse.* Canada: Health and Welfare.

Sobsey, D., & Varnhagen, C. (1988). *Sexual abuse, assault, and exploitation of people with disabilities.* Ottawa: Health and Welfare Canada.

Sobsey, D., Wells, D., & Gray, S. (1989). *Sexual assault and abuse of people with disabilities: Networking directory.* Edmonton: University of Alberta Department of Educational Psychology Severe Disabilities Program.

Stavis, P., & Tarantino, L. (1986, Oct.–Nov.). Sexual activity in the mentally disabled population: Some standards of the criminal and civil law. *Quality of Care,* pp. 2–3.

Stiggall, L. (1988). AIDS education for individuals with developmental, learning or mental disabilities. In M. Quackenbush & M. Nelson (Eds.), *The AIDS challenge: Prevention education for young people* (pp. 405–418). Santa Cruz, CA: Network Publications.

Sumarah, J., Maksym, D., & Goudge, J. (1988). The effects of a staff training program on attitudes and knowledge of staff toward the sexuality of persons with intellectual handicaps. *Canadian Journal of Rehabilitation 1*(3), 169–175.

Swedish Institute for the Handicapped. (1986). *Sexuality and disability: A matter that concerns all of us.* Broma: Swedish Institute for the Handicapped. (ERIC Document Reproduction Service No. ED 281 334).

Tasch, V. (1988). Parenting the mentally retarded adolescent: A framework for helping families. *Journal of Community Health Nursing, 5*(2), 97–108.

Unkovic, C. M., & Klingman, J. A. (1980). The continued neglect of the mentally retarded offender. *Corrections Today, 42,* 38–39.

Varner, N., & Freeman, M. (1976). *Some things about sex for both men and women.* Atlanta: Emory University Press.

Watson, J. D. (1984). Talking about the best kept secret: Sexual abuse and children with disabilities. *Exceptional Parent, 14*(6), 15, 16, 18–20.

Whitman, B. Y., & Accardo, P. J. (1990). *When a parent is mentally retarded.* Baltimore: Paul H. Brookes Publishing Co.

Whitman, B. Y., Graves, B., & Accardo, P. J. (1990). Parents Learning together I: Parenting skills training for adults with mental retardation. In B. Y. Whitman & P. J. Accardo (Eds.), *When a parent is mentally retarded* (pp. 51–65). Baltimore: Paul H. Brookes Publishing Co.

Wolfensberger, W. (1972). *The principle of normalization in human services.* Toronto: National Institute of Mental Retardation.

Worthington, G. M. (1984). Sexual exploitation and abuse of people with disabilities. *Response to Victimization of Women & Children, 7*(2), 7–8.

Zantal-Weiner, K. (1987). *Child abuse and the handicapped child.* Reston, VA: ERIC Clearinghouse on Handicapped & Gifted Children Digest No. 446. (ERIC Document Reproduction Service No. ED 287 262).

Zelman, D. B., & Tyser, K. M. (1979). *Essential adult sex education for the mentally retarded (EASE).* Santa Monica, CA: James Stanfield Film Associates.

Index

Page numbers in italics indicate figures; those followed by "t" indicate tables.